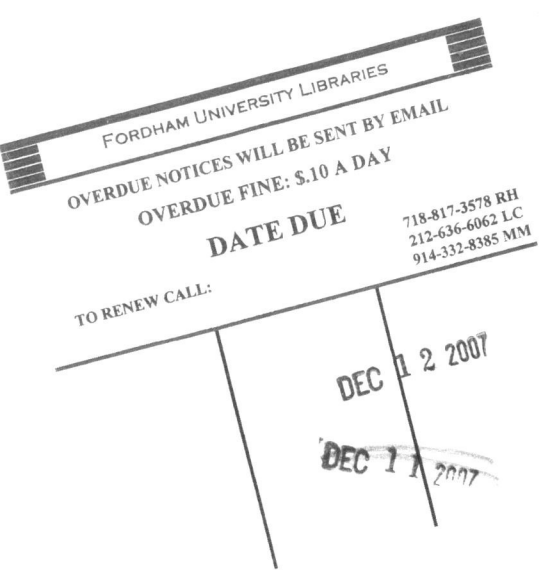

The Courts, the Constitution, and Capital Punishment

The Courts, the Constitution, and Capital Punishment

Hugo Adam Bedau
Tufts University

Lexington Books
D.C. Heath and Company
Lexington, Massachusetts
Toronto

Library of Congress Cataloging in Publication Data

Bedau, Hugo Adam.
 The courts, the Constitution, and capital punishment.

 Includes bibliographical references and index.
 1. Capital punishment—United States—Addresses, essays, lectures.
 2. United States—Constitutional law—Addresses, essays, lectures. I. Title.
 KF9227.C2B39   345'.73'077   77-6552
 ISBN 0-669-01290-4

Copyright © 1977 by D.C. Heath and Company.

All rights reserved. No part of this publication may be reproduced or transmitted in any form or by any means, electronic or mechanical, including photocopy, recording, or any information storage or retrieval system, without permission in writing from the publisher.

Published simultaneously in Canada.

Printed in the United States of America.

International Standard Book Number: 0-669-01290-4

Library of Congress Catalog Card Number: 77-6552

To Jan

Contents

	List of Tables	ix
	Acknowledgments	xi
	Introduction	xiii
Chapter 1	The Issue of Capital Punishment	1
Chapter 2	The Courts, the Constitution, and Capital Punishment	11
	i An Impartial Jury	15
	ii Equal Protection of the Laws	21
	iii Due Process of Law	27
	iv Cruel and Unusual Punishment	32
	v The Right to Life	42
	vi A Mandate for Judicial Repeal	43
Chapter 3	Deterrence and the Death Penalty	45
Chapter 4	The Death Penalty in America: Review and Forecast	59
Chapter 5	The Politics of Death	75
Chapter 6	Challenging the Death Penalty	81
Chapter 7	New Research and Literature Since *Furman*	91
Chapter 8	Are Mandatory Capital Statutes Unconstitutional?	103
Chapter 9	New Life for the Death Penalty	111
Chapter 10	Epilogue: A Right to Die by Firing Squad?	121
	Notes	127
	Index	155
	About the Author	167

List of Tables

1-1	Murder in the United States, 1960-1965	2
1-2	Executions in the United States, 1960-1966	3
1-3	Death Sentences in the United States, 1960-1967	3
1-4	Abolition of Death Penalties in the United States, 1846-1966	5
4-1	Executions, Commutations, and Death Sentences in the United States, 1961-1971	60
4-2	Persons Under Death Sentence in the United States, 1971	61
9-1	Persons Under Sentence of Death by State, Sex, Race, and Crime, 1976	112

Acknowledgments

These essays have profited from the advice and assistance of several persons. Jack Himmelstein, while he was a staff attorney for the NAACP Legal Defence and Educational Fund, was more than helpful in explaining the current activities of the litigation campaign and the effect upon it of various Supreme Court rulings. The essays reprinted in Chapters 4, 5, and 7 owe much to his advice. His successors at the LDF, Peggy Davis and David E. Kendall, have been helpful as he was, and the essay in Chapter 9 is the better for it. Some of the revisions in this chapter were suggested to me by an unpublished address by Ms. Davis. Lou Brin, associate editor of *The Jewish Advocate*, and Robert Hatch, executive editor of *The Nation*, have always welcomed my submissions, including the essays that reappear here in Chapters 5, 8, and 9. Howard Blatchford, a student of mine at Tufts, gave me prompt and indispensable clerical assistance in preparing the manuscript. Most of all, I am grateful for unstinting editorial assistance in revising all these essays for publication here, especially in Chapters 5 and 7, as well as in the initial versions of Chapters 8, 9, and 10, and the introduction.

Chapter 1 appeared originally as "The Issue of Capital Punishment," in *Current History* 53, no. 312 (August 1967): 82-87, 116. Copyright © 1967, by Current History, Inc. Reprinted with permission.

Chapter 2 appeared originally as "The Courts, the Constitution, and Capital Punishment," in *Utah Law Review* 1968, no. 2 (May 1968): 201-239. Copyright © 1968, Utah Law Review Society. Reprinted with permission.

Chapter 3 appeared originally in two journals under slightly different titles and in slightly different versions: (1) "The Death Penalty as a Deterrent: Argument and Evidence," *Ethics* 80, no. 3 (April 1970): 205-217. Copyright © 1970, The University of Chicago. Reprinted with permission. (2) "Deterrence and the Death Penalty: A Reconsideration," *The Journal of Criminal Law, Criminology and Police Science* 61, no. 4 (December 1970): 539-548. Copyright © 1971, by Northwestern University School of Law. Reprinted with permission. Errata published in "A Concluding Note," *Ethics* 81, no. 1 (October 1970): 76 are incorporated.

Chapter 4 appeared originally as "The Death Penalty in America: Review and Forecast," in *Federal Probation* 35, no. 2 (June 1971): 32-43.

Chapter 5 is based on two essays: (1) "The Politics of Death," *Trial* 8, no. 2 (March/April 1972): 44-46. Copyright © 1972, by The Association of Trial Lawyers of America. Reprinted by permission. (2) "Supreme Court Challenged by 8th Amendment Death Penalty Pleas," *The Jewish Advocate*, 3 February 1972, p. 3. Copyright © 1972, The Jewish Advocate. Reprinted with permission.

Chapter 6 appeared originally as "Challenging the Death Penalty," in *Harvard Civil Rights-Civil Liberties Law Review* 9 (May 1974): 626-643.

Copyright © 1974, by the Harvard Civil Rights-Civil Liberties Law Review. Reprinted with permission.

Chapter 7 is based on two essays: (1) "Social Science Research in the Aftermath of *Furman v. Georgia*: Creating New Knowledge About Capital Punishment in the United States," in *Issues in Criminal Justice: Planning and Evaluation*, ed. Marc Riedel and Duncan Chappell, New York, Praeger Publishers, Inc., 1976, pp. 75-86. Copyright © 1976, by the American Society of Criminology. Reprinted by permission of the publisher. (2) "Capital Punishment: The Literature Still Says No," *The Civil Liberties Review* 2, no. 3 (Summer 1975): 125-133. Copyright © 1975 by the American Civil Liberties Union, Inc. Reprinted by permission.

Chapter 8 originally appeared as "Are Mandatory Capital Sentences Inherently Discriminatory?" in *The Jewish Advocate*, 22 May 1975, section two, p. 1. Copyright © 1975, The Jewish Advocate. Reprinted by permission.

Chapter 9 originally appeared as "New Life for the Death Penalty," in *The Nation* 223, no. 5 (28 August 1976): 144-148. Copyright © 1976, by the Nation Associates, Inc. Reprinted with permission.

Chapter 10 originally appeared as "The Right to Die by Firing Squad," in *The Hastings Center Report* 7, no. 1 (February 1977): 5-7. Copyright © 1977, by the Institute of Society, Ethics and the Life Sciences. Portions appearing originally in my editorial, "Should we let Gilmore decide his own fate?" in *The Boston Globe*, 19 November 1976, p. 23, are reprinted here courtesy of The Boston Globe. Copyright © 1976, The Boston Globe.

Introduction

Just ten years ago, the noted criminologist, Thorsten Sellin, published his selection of essays, *Capital Punishment*, and the revised edition of my book, *The Death Penalty in America*, appeared. Together these two volumes made generally available a harvest of research, evidence, and argument on the death penalty controversy that served as the baseline for future investigations. In the same year, the President's Commission on Law Enforcement and the Administration of Justice completed its work and published its report. The Commission all but ignored capital punishment as an acceptable and effective weapon against crimes of violence. At a press conference, also in 1967, Attorney General Ramsey Clark expressed opposition by the Department of Justice to the death penalty. This brought to public notice a sentiment in favor of abolition that had been gaining momentum in the Department for several years. Concurrently, the NAACP Legal Defense and Educational Fund (LDF) and the American Civil Liberties Union (ACLU) were bringing state and federal death sentences under attack on constitutional grounds, an unprecedented challenge to capital punishment. Executions were in decline: one in 1966, two in 1967—and then 1968 became the first year in our history in which none occurred anywhere in the nation.

We can see now that the mid-1960s was a decisive period in which a new strategy was developed to attack the death penalty and new hope awakened among its opponents. During the 1950s, the abolitionist effort had two main goals: lobbying in the legislatures for repeal of capital statutes, and desperate maneuvers to obtain commutation of death sentences. Efforts of both sorts failed more often than they succeeded. After the mid-1960s, such challenges took distinctly second place to the work of lawyers who were pressing federal constitutional objections against the death penalty in appellate courts. The highwater mark of this phase was 29 June 1972, the day the Supreme Court announced its decision in *Furman v. Georgia*. In its ruling in *Furman*, the Court in effect abolished the death penalty throughout the nation on the ground that, as then administered, it was "cruel and unusual punishment," prohibited by the Eighth Amendment and therefore unconstitutional.

Now, more than four years later, it is clear that this phase of the struggle to abolish the death penalty has come to an end. The first blow was the Supreme Court's decision on 2 July 1976, upholding the constitutionality of the death penalty in *Gregg v. Georgia*. A decade of effort to persuade the federal courts to repeal the death penalty, though not an outright failure—no litigation campaign that permanently narrowed the scope of capital statutes and nullified hundreds of death sentences can be counted as a failure—had not been crowned with success. As this is being written, the authorities in one state after another are moving toward setting execution dates for many of the hundreds of persons currently under death sentence. The second blow came on 17 January 1977, as nearly ten years without any executions came to a violent end. On that day, a firing squad executed Gary Mark Gilmore in Utah. The way was thus opened for a return to the situation of earlier years, with its uphill political struggle against this most ancient of punishments. It seems a good time, therefore, to pause and reflect on this eventful decade in the capital punishment controversy. That is what this book enables the reader to do.

Since 1967 I have had many occasions to put on paper my thoughts about capital punishment—the politics, law, and morality of its abolition, and the state of the evidence on particular questions of fact. I have prepared testimony for several legislative committees and legislative commissions. I was able to be present at the oral arguments before the Supreme Court in the three leading recent death penalty cases, *Furman v. Georgia, Fowler v. North Carolina*, and *Gregg v. Georgia*, and to report what transpired. Scholars and social scientists engaged in research on capital punishment have shared their ideas with me, and I have been able to learn much from reading and commenting on their work. Above all, I have had the good fortune to work closely with the two leading national civil liberties and civil rights organizations that placed abolition of the death penalty high on their agendas, the ACLU and the LDF. The essays in this book are the product of these experiences—and they consist of information, reflections, predictions, explanations, conjectures, and interpretations from the past decade, almost year by year, on the vicissitudes of a struggle whose end is not yet in sight.

In the opening chapter, I have described the situation and identified the main issues as I saw them in the early months of 1967. With one exception, all of the themes to be pursued in greater detail in the later chapters are mentioned here. The exception is nothing less than the developing constitutional challenge to the death penalty—the central theme of the whole book! Although the policy of opposition to the death penalty by both the ACLU and the LDF is cited, the campaign to end the death penalty through constitutional litigation is not. The reason is that, like most observers at the time, I was simply unaware of it. After 1968, this campaign begins to dominate the scene, so much so that other aspects of the struggle to abolish the death penalty are no more than mentioned in passing.

The major essay in the book is Chapter 2, in which I survey all the possible constitutional objections to the death penalty as they appeared to me a decade ago. This essay was the first comprehensive constitutional critique of capital punishment published. It had its origin in 1960, when I received a proposed brief against capital punishment confined essentially to one thesis: the death penalty is inconsistent with the Eighth Amendment to the federal constitution, since that amendment prohibits "cruel and unusual punishment," and this is precisely what the death penalty had become. This brief, prepared on behalf of the Southern California affiliate of the ACLU, was the work of Gerald H. Gottlieb, a lawyer practicing out of Beverly Hills. Gottlieb was the first legal thinker to spell out a frontal attack on capital punishment as a "cruel and unusual" punishment, a line of objection that had always had considerable appeal to many critics of the death penalty unschooled in constitutional litigation and unintimidated by doctrines of federalism and judicial restraint. A year or so later, while on a fellowship at Harvard Law School, I undertook to restate Gottlieb's argument and conjoin it with other constitutional objections of a procedural sort. The first clear sign that there might be some hope for one or another of these arguments against the death penalty came in October 1963, in the dissenting opinion written by Justice Arthur J. Goldberg in *Rudolph v. Alabama*, a case involving rape but not murder. The scholarly community took little notice of the *Rudolph* dissent; it provoked no rash of speculation among legal scholars on whether the death penalty might, after all these decades, be in violation of one or more provisions of the Bill of Rights. Even so, there were encouraging developments during the early 1960s tending in this direction, and in 1967 I undertook to rewrite, update, and expand my thoughts. The resulting essay appears as Chapter 2.

Probably no one today would set out the constitutional possibilities for outlawing the death penalty in the fashion I did ten years ago. One reason, of course, is that during the interval, in a series of important decisions, the Supreme Court tested and, one by one, rejected most of these possibilities. The essays in this book after Chapter 3 examine all of these important decisions. But there is another reason. Lawyers studying the prospects for abolition in the mid-1960s would have seen the constitutional possibilities rather differently than I did, right from the start. Where I proceeded abstractly and without concern for litigational strategy, this is what would have been uppermost in a lawyer's mind, and properly so. A good example of the precedent-oriented, case-by-case approach favored by lawyers (and, no doubt, appellate courts) can be found in a brief article published a few months after mine.[1] The authors were Jack Greenberg, executive director of the LDF, and Jack Himmelstein, the staff attorney chiefly responsible for the day-to-day management of the LDF's anti-capital punishment campaign. Their viewpoint is set out in greater detail by Michael Meltsner, another of the former litigating attorneys on the LDF staff, in his superb book, *The Supreme Court and Capital Punishment* (New York, Random House, 1973). Looking back now, one might still say in favor of my approach that it approximates how the general reader, thumbing through the Bill of Rights, might also ponder the question of whether capital punishment is unconstitutional.

Whenever the death penalty is debated, the dominant empirical issue under dispute is the question of deterrence. In 1968, the social philosopher Ernest van den Haag published an essay in which he both attacked arguments against capital punishment and constructed a few for it. The gist of his views is now conveniently available in his recent book, *Punishing Criminals* (New York, Basic Books, 1975). Van den Haag's essay remains one of the few written by a serious academic thinker willing to give his support to capital punishment in our society. Because I thought his argument rested to a considerable extent on faulty reasoning and confusions about deterrence, I wrote a reply. Since van den Haag published his remarks in a scholarly journal,[2] I decided to respond in the fashion philosophers are wont to deploy on disputed questions in epistemology or Cartesian metaphysics. The result was the somewhat ponderous and polemical essay that appears as Chapter 3. In the several years since my exchange with van den Haag, the academic community has been absorbed with trying to evaluate some new research, discussed briefly in Chapter 8, purporting to show that there is a measurable deterrent effect from executions. Without opening up that argument here, it is pertinent to report that the authors of a recent comparison of this new research with the older research by Sellin and others—on which I relied in my criticisms of van den Haag—conclude that "more credibility" attaches to Sellin's negative conclusions of no deterrent effect than to these newer positive conclusions.[3] I concur.

By 1970, it was fairly clear that if the death penalty was to be ruled unconstitutional, it would have to be because it was held to violate either the "equal protection" clause or the "cruel and unusual punishment" clause of the federal constitution. The equal protection argument was rejected by the Supreme Court in the spring of 1971 in *McGautha v. California*. Chapter 4 was written just before that disappointing ruling was announced, and it reviews political and legal developments as of the end of 1970 relevant to abolition. I also undertook a brief assessment of the status of empirical knowledge on five general issues: public opinion, deterrence, miscarriages of justice, legislative repeal, and constitutional litigation. Even in 1970, as this quintet of topics shows, it seemed to many opponents of the death penalty that judicial repeal of executions on constitutional grounds was not the only hopeful prospect ahead.

Because of the way several writers in recent years seem to have misunderstood something I wrote in this essay,[4] a few words of further comment are appropriate here. In 1971 I said, "it is ... a false sentimentality to argue that the death penalty ought to be abolished because of the abstract possibility that an innocent person might be executed, when the record fails to disclose that such cases occur." I still think this is true, though I never thought it was the whole truth. The "record" to which I referred was the legal and historical research published after my own essay on this subject ("Murders, Errors of Justice, and Capital Punishment"), written in 1962 and revised in 1966 for inclusion in *The Death Penalty in America*. As of 1971, this record showed that entirely innocent persons had been erroneously *accused* and *convicted* of murder and other capital crimes, and that some of them had been *sentenced* to death. It was also true, I believed, that entirely innocent persons had been *executed*, and that this was not merely an "abstract possibility." But it is not so clear that the "record" attests to this. For example, I believe (and did, in 1971) that Julius and Ethel Rosenberg were innocent of the crime for which they were executed in 1953. I believe not only that the government did not prove its case beyond the proverbial reasonable doubt, but that the Rosenbergs were simply *not guilty* of any capital crime. But the record, even now, insofar as it is constituted by postexecution legal proceedings, does not establish this. At most, historical research, notably by Walter and Miriam Schneir in their fascinating book, *Invitation to an Inquest* (New York, Doubleday, 1965), gives one ample ground for thinking that these executions were entirely in error.

Today, much research still needs to be done to establish the record where miscarriages of justice and capital punishment are involved. A sophisticated approach to this whole problem, though not one based on exposés of particular cases where justice miscarried, may be found in the penetrating essay by Charles L. Black, Jr., *Capital Punishment: The Inevitability of Caprice and Mistake* (New York, W.W. Norton, 1974). It is strongly recommended to those who naively argue from the absence of a frequent and incontestable record of innocents hanged, electrocuted, or gassed to the conclusion that it has not happened and cannot happen. It is more than ironic that those most skeptical about the execution of the innocent are often the most eager to insist that we will never know how many murders the death penalty has prevented, and therefore that it is only prudent to keep it available despite the absence of compelling evidence of its deterrent effect.

When oral argument before the Supreme Court was scheduled for January 1972 in what was to become the landmark case of *Furman v. Georgia*, the editors of *The Nation* and of *The Jewish Advocate* accredited me as their representative. I sat in the correspondents' section of the Court throughout that day as Anthony G. Amsterdam, the chief architect of the LDF's litigation campaign, and Jack Greenberg presented their arguments. An observer could not have asked for a better perch from which to watch history unfold. For a participant in the abolition struggle whose pleadings would never be presented directly in any judicial forum, the proximity afforded by being in the press box gave an altogether gratifying feeling of involvement. Chapter 5 focuses on the arguments presented that day in court.

Where the long essay in Chapter 2 provides the reader with a comprehensive survey of constitutional possibilities for outlawing the death penalty, the essay in Chapter 6 offers my reaction to the legal campaign that the LDF actually waged and that culminated in the *Furman* ruling. The occasion for such an essay was an invitation to review Michael Meltsner's book (mentioned earlier), *The Supreme Court and Capital Punishment*. I used the opportunity to cast a backward glance over the whole decade that preceded *Furman*, and especially to the situation in 1962, ten years earlier, to help put the LDF's accomplishments into its proper perspective. As I have noted already, the LDF's contributions to the effort to end the death penalty in this country have tended to overshadow all other activities moving in the same direction. One reviewer of Meltsner's book was moved to comment somewhat unadmiringly that since 1967 there had been other "significant abolitionist forces at work ... which had nothing to do with anyone's grand 'strategy.' There has been and remains a profound antipathy for capital punishment in the system of criminal justice itself."[5] This is entirely true. Yet it is difficult to imagine how the abolition effort could have proceeded as rapidly and as effectively as it did in the federal courts, in the South, and in the media without the acknowledged initiatives of the LDF. Richard Kluger, in his absorbing volume, *Simple Justice*, has shown how some of the first legal cases brought to the NAACP in its earliest years involved black defendants, white justice, and the hangman's noose.[6] Nothing is more fitting, in my view, than for the LDF, half a century later, to have become recognized as the organization responsible for the major initiatives in using constitutional litigation in the attempt to limit and abolish the death penalty.

In January 1973, a grant from the Russell Sage Foundation enabled me to try to interest social scientists in undertaking research on the full range of unanswered empirical questions affecting the future of capital punishment in the aftermath of *Furman*. The focus was on questions where the professional interests of social scientists naturally converged on the identifiable concerns of the courts. The main results of these investigations did not appear until three years later. Then, almost on the day of the fourth anniversary of *Furman* and coincident with the Supreme Court's first post-*Furman* death penalty rulings, *Capital Punishment in the United States* (New York, AMS Press, 1976) appeared, sponsored by the American Orthopsychiatric Association and jointly edited by Chester M. Pierce and me. This volume presented the research results of over two dozen scientific inquiries, many addressed to questions never before examined. The circumstances, initial accomplishments, and subsequent developments of the Russell Sage project are discussed in Chapter 7. It provides some insight into how social science research can be organized to pursue questions in the public interest.

Chapter 7 also includes my evaluation of other research and writing on capital punishment that appeared after the *Furman* ruling. Published too late for mention in the essays that make up this chapter was one volume worth special note here, Philip English Mackey's *Voices Against Death: American Opposition to Capital Punishment, 1787-1975* (New York, Burt Franklin, 1976). In the twenty-six selections Mackey has assembled, we are presented with an unexcelled opportunity to examine nearly two hundred years of argument by critics of the death penalty in this country. Ideologically, the abolition movement has exhibited the widest diversity: religious and secular, conservative and radical, utilitarian and contractarian, egoist and altruist—both sides of these familiar dichotomies have had their representatives in the two centuries of opposition to punishment by death. Thanks to Mackey's careful winnowing of a varied literature, we have the materials before us for a closer look at the abolitionist cause, its leading spokesmen, and their several arguments.

In April 1975, the Supreme Court heard oral argument in *Fowler v. North*

Carolina, the first death penalty case to reach the Court subsequent to *Furman*. I was again fortunate to be present for the argument, and the essay reprinted as Chapter 8 was prompted by my second visit to the Court as a correspondent. Although no one could have foretold it at the time, *Fowler* was not destined to become a source of important new constitutional law. Decision was delayed throughout 1975, owing first to the illness of Justice William O. Douglas and then to the search for his successor. It was not reported until the summer of 1976, when it became one of the many footnotes to the major ruling in *Woodson v. North Carolina*.

On 2 July 1976, the Supreme Court announced its long-awaited clarification of *Furman* in a group of five new decisions, led by *Woodson* and *Gregg v. Georgia*. Although the *Woodson* ruling gratifyingly struck down mandatory capital statutes, *Gregg* dashed the hopes of the decade. The ruling in that case upheld capital punishment as not "cruel and unusual punishment," provided the death penalty statutes "individuate" the sentencing decision and thereby avoid the admittedly "arbitrary" and "freakish" imposition of the death sentence against which the Court had ruled in *Furman*. Within a week, the ACLU had convened a group of lawyers and representatives of civil liberties and civil rights organizations to review the likely effects of these rulings and to organize a new National Coalition Against the Death Penalty.[7] The essay reprinted as Chapter 9 was written shortly after I attended this conference.

During the autumn and early winter of 1976, Gary Mark Gilmore captured the nation's attention, as he fought not to evade or delay his date with the executioner but to meet it on schedule. And he eventually did, thereby ending the decade of *de facto* abolition with extraordinary symmetry. The last person to be executed before Gilmore, Luis Monge in June 1967, had also refused all efforts to appeal his conviction or sentence and eagerly sought death. More deserves to be said about Gilmore and others like him than I have written in my short essay, reprinted here as Chapter 10. We need to acknowledge the frustration Gilmore must have felt as others fought to stave off his execution, and the way this must, understandably, have enraged him. One must confront the possibility that Gilmore had reached a sober and rational self-judgment of his wretchedness and of the worthlessness of his own life, at least in his eyes. He knew he had killed two innocent men for no reason whatsoever. What, in all honesty, *is* one to say to himself after doing that? These and other themes found no place in my essay, but not because I thought they were irrelevant or superficial. In any case, it is fitting that a book such as this should end with a comment on the first legal execution in the United States in ten years. It will probably not be the last.

Since these essays were originally prepared for widely different audiences, they vary considerably in length, style, amount of documentation, and detail. All but one were occasional pieces, prompted by immediate events and the needs of a particular audience. Apart from a few scholars with a special interest in the subject, no one has seen them all before. Many appeared in relatively inaccessible publications, and that is one reason for bringing them together now. Because it is my intention to share with the reader my own grasp of the diverse issues that make up the death penalty controversy in our time, I have arranged these essays essentially in chronological form. And though I would now put many things differently, I have thought it best to leave my remarks by and large unchanged from what they were when originally published. In that way, they show best the ideas and themes of main concern to me in the form in which they actually emerged. Accordingly, in revising the text and notes of the essays reprinted here, I have confined myself to such changes as were required to remove plain error, gross infelicities, and redundancies. Throughout, I have denied myself the pleasures of displaying the wisdom of hindsight, in order to let the reader experience the thoughts and feelings much as I had them at the time, of sobering defeats, unfolding possibilities, new ideas, alarming developments, and urgent needs. Reexamining tentative ventures through the underbrush and putative landmarks for the course ahead, as this book does, seems to me not less valid and interesting than a guided tour down the well-tended paths of a carefully landscaped park.

February 1977   *Hugo Adam Bedau*

The Courts, the Constitution, and Capital Punishment

1 The Issue of Capital Punishment

In February 1967, the President's Commission on Law Enforcement and Administration of Justice published its report, *The Challenge of Crime in a Free Society*. Supported by a third of a million words and dozens of graphs and tables, the commission advanced more than 200 specific recommendations touching every aspect of crime and criminal justice in the country. Many readers of the report will be shocked to discover that the perennial problem of capital punishment has been disposed of in barely one page! The commission's solitary recommendation could hardly have been briefer:

> The question whether capital punishment is an appropriate sanction is a policy decision to be made by each State. Where it is retained, the type of offenses for which it is available should be strictly limited, and the law should be enforced in an evenhanded and nondiscriminatory manner, with procedures for review of death sentences that are fair and expeditious. When a State finds that it cannot administer the penalty in such a manner, or that the death penalty is being imposed but not carried into effect, the penalty should be abandoned.[1]

There is some irony in the disproportionate public attention lavished upon the crime of murder and the issue of capital punishment (widely dramatized recently in the best-selling "nonfiction novel" by Truman Capote, *In Cold Blood*) and the near dismissal of the entire subject in the commission's report. Yet this relative neglect of a major social issue by the most distinguished group of public servants ever assembled under a mandate to scrutinize crime and punishment in America is not really surprising, if one is aware of the relevant facts over the past several decades. All one must do is review the practice of capital punishment in terms of the volume of capitally punishable crimes, the annual number of executions, the trends toward final disposition of death sentences and toward abolition of death penalties, and the attitudes of the public and responsible spokesmen.[2] Once these facts are grasped, the position of the commission and the familiar arguments for and against abolition can be viewed in a somewhat more intelligible light.

Murder, first of all, is by no means the only capital crime: treason, rape, kidnapping (with or without ransom), robbery, burglary, carnal knowledge, perjury in a capital case, and some two dozen other crimes (against property, persons, or the state) are all punishable by death somewhere in the United States. Few, however, carry a mandatory death penalty; nowhere today is either murder or rape, for instance, punishable by death except at the discretion of the court. Nor are all kinds and degrees of murder subject to the death penalty. Whatever may once have been meant by the Biblical injunction, "life for life, eye for eye, tooth for tooth," (*Exodus* XXI: 23-24), today at most it is first degree ("wilful, deliberate and premeditated") murder that carries the death penalty.

How frequently do capital crimes occur? In contrast to the rate and volume of crime generally, "crime and arrest data ... indicate no substantial increase in aggressive crimes during recent years."[3] This judgment is borne out by the statistics on "murder and nonnegligent manslaughter" as released by the FBI in its annual *Uniform Crime Reports* (see Table 1-1). No annual criminal statistics are reported on kidnappings; this itself is a measure of how infrequently this crime occurs. The annual statistics on rape show essentially the same trend as murder, namely, a fairly constant rate. In sum, crimes of personal violence (for which the death penalty is most typically imposed and thought to be justified) are moderate in volume for a population of nearly 200 million, and show no marked tendency to increase at present.

A reasonable estimate of the legal executions carried out in the United States since 1900 would put the total somewhere over 7,000. The greatest number in any one year—199—occurred in 1935.[4] These 199 were a typical sample of the total execution population. All but a few (3) were *male* (of the 3,857 persons executed since 1930, only 32 have been female). Most (119) were *white*, though the proportion of nonwhites (mainly Negroes) executed far exceeds the white/nonwhite ratio in the general population (exactly half of all executions between 1930 and 1966 have been of Negroes). The vast majority (184) were for the crime of *murder*; most of the rest (13) were for rape (since 1930, executions have actually been carried out for only seven crimes: murder, rape, armed robbery, kidnapping, burglary, espionage, and aggravated assault).

Last year, however, only *one* person was executed, by far the lowest figure in our history. Although all except six states have executed at least one criminal

Table 1-1
Murder in the United States, 1960-1965

Year	Number of Murders	Rate per 100,000 of Population
1960	9,140	5.1
1961	8,600	4.7
1962	8,400	4.5
1963	8,500	4.5
1964	9,250	4.8
1965	9,850	5.1

Source: *Uniform Crime Reports, 1960-1965.*

since 1930, the sharp decline (especially since 1960) in total executions and in the number of jurisdictions carrying out executions is evident (see Table 1-2).

However, in every year, the courts hand down far more death sentences than the prisons carry out. In the current decade, this gap has grown to disturbing proportions (see Table 1-3). These figures show that the trial courts have by no means ceased to hand down death sentences, and that with the decline in executions, the total number of persons under sentence of death has steadily mounted. Over the same period, the median time endured by those under sentence of death has stretched from roughly seventeen months to nearly *four years!* The explanation for this increasing delay is the development of postconviction remedies—thanks to the Supreme Court—that permit (some

Table 1-2
Executions in the United States, 1960-1966

Year	Total Executions	Total Executing Jurisdictions
1960	56	20
1961	42	18
1962	47	18
1963	21	13
1964	15	8
1965	7	4
1966	1	1

Source: *National Prisoner Statistics*, "Executions 1930-1966."

Table 1-3
Death Sentences in the United States, 1960-1967

Year	Total Death Sentences Issued	Total Persons Under Death Sentence at Beginning of Year
1960	113	189
1961	136	219
1962	99	266
1963	91	268
1964	98	298
1965	67	322
1966	113	351
1967	102	415

Source: *National Prisoner Statistics*, "Executions 1930-1968."

would say "encourage") appeal of felony convictions, particularly under *habeas corpus* proceedings. Lawyers across the nation, spurred by concern over civil liberties and civil rights, have managed to delay if not defeat almost every death sentence where they have made such an effort. As the President's Commission understandably put it, "All the members of the Commission agree that the present situation in the administration of the death penalty in many States is intolerable...."[5] Yet nothing in sight, short of outright abolition itself, promises to relieve this expensive and interminable process of appellate litigation.

The laws of the several dozen United States jurisdictions competent to impose the punishment of death—the fifty states, the District of Columbia, the Commonwealth of Puerto Rico, the Virgin Islands, and the federal government under civil law (extending to territorial, maritime, and interstate matters) and military law—have been so changeable that at no time in the past century have all these jurisdictions ever imposed the death penalty for a given crime (much less actually carried out an execution) in any given year. As early as 1794, Pennsylvania limited the death penalty to first degree murder. In 1846, the Territory of Michigan became the first English-speaking sovereignty to abolish the death penalty for murder. To date, nearly half the states of the union have experimented with abolition of the death penalty (see Table 1-4).

Much of the recent strength of the abolition movement stems from the decisive repeal of all death penalties in Oregon by public referendum in November 1964, by a vote of 455,654 to 302,105. Within six months, Vermont, Iowa, West Virginia and—most significantly—New York also abolished it for first degree murder (though with some exceptions; see the notes to Table 1-4). This brings to thirteen the number of states nominally at present without the death penalty, the greatest number and regional distribution of abolition jurisdictions at any one time in our history. Today, more Americans live without the threat (or protection) of capital punishment than ever before.

In the thirty years between the first Gallup Poll on capital punishment of April 1936, and the most recent Harris Survey of July 1966, public approval of the death penalty has dwindled from 62 percent to 38 percent, whereas abolition sentiment has grown from 33 percent to 47 percent. In the intervening years, other polls taken by the Gallup and the Roper organizations record considerable fluctuation; but they are consistent with the overall impression that the nation has changed within a generation from overwhelming support for the death penalty to a near majority in opposition to it. How stable this majority will prove to be, or how large and how rapidly it will grow, remains to be seen. But there is no doubt, if we may trust the polls, that the days of easy public acquiescence to capital punishment are over.

At the same time, several groups with a national constituency have taken public stands in favor of abolition. Most of the major Protestant denominations (Episcopal, Methodist, Congregational, Lutheran, Presbyterian, American Baptist) have been on record against the death penalty for several years. So have the Conference of American Rabbis and prominent Roman Catholic spokesmen,

Table 1-4
Abolition of Death Penalties in the United States, 1846-1966

Jurisdiction	Date of Abolition	Date of Restoration	Date of Reabolition
Michigan	1846[a]		
Rhode Island	1852[b]		
Wisconsin	1853		
Iowa	1872	1878	1965
Maine	1876[c]	1883	1887
Colorado	1897	1901	
Kansas	1907[d]	1935	
Minnesota	1911		
Washington	1913	1919	
Oregon	1914	1920	1964
North Dakota	1915[e]		
South Dakota	1915	1939	
Tennessee	1915[f]	1919	
Arizona	1916	1918	
Missouri	1917	1919	
Puerto Rico	1917	1919	1929
Alaska	1957		
Hawaii	1957		
Virgin Islands	1957		
Delaware	1958	1961	
West Virginia	1965		
Vermont	1965[g]		
New York	1965[h]		

Source: *National Prisoner Statistics, 1930-1970.*

[a] Death penalty retained for treason until 1963.

[b] Death penalty restored in 1882 for any life term convict who commits murder.

[c] In 1837 a law was passed to provide that no condemned person could be executed until one year after his sentencing and then only upon a warrant from the governor.

[d] In 1872 a law was passed similar to the 1837 Maine statute (see note c above).

[e] Death penalty retained for murder by a prisoner serving a life term for murder.

[f] Death penalty retained for rape.

[g] Death penalty retained for murder of a policeman or guard or by a prisoner guilty of a prior murder.

[h] Death penalty retained for murder of a police officer on duty, or of anyone by a prisoner under life sentence.

such as Richard Cardinal Cushing of Boston. Until recently, the major civil liberties, civil rights, and correctional organizations refused to take such a stand. Within the past two years, however, the American Civil Liberties Union, the NAACP Legal Defense and Educational Fund, the National Council on

Crime and Delinquency, and the American Correctional Association have publicly joined forces with the abolition movement, which has been led for forty years by the American League to Abolish Capital Punishment.

No less noteworthy has been the shift in public posture within the Department of Justice in Washington. For many years, the most outspoken defender of capital punishment in the country was Director of the FBI J. Edgar Hoover; his views on the subject were often released to law enforcement personnel through official FBI publications.[6]

But two years ago, in a letter to Congress, Ramsey Clark (later Attorney General), wrote:

We favor the abolition of the death penalty. Modern penology, with its correctional and rehabilitative skills, affords greater protection to society than the death penalty, which is inconsistent with its goals.[7]

He reiterated these views at his first official press conference in March 1967. Such sentiments, expressed by a government official so close to the White House, indicate clearly the changing climate of American opinion.

Arguments over the death penalty are legion; a recent tabulation listed no less than sixty-five for and eighty-seven against capital punishment![8] Despite their variety, they fall into two groups: those based essentially on empirical, utilitarian, or pragmatic considerations; and those reflecting essentially religious or moral convictions.

Among the arguments of the latter sort are these: the death penalty is the only punishment proportionate to the gravity of the offense; the death penalty is the only punishment whereby the murderer can expiate his crime; the death penalty is more humane than life imprisonment; in capital punishment the state indulges the very lust for vengeance it denies to its citizens; capital punishment violates the sanctity of human life; life imprisonment is more humane than capital punishment; and so on. Clearly, neither abolitionist nor retentionist has any monopoly on these nonempirical arguments.

But the questions that have drawn the most controversy are whether capital punishment can be equitably administered, whether it is an effective deterrent, and whether there is any viable alternative. These arguments raise issues to which evidence is directly relevant, even if it is not wholly conclusive.

It has been argued (with considerable basis, as shown above) that nonwhites bear a disproportionate share of all death penalties, and that capital punishment shows the effects of racial discrimination at every point. Two recent studies are specially pertinent here. One shows that the vagaries of appellate review of death sentences in Virginia have led to fifty-six executions for rape; in every case the convict was nonwhite.[9] Another study shows that the absence of any standards to guide the trial jury in its deliberations over the sentence of a person found guilty of first degree murder in New Jersey tends to allow racial prejudice to tip the scales against the Negro offender.[10] These are only indications of what fuller studies would probably reveal.

Quite apart from the way capital punishment works unfairness toward nonwhites, there is the ever-present danger of executing an innocent man. A tally in 1962 of all known cases where miscarriage of justice in murder cases had been alleged show that they occured at about the rate of one per year.[11] True, very few involved the actual execution of a demonstrably innocent person. But there were two dozen cases where the death sentence was averted and where the innocence of the convict was subsequently established beyond doubt.

Those in favor of the death penalty will, of course, argue that the risk of executing an innocent person is overestimated, and that such risk must be accepted if society is to have the fullest protection of the criminal law. Abolitionists will reply that unless some deterrent benefit from capital punishment can be clearly shown, there is no justification for risking an irreversible mistake.

But by far the greatest objection to the death penalty in terms of its inequities is simply this: given the fact that each year roughly 10,000 murders are committed, is there any reason to believe that the 100 or so sentenced to death and the handful finally executed were those who committed the most vicious crimes, were the most depraved and beyond rehabilitation, and had the benefit of counsel as skillful as the great majority who are never sentenced to death at all? Abolitionists question such comforting assumptions.

Although the President's Crime Commission Report (as quoted earlier) is not squarely in favor of abolition, it is unambiguous in its appraisal of the evidence over the crucial issue of deterrence.

It is impossible to say with certainty whether capital punishment significantly reduces the incidence of heinous crimes. The most complete study on the subject, based on a comparison of homicide rates in capital and non-capital jurisdictions, concluded that there is no discernible correlation between the availability of the death penalty and the homicide rate. This study also revealed that there was no significant difference between the two kinds of States in the safety of policemen. Another study of 27 states indicated that the availability of the death sentence had no effect on the rate of assaults and murders of prison guards.[12]

The results summarized here have been widely discussed wherever the death penalty has been seriously examined. They derive from the statistical tabulations drawn up by Thorsten Sellin and his associates at the University of Pennsylvania a decade or so ago and have been frequently reprinted and are readily available.[13] In each case, Sellin's evidence tends to show not that capital punishment is no deterrent, but that there is no evidence that capital punishment is a deterrent superior to imprisonment.

Since all the statistical data essentially reinforces this point, abolitionists are understandably confused by the undiminished confidence with which many retentionists cling to the doctrine of the unique deterrent efficacy of the death penalty. For instance, the Report of the New Jersey Commission to Study Capital Punishment stated, in support of its recommendation not to abolish the death penalty, that "those most intimately concerned with law enforcement gave evidence and their conclusion is that capital punishment is a deterrent in some cases."[14] Such a statement blurs the distinction between (1) whether the death penalty is or is not a deterrent, and (2) whether it is a more effective deterrent than the alternative of imprisonment. Moreover, the judgment quoted above rests essentially not on statistical but on anecdotal evidence, and there are anecdotes to the contrary as well; they are in the nature of the case inconclusive. It is safe to say that the vast majority of those who have studied Sellin's data concerning the alleged deterrent efficacy of capital punishment have rendered a Scottish verdict: "Not proven."

Whereas many Americans are apprehensive lest the rehabilitative ideal in penology turn our prisons into country clubs, most Europeans are aghast at the draconian punishments commonly inflicted under our statutes. European penologists have long been adjusted to the idea that no class of offender should be permanently barred from the possibility of eventual release; and that, moreover, prison terms should be as short as possible (for the crime of murder, very often no more than five to ten years).[15]

Yet one of the major obstacles to abolition of the death penalty has been the question whether murderers can be safely imprisoned and eventually released without again preying upon the public. Actually, murderers probably have less tendency to repeat their crime (either inside prison or outside, after release) than any other class of offender. A study of some 1,158 released and paroled murderers in eight states (California, Connecticut, Maryland, Massachusetts, Michigan, New York, Ohio, Rhode Island) over the past several decades showed this: six committed another murder, nine others committed a crime of personal violence or some other felony.[16] This is not, to be sure, a perfect record. Yet it does show that public confidence in parole boards, release procedures, and programs of rehabilitation, however faulty they may be in fact, is not misplaced.

Retentionists, if they are to be consistent, must argue that it is better for a thousand murderers to be executed (even though they can be safely released) than for the lives of half a dozen innocent persons to be sacrificed. Abolitionists find this unacceptable.

The argument against capital punishment and in favor of abolition is by no means conclusively established. Not only capital punishment but all criminal justice is liable to the complaint that it is riddled with inequities. It seems a moral certainty, furthermore, that sometimes at least the death penalty must have served to deter crime where life imprisonment would have failed. Nor can anyone claim, finally, that life imprisonment (which, of course, does not mean "life" at all) offers complete protection to society. Yet the trends in public opinion, the views of government spokesmen, the unmistakable decline in executions, and the piecemeal abolition of death penalties across the nation—all these are clear signs that whatever the facts and the consequences, the death penalty is now in the twilight of its historical role as a mode of social defense against crime in America.

2

The Courts, the Constitution, and Capital Punishment

Whenever legislatures refuse to modify the law in response to demands for reform, other governmental institutions through which these demands can be satisfied should be explored. In our nation, reform denied in the legislature can sometimes be obtained through the appellate courts because legislative action can be limited by the rule of constitutional law with its provision for basic rights and liberties, and because final interpretation rests with an independent judiciary empowered to review and nullify statutory enactments. During the 1950s and early 1960s, it was not the Congress but the Supreme Court that instructed the nation in the meaning of "equal protection of the laws" under the Constitution as it applies to all Americans in schools and other public facilities. A few state legislatures anticipated the court decisions by repealing the inherited segregationist laws or by passing antidiscrimination legislation, but many other legislatures turned a deaf ear to the demands for reform. One could cite other instances where legislative inertia has been overcome only by judicial initiative. To mention but one other contemporary example, the "loyalty oaths" imposed on public employees, including teachers, have at last been falling in state after state thanks to court decisions which have found these oaths invalid and unconstitutional. In no case, however, has a legislature itself undone its misguided enactments in this area; the work of reform has been accomplished almost entirely by the judiciary.

In the United States today, one is tempted to guess that repeal of the death penalty is roughly at the same point that abolition of slavery would be had there been no Emancipation Proclamation and no Civil War. This country's slow and uneven progress toward abolition of capital punishment has depended upon the fitful attention of the several state legislatures, rarely noted for their preoccupation with the task of penal reform. Given the affront to human dignity of this anachronistic penalty, one naturally wonders whether the lethargy of the legislatures might not be effectively outflanked by recourse to the courts and the Constitution. In another place, I have proposed that eventually there ought to be a constitutional prohibition of the death penalty.[1] Although this would not be a specially plausible political tactic for abolitionists to pursue, it would be a fitting way to record society's total repudiation of this mode of punishment. But before this idea is pursued, a prior strategy commends itself. Why not try to establish the unconstitutionality of the death penalty under the Constitution as it already stands, and rid ourselves of this blight in the same way we are ridding ourselves of legally protected racial discriminations and legally imposed tests of "loyalty"? With one eye on the resources of the existing Constitution and its possible interpretation by the courts, why not reformulate the argument against the death penalty to establish that it is a violation of civil rights and civil liberties? So might speculation run. After all, is this not precisely what reformers envisioned and then persuaded the Supreme Court to do in *Brown v. Board of Education*, when racial segregation in the public schools was struck down as "inherently unequal" under the Fourteenth Amendment?

Death penalties have, of course, long been attacked on constitutional grounds, and often successfully. Many a man sentenced to death has owed his life to state or federal Constitutions as interpreted by the higher courts. When a death sentence has been voided, it is usually by setting aside the *conviction* on which the sentence rests—for example, by holding that the trial court failed to grant the defendant "due process of law" as required under the Fifth and Fourteenth amendments. Rarely if at all has it been determined that even though no error undermined the conviction, some constitutionally prohibited flaw attached to the imposition of the *sentence* itself. And in no case has any appellate court, state or federal, ever voided a death sentence on the ground that the *penal law* which prescribed this punishment was itself unconstitutional. It is precisely and solely the arguments necessary to reach this latter conclusion that concern us here.

That no court has yet read the Constitution in this way does not of itself prevent such a development in the future. A century ago, the members of the Supreme Court thought that the Bill of Rights could not be used to interfere with *any* of the practices a state might choose to impose in its own jurisdiction under its own laws! A generation ago, few constitutional lawyers would have predicted that the Supreme Court would ever scrutinize unequally apportioned congressional districts and judge them to violate the Constitution; such a matter was clearly a "political question" beyond the power of judicial review. Clearly, the history of the federal Constitution, with its continuing interpretation by the Supreme Court, shows that it has the capacity for growth and can, with imagination, be kept relevant to the changing needs of society. So the death penalty, at one time taken for granted by all men (save for a few eccentrics and visionaries) as a bulwark of social order, may itself be on the verge of assault from a quarter hardly imaginable a few years ago.

Today, there is more than mere speculation behind these suggestions. From at least three directions this course of events has now begun to unfold. In October 1963, three members of the Supreme Court, in a dissenting opinion written by Justice Arthur J. Goldberg, reasoned that the Court ought to hear argument on the question whether "the imposition of the death penalty on a convicted rapist who has neither taken or endangered human life" is in violation of the Constitution, particularly if "the permissible aims of punishment (e.g., deterrence, isolation, rehabilitation) [can] be achieved as effectively by punishing rape less severely than by death (e.g., by life imprisonment) . . . ."[2] This opinion signalled that more than one member of the Court was willing to hear argument that most observers would have doubted the Court would ever consider. A year and a half later, in April 1965, the American Civil Liberties Union (ACLU), after wrestling with the problem for several years, revised its position on capital punishment and introduced its new policy with these words:

> ... capital punishment is so inconsistent with the underlying values of a democratic system that the imposition of the death penalty for any crime is a denial of civil liberties. We believe that past decisions to the contrary are in error, and we will seek the repeal of existing laws imposing the death penalty, and will seek reversal of convictions carrying a sentence of death.[3]

This policy statement is significant primarily because it comes from the one national organization devoted to interpreting and securing enforcement of the Bill of Rights as a living force in American life. If the ACLU thinks capital punishment is unconstitutional, perhaps it is. During August 1967, in two class actions, *Adderly v. Wainwright* and *Hill v. Nelson* (argued by the NAACP Legal Defense and Educational Fund (LDF) and the ACLU attorneys), injunctions staying all executions were granted to enable the lower federal courts to decide whether the death penalty violates the Constitution.[4] This is unprecedented recognition by the courts of the possible conflict between civil liberties and capital punishment.

In the United States today there are forty-three jurisdictions (forty-one states, the District of Columbia, and the federal government) in which one or more crimes are punishable by death, and the capital laws in these jurisdictions total several hundred. The status of these laws is best understood in terms of three pairs of distinctions: statutory as opposed to constitutional, state as opposed to federal, and discretionary as opposed to mandatory. In 1968, few state and no federal death penalties are constitutionally imposed. With the exception of Oregon, where between 1920 and 1964 the death penalty for first degree murder was imposed by the state constitution,[5] all executions in modern times have been authorized by *statutory* law. All but a few of these death sentences have, in turn, been imposed under *state* law. Less than 1 percent of all persons executed since 1930 were convicted of federal crimes. In addition, the vast majority of all death sentences have issued under the *discretionary* sentencing authority of the court (usually the jury). Of the nearly 4,000 executions in this country since 1930, no more than 10 percent have been for crimes that carry a mandatory death penalty. (Moreover, 95 percent of all executions during this period have been for the crime of first degree murder.) The issue before us, then, reduces for all practical purposes to this: how might the Supreme Court conclude that the capital statutes in the states that give sentencing discretion to the jury are unconstitutional under the federal Constitution?

Let us begin by considering which clauses in the Constitution might conceivably bear the required interpretation. There are at most five passages that might be used to reach the desired conclusion. Given appropriate supporting argument, the courts conceivably could conclude that: (A) any attempt to "deprive" a person of his "life" involves a violation of "due process of law" (Fifth and Fourteenth Amendments); (B) it is not possible to try a defendant by an "impartial jury" where the death sentence is involved (Sixth Amendment); (C) the death penalty is a "cruel and unusual punishment" (Eighth Amendment); (D) the death sentence violates "certain rights ... retained by the people" (Ninth Amendment); (E) anyone sentenced to death has been denied "equal protection of the laws" (Fourteenth Amendment). More than one line of reasoning could be developed on behalf of each of these interpretations. Indeed, theoretically, there are an infinite number of different arguments which could serve to establish any of these results. But they would all be variations on one or more of these five constitutional themes.[6]

Before turning to examine this quintet of possibilities one by one, a few preliminary observations may help to set them in the proper perspective. First, none of these constitutional interpretations could be supported by historical research into the original intention of the Congress or the states in proposing and ratifying these amendments. During the debates prior to adoption of the Bill of Rights in 1789 and the Fourteenth Amendment in 1865, there seems to have been no attempt to discuss a possible application of these constitutional provisions to the issue of capital punishment. At least we have no record of such discussions, with one exception. In debating the Eighth Amendment, a possible future application to bar the death penalty was anticipated, and this was urged at the time as one of the reasons *against* adopting it. "[I]t is sometimes necessary to hang a man, villains often deserve whipping ... ," one congressman argued, "but are we, in future to be prevented from inflicting these punishments because they are cruel?"[7] What inferences we may draw consistent with the amendment's ensuing adoption remains to be seen. Here, we may content ourselves by observing that our interest today in the "original intent of the framers," if it is to be more than an exercise in historical scholarship, must take its dominant cues from the constitutional (structural, fundamental) needs of our society and our ideals and aspirations as they are understood today. Justice Hugo L. Black was quite right when he denied that "our ultimate constitutional freedoms are no more than our English ancestors had when they came to this new land to get new freedoms."[8] It is equally mistaken to let these ultimate constitutional freedoms rest upon the presumed intentions and understandings of our earliest constitutional deliberations, except as those deliberations help us to penetrate into the farthest limits of our rights.

Second, although to date the federal and state appellate courts have not advanced any of the five constitutional interpretations suggested above, it is settled law that both state and federal courts accept the applicability of the Fifth, Sixth, Eighth, and Ninth Amendments to state penal codes, at least in those respects pertinent to the arguments considered here.[9] True, the theory of constitutional interpretation under which these amendments to the *federal* Constitution apply to the *states* is something on which constitutional lawyers and even the justices of the Supreme Court themselves continue to differ. But there is no disagreement as to the fact of application. No bar to our arguments, then, can arise from this quarter, though as recently as a generation ago it would have been the source of a fatal objection.

Third, we should note that the five arguments fall into two categories. Some of the arguments, viz., (A), (B), and (E), attack the death penalty collaterally, through faulting the procedures under which it is administered; while the other two attack it directly, through faulting the substance of such a penalty no matter how it is (actually or conceivably) administered. Of these five arguments, to date only two, (A) and (E), have already been successful in obtaining reversals of death penalty convictions in particular cases. So, what we are envisioning here is an enlargement of these arguments to attack not only particular convictions or sentences but entire statutes.

Perhaps the most convenient way to discuss the arguments before us is to examine the three procedural ones first, and to appraise them in the order in which the issues raised follow the sequence of events in a criminal trial. Then we may consider the two remaining nonprocedural arguments. Accordingly, I shall take up the five arguments in this order: (B), (E), (A), (C), and (D).

i An Impartial Jury

Gallup, Roper, and Harris public opinion polls over the past thirty years indicate a steady decline in approval of the death penalty by the general public. Between the first national poll on capital punishment in April 1936, and the most recent one in July 1966, public approval of the death penalty has dwindled from 62 percent to 38 percent, while abolition sentiment has increased from 33 percent to 47 percent. In the intervening decades, other polls taken record considerable fluctuation; but they are consistent with the overall impression that within a generation the nation has changed from widespread support for the death penalty to near majority opposition to it. Today, it looks as if not even half the population is willing to see *anyone* executed in punishment for murder. Or so the polls indicate.

We may prefer to rely instead on the evidence afforded by jury impanelling in capital cases. In recent years, probably a majority of the prospective jurors in capital trials have been disqualified on the ground that they declare conscientious opposition to the death penalty under any circumstances. The average citizen, faced with the actual prospect of trying a case where the defendant's life is in the balance, is frequently unwilling to accept the task. We do not, to be sure, have any statistics on this point. But I do not think experienced students of criminal trials will deny that it is difficult and occasionally impossible to impanel a so-called "death-qualified" jury. Two examples, one extreme and one typical, will illustrate the problem. In New Jersey, the prosecutor in one case found himself, though "reluctant," urging the court to accept the defendant's plea of no defense (*nolo contendere*—tantamount to a plea of guilty) because "two days of interrogation of thirty-seven prospective jurors failed to seat even one." The prosecutor attributed this failure to "a general reluctance on the part of all talesmen to ask for the death penalty."[10] Nothing about the defendant, his victim, the court, the local population, or New Jersey's official attitude toward capital punishment would have led anyone to expect that a jury could not even be impanelled. More typical is a Texas case where eighty-eight prospective jurors were examined before a dozen were impanelled. What is the explanation?

Forty-two ... were challenged for cause by the prosecution and excused from service by the trial judge because of scruples against capital punishment. Moreover, the prosecution exercised eleven *peremptory* challenges [differing from challenges for *cause* in that no reason need be given for their exercise] for the apparent purpose of eliminating other jurors who, while affording inadequate basis for a challenge for cause none the less evinced a "weakness" on the death penalty.[11]

So, on these two occasions, when directly confronted with the issue of capital punishment, these members of the public voted thirty-seven to zero and (at least) fifty-three to thirty-five against it. Cynics will argue that almost all prospective jurors are only too anxious to avoid jury duty, and that many will plead conscientious scruples (which they really do not have) in the knowledge that this will excuse them. Yet the opinion poll evidence reinforces the evidence from the jury box.

These facts about community sentiment and the composition of every capital jury raise three questions, each of which has constitutional overtones because each touches on the notion of an "impartial jury," as that term has been interpreted by the courts: (1) How can a death-qualified jury be impartial on the question of sentence? (2) How can a death-qualified jury be a true "jury of one's peers"? (3) How can a death-qualified jury be unbiased on all factual issues disputed in court upon which determination of the defendant's guilt itself rests? No one can dispute the ACLU's succinct conclusion that "the state is protected from a jury biased against the death penalty, but the defendant is not protected against a jury biased in favor of the death penalty."[12] In perhaps the only case so far decided in which this challenge was squarely faced, the Oregon Supreme Court, claimed that such an objection as this

rests upon the false premise that a person who believes in capital punishment, or at least one who has no conscientious scruples against it, is apt to be unfair and vindictive. This is practically an indictment of the people of Oregon, for it is by their will that capital punishment is authorized in this state .... The Constitution and the statutes assume, as well they may, that a man or a woman may have no conscientious scruples against capital punishment and yet be a fair and impartial juror.[13]

But surely this "assumption" *is* highly implausible as an answer to the objections (1) and (2). As to (1), the death-qualified jury is bound to be death-inclined on the question of punishment. That a jury, composed of individuals who expressed no unwillingness to impose this penalty in at least some hypothetical case, should be wholly free from bias in the actual case before it, is not a plausible assumption at all. It is preposterous to assume that such a jury, evidently composed of some of the most vindictive of eligible jurors, would restrain its collective attitude and consider an alternative penalty without bias either way. It would be more reasonable to say that "those who survive the examination, and thus man the jury box, become almost *volunteers*—that they are not merely impartial on the death penalty, but affirmatively support it."[14] It is no reply to remind us that death-qualified juries often do not bring in a death sentence. One might as well argue that confessions extracted by third degree methods ought to be allowed in evidence because juries would not always believe them.

As to (2), there is a legitmate presumption that the jury is not "impartial" if it is not a "jury of one's peers"; and there is a legitimate presumption that it is not of one's peers if it is not a representative jury, "a body truly representative of the community."[15] But given the public's hostility to the death penalty, how can anyone indicted for a capital crime ever be tried by a jury of *his* peers, by "a body truly representative of the community," so long as his jury must be death qualified? The objection was lodged before the California courts in a 1965 case in these words:

What the state is interested in is having the fate of the defendant left to the "absolute discretion" of a representative jury . . . . If the People cannot "prefer" the death penalty, and if the question of life or death is left to the "absolute discretion" of a representative jury, then there can be no justification for permitting the People's representative, the prosecutor, to demand as a matter of right a jury purged of all those who do not believe, for one reason or another, that capital punishment ought to be imposed.

Today, a large number of appellants' "peers" believe that the death penalty cannot be justified in the light of humanity and modern penology. There is no such thing as a representative jury from which all opponents of the death penalty have been excluded. To permit the court to excuse those jurors for cause is to deprive the accused of his constitutional rights to a jury trial . . . .[16]

When we turn to (3), we reach the only truly open question of the three. Is there any reason to believe that a death-qualified jury is more likely than a truly representative jury to convict on a given body of evidence? Is it less likely, for instance, to accept the defendant's plea of insanity? Is it more likely to decide all or some disputed factual issues adversely to the defendant? (One is reminded of the lady juror in an old *New Yorker* cartoon. After the judge's admonition to ignore a witness's prejudicial remarks, she turned to her neighbor and snapped, "Well, I don't intend to 'strike that' from *my* record!") In the nature of the case there is no direct evidence in point because no capital defendant has ever been tried by both kinds of juries.

There is some indirect evidence, however, in research undertaken by Walter Oberer and Cody Wilson. Oberer argued that in his experience the prosecutor seeks a death-qualified jury even when he has no intention of seeking the death penalty because in this way, he "expects to get a 'better' jury for its purpose—one that will be more responsible to the prosecution's case on the guilt-innocence issue...."[17] Through a test to determine an individual's proneness to find a verdict under different hypothetical fact-situations, Oberer and Wilson learned that those "who believed in capital punishment more often felt that the defendant in simulated capital cases was guilty than did those ... who did not believe in capital punishment."[18] Also, the former "were more confident of their decisions about guilt and innocence." In addition, they were "more likely to impose harsher penalties on a person convicted of crime—even when the death penalty was not considered."[19] These results were only the preliminary findings of their research; unfortunately, the project was abandoned before completion.[20] If substantiated, these results would raise serious doubt over the assumption against bias which the courts have so far placed beyond rebuttal.

In 1966, Robert F. Crosson reported research tantamount to a partial test of the Oberer-Wilson hypothesis. Drawing the experimental and control groups from the *voir dire* of Cuyahoga County Criminal Court (Cleveland, Ohio), the author showed that (a) the death-qualified (DQ) jurors were "significantly ... more conservative in their political attitudes" than the "death scruple" (DS) jurors, and thus exhibit the marked cluster of traits commonly known to social psychologists as the "authoritarian personality." The result is that "more of the humanitarian jurors appear to be denied representation on ... [the] jury."[21] His investigation also showed that (b) the DS jurors were "better able to think critically and evaluate verbal arguments" than the DQ jurors, though (a) was confirmed less significantly than (b). Crosson's overall conclusion was that "the results of this study suggest that removal of the death qualification from the capital *voir dire* would be a step in the direction of fairer representation which might better serve justice rather than just the prosecution."[22] So far, of course, the evidence supplied by Oberer, Wilson, and Crosson is far from conclusive, and probably would not suffice to persuade any court to reverse a death penalty conviction, much less to invalidate an entire statute, on the ground that in all capital cases the death-qualified jury is biased against the defendant even on issues having nothing directly to do with sentence. Yet this sort of evidence is relevant to that conclusion, and one would expect to see it confirmed by further research.[23]

Now, let us suppose *arguendo* that one or more of the three objections, (1)-(3), is both plausible on the evidence and suitably brought on appeal before the Supreme Court.[24] How would a ruling against death-qualified juries affect capital punishment? Even if the Court ruled that death-qualified juries are improperly "partial," all capital statutes would remain intact and untouched. At most, abandonment of the present practice, which permits the prosecution to challenge any juror for cause because of his conscientious scruples, would severely handicap the prosecution in obtaining death sentences. A prosecutor could still count on a limited number of peremptory challenges to help him keep those he thought most likely to oppose the death penalty off the jury. But peremptory challenges alone would rarely suffice to remove from a jury all who were conscientiously opposed to capital punishment. A decade ago, the California Supreme Court bluntly stated that to depart from the prevailing practice "would in all probability work a *de facto* abolition of capital punishment."[25] Although this view is not shared by all the courts,[26] it is possibly correct, and it is worth seeing why.

Since the typical capital jury would then include one or more members opposed to the death penalty under any circumstances, either the jury would be certain to agree upon a recommendation of mercy, since the unanimity required for the death penalty would be beyond reach, or the prosecutor would have to face the prospect of a hung jury, unable to agree on any verdict, as his price for resolutely seeking the death penalty. Any legislature wishing to provide for the regular enforcement of its capital statutes under these conditions would confront a serious dilemma. Legislatures could abandon death qualification if (but only if) they could also revise the rule of unanimity. There is little likelihood that legislatures could, by statutory enactment, effect this expedient. The rule of unanimity in jury verdicts, especially in serious felony cases, is firmly rooted in tradition and practice. The Supreme Court itself has said:

Unanimity in jury verdicts is required where the Sixth and Seventh Amendments apply. In criminal cases this requirement of unanimity extends to all issues— character or degree of the crime, guilt and punishment—which are left to the jury.[27]

Legal scholars would agree that the unanimity rule was intended to, and does in fact, afford a considerable protection to the defendant. It is very doubtful that appellate courts would hold that it should be waived solely for the purpose of making it easier for the state to execute criminals. Even though the courts have not ruled out "blue ribbon" juries because they are conviction-prone,[28] we could hardly expect them to look with equal tolerance upon execution-prone juries.

Another alternative theoretically open to a legislature so inclined would be to repeal all its discretionary death penalties in favor of mandatory ones—a return to the practice of a century ago. Yet even this would not guarantee against *de facto* abolition. Juries could evade the intended effect by finding defendants guilty of second degree murder or manslaughter, rather than of first degree murder (which alone carries the death penalty). Cases during the past century have been reported where juries did precisely this.[29] So, nothing less than abandoning both jury sentencing discretion and the distinction of degrees of murder would suffice to preserve the regular enforcement of capital punishment. It is difficult to believe that any legislature would undertake such extreme measures. To do so would be to risk paralyzing the criminal courts. Today, it is possible to have statutes that impose a mandatory death penalty only if no one is ever indicted—for example, treason or perjury in a capital case—as any legislature that contemplated turning back the clock in this fashion would quickly discover.

Perhaps as a last resort the legislatures might increase the permissible number of peremptory challenges from a few to several dozen. But it is doubtful that if the courts did prohibit the use of death-qualified juries, they would permit them to reenter the jury box, as it were, by the back door. One is tempted to conclude that ending the nearly universal practice of using death-qualified juries in capital cases might indeed result in *de facto* abolition.

Two interesting developments that may initiate a trend in this direction have recently occurred. In 1965, the Supreme Court of New Jersey simply notified all its lower criminal courts that, henceforth, in capital cases where the prosecutor did not intend to seek the death penalty and so notified the court and defense counsel, he would be forbidden from inquiring into the attitudes toward capital punishment of prospective jurors.[30] The court's reason for this ruling was the need to expedite cases at trial. The court's maneuver is bound to encourage New Jersey prosecutors to spare their energy and the county treasury by abandoning any intention of seeking the death penalty in cases where the prospects of success are marginal. By risking the disapproval of the most vindictively minded citizens, the prosecution runs a good chance of getting a conviction without subsequent endless appeals and the definite possibility of reversal. Yet the effect of such a procedure, if widely followed elsewhere, can only be to emphasize the biased character of death-qualified juries that do bring in death sentences. This, in turn, will pave the way for a reversal on appeal in some or even all such cases.

Much more interesting than the New Jersey court's 1965 ruling is the Maryland statute enacted in April 1967, which reads: "Hereafter no person shall be disqualified for service as a juror of this State by reason of his beliefs against capital punishment."[31] This statute abolishing death-qualified juries by legislative action is unprecedented.

The effect of such changes as these in New Jersey and Maryland upon the death penalty is not precisely calculable. How near to *de facto* abolition these rulings will bring these two states is also not clear. Opponents of the death penalty dare not be too sanguine. They should know that during the seventy years Iowa was without death-qualification of its capital juries, from the execution of Lee in 1894 to legislative abolition of the death penalty in 1965, thirty-nine executions—about one every two years—were recorded under state law.[32]

ii Equal Protection of the Laws

"The discretionary use of the death penalty requires a decision which no human should be called upon to make."[33] So conclude Harry Kalven and Hans Zeisel, authors of the first scientific study of the American criminal trial jury. Yet juries throughout the country have been making just such decisions almost daily. Students of the criminal law deserve to be disturbed by this practice for at least two reasons. First, none of the statutes authorizing jury discretion in capital punishment specifies any standards for a jury to follow in arriving at its decision; few of the statutes even require, as does New Jersey's, that the jury reach its decision "upon and after the consideration of all the evidence." In only a few states may evidence be introduced if it is relevant solely to the issue of punishment. A more typical practice has been explained by the California Supreme Court:

[T]he legislature fixed no standards for the guidance of the jury in determining whether a defendant should suffer the penalty of life imprisonment or death, and to that extent left the function of the jury in a somewhat nebulous state.[34]

Section 190 [prescribing the punishment for first degree murder] ... imposes neither death nor life imprisonment, but with a perfectly even hand presents the two alternatives to the jury. The legislature, perhaps because of the very gravity of the choice, has formulated no rules to control the exercise of the jury's discretion.[35]

This absence of standards has been rationalized on the implicit ground that the jury, in recommending mercy, in effect is exercising a prerogative strictly analogous to executive clemency. No one claims the chief executive's exercise of the clemency power should be controlled by statutory-based standards; so why should the trial jury's? This view, it must be said, quite ignores the well-established position that the exercise of sentencing discretion is wholly a judicial responsibility, no matter whether exercised by judge or jury, and that, therefore, standards and not caprice must govern the discharge of this task. Second, the jury's sentence, once decided, is all but unaccountable to any higher judicial authority. Only in four states (as of 1953) could the trial judge refuse to follow the jury's recommendation. Appellate courts have rarely been willing to review the jury's exercise of its discretion. Typical is this judgment from the Pennsylvania Supreme Court: "The jury ... imposed the penalty of death and, since it is they in whom the statute . . . vests discretion to fix the penalty, it is not for this Court to review their decision."[36] In its latest dictum on the matter, the Supreme Court itself has noted: "[W]e intend to cast no doubt whatever on the constitutionality of the settled practice of many States to leave to juries finding defendants guilty of a crime the power to fix punishment within legally prescribed limits."[37]

Especially in capital cases, it has been believed for some time that juries have yielded to prejudice against certain classes of defendants and sentenced them more severely. Of course, some of the things that typically offend juries, and therefore dissuade them from a recommendation of mercy, justifiably do so. But no one can argue that such justifiable indignation is always what lies behind the jury's imposition of the death penalty. It is, for example, impossible to account in this way for the fact that in six jurisdictions since 1930, a total of sixty-seven nonwhites have been executed for rape, but not a single white; and that throughout the South, execution for rape has claimed nearly ten times as many blacks as whites.[38] Given the chronic racial sickness from which this nation suffers, and the studied practice in most communities whereby even the courts have been an instrument of white supremacy, one would expect that the unguided and irrevocable sentencing discretion of capital juries would be used in a racially biased way, and that blacks could be shown to have received a statistically significant disproportion of all death sentences for murder as well as for rape, the two crimes that have accounted for 98 percent of all executions since 1930. A close scrutiny of appealed cases has shown that, despite the ostensible policy of nonreview of sentences, the federal courts have in fact reviewed and revised state court sentences insofar as the defects could be attributed to unconstitutional faults in the sentencing procedure. Could it not be argued that the very statutes that fail to provide standards for and review of the exercise of jury discretion in capital cases, and that demonstrably result in racial discrimination, contain an unconstitutional procedural fault because they fail to provide for the "equal protection of the laws"? Let us consider this proposition in detail, first with respect to murder, and then to rape.

In 1961, it was argued on appeal in a New Jersey case that the state's jury discretion statute for first degree murder was unconstitutional because the lack of standards required the jury to make "arbitrary and invidious discriminations," with the result that "persons belonging to minority groups" were "necessarily subject" to "greater and more severe punishment than others in similar circumstances."[39] To this allegation, the New Jersey Supreme Court replied in the language common to all courts to date on this issue: "A determination of what circumstances make the imposition of capital punishment unjust or unwise is left to the collective discretion and judgment of the jury . . . ."[40] A year later, the Kansas Supreme Court rejected a similar argument in the same way. The New Jersey court did not review the factual basis for the allegations in the appellant's brief, and the United States Supreme Court refused to hear argument. Not until four years later was the evidence published elsewhere and made generally available,[41] and even then it went largely unnoticed. The evidence showed that the death sentence, as it had been imposed in New Jersey between the years 1937 and 1961, could be statistically correlated to a significant degree with only one important variable—the race of the defendant. Convict a black man of first degree murder and, quite apart from whether his crime occurred in the course of committing another felony, or whether it was committed in an especially brutal manner, he was more likely than a white murderer to receive a death sentence. An admitted weakness in the research was the control of too few of the relevant variables. Noticeably neglected were the status of the victim ("cop killers" tend to be sentenced to death) and the status of defendant's counsel (convicts with court-appointed counsel are more likely to be sentenced to death).[42] This study is the only one currently available on this extremely important issue, and, despite its limitations, there is no reason to doubt that comparable results would be reached for other jurisdictions if only the data were gathered and examined. No appellate court to date has really been forced to assess this evidence of racial discrimination in jury sentencing discretion.

Beginning in 1965, the LDF sponsored an investigation of jury-imposed capital punishment for rape in eleven of the sixteen states still punishing this crime with death. The results of this investigation, although far from completely reported as of this writing, have already been brought into litigation in several cases. The details of the research, so far as they affect the punishment for rape, are reviewed in the decision of the federal district court in the Arkansas case of *Maxwell v. Bishop* and in more detail in Maxwell's appeal brief before the Eighth Circuit Court of Appeals. The district court fairly summarized the results of the research, which had been designed, interpreted, and reported to the court by Marvin E. Wolfgang, a nationally known criminologist.[43] The court's summary deserves to be quoted in its entirety:

As far as Arkansas is concerned, Dr. Wolfgang caused Mr. John Monroe, a qualified statistician, to select a representative sample of Arkansas counties with reference to which the study would be made. The sample drawn by Mr. Monroe, who testified at the hearing, consisted of 19 counties in the State.

During the summer of 1965 law students interested in civil rights problems were sent to Arkansas to gather basic data with respect to all rape convictions in the sample counties for a period beginning January 1, 1945, and extending to the time of the investigation. Data obtained as to individual cases were recorded on individual case schedules. When the work was completed, the individual schedules were turned over to Dr. Wolfgang for evaluation.

The investigation brought to light 55 rape convictions during the study period involving 34 Negro men and 21 white men. The offenses fell into three categories, namely: rapes of white women by Negro men; rapes of Negro women by Negro men; and rapes of white women by white men. No convictions of white men for raping Negro women were found.

Dr. Wolfgang found that of the 34 Negroes convicted of rape 10 had been sentenced to death and 24 had been sentenced to life imprisonment; the corresponding figures for the white offenders were 4 and 17. The witness did not consider that particular variation to be of great significance. But he did attach great significance to the fact that of the 19 Negroes convicted of raping white women 9, or nearly 50 percent, had been sentenced to death, whereas in other racial situations only 5 death sentences had been imposed, those 5 sentences representing only about 14 percent of the total sentences imposed in those situations.

Using recognized statistical procedures Dr. Wolfgang undertook to determine whether the differential in the imposition of the death sentence was due to some factor other than the association between Negro offender and white victim. He concluded, and the Court agrees, that the differential could not be due to the operation of the laws of chance.

The witness then proceeded to consider race in relation to certain variables appearing in rape cases, and also to consider sentences imposed in relation to such variables. He found that race had significant associations with certain variables but not with others, but he also found that in general the sentences imposed had nothing significant to do with the variables, other than the combination of Negro offenders and white victims.

Without stopping to go into further detail, the Court will state that it understands Dr. Wolfgang's conclusion to be that a Negro man who is convicted of raping a white woman has about a 50 percent chance of receiving a death sentence, regardless of the facts and circumstances surrounding the crime, whereas a man who is convicted of criminally assaulting a woman of his own race stands only about a 14 percent chance of receiving the death sentence.

Petitioner has made no effort here to show that the individual jury which tried and convicted him acted in his particular case with racial discrimination. Rather, petitioner urges that a showing of a pattern of racial discrimination in the imposition of the death penalty makes a prima facie showing of such discrimination in a particular case; that a failure of an Arkansas jury to assess punishment at life imprisonment in a capital case is tantamount to an assessment of the death penalty; and that it is unconstitutional for a jury to permit a death sentence to be imposed on a Negro man convicted of raping a white woman if it would have assessed a penalty of life imprisonment had the defendant been white and had he raped the same women in the same or similar circumstances.[44]

The court refused to reverse Maxwell's sentence and offered several reasons: the statistical evidence was not sufficient to establish that the jury which convicted and sentenced Maxwell did so because of bias against him on account of his race; the statistical evidence of itself was not "sufficiently broad, accurate, or precise as to establish satisfactorily that Arkansas juries in general practice unconstitutional racial discrimination in rape cases involving Negro men and white women...."; the evidence was based merely on a sample of all rape cases in Arkansas and an unrepresentative sample at that; and, finally, "such discrimination...can[not] be detected accurately by a statistical analysis such as was undertaken here. Statistics are elusive things at best, and it is a truism that almost anything can be proved by them."[45] If the appellant's argument in *Maxwell* is not ultimately to prevail, one hopes it will be because the higher courts have improved on this district court's criticisms.

The arguments reviewed above were originally designed only to secure reversals of particular convictions. Nevertheless, they succeed in posing at least two "equal protection" objections to the statutory procedures through which capital punishment is currently employed: (1) the absence of standards by which the exercise of jury discretion in capital cases can be evaluated is itself unconstitutionally unfair; and (2) the use in practice of this arbitrary discretion affords demonstrably discriminatory treatment of nonwhite convicts and this is a failure of equal protection. Let us assume that at least one of these objections is well taken, and that the factual support outlined above in the 1961 New Jersey murder case and the 1966 Arkansas rape case are bolstered by further evidence of the same sort. What would be the effect upon capital punishment if the courts were to accept either (1) or (2)? Would it constitute judicial abolition of capital punishment? The answer is, once again, "No." Legislatures could obviate the entire problem of sentencing standards in capital cases by restoring mandatory capital punishments. No question of jury discretion in sentencing could then arise. To be sure, it is possible that a quite parallel question of "unequal protection" could arise under mandatory death penalties, based on a discriminatory pattern of convictions and acquittals (or convictions of lesser vs. graver crimes, or even indictments on lesser vs. graver charges). Nevertheless, mandatory capital punishments once again provide a theoretically possible, though unlikely and undesirable, way to prevent unconstitutional procedural faults from resulting in judicial abolition of capital punishment.

The more interesting route to consider to avoid this result is for the legislatures to undertake to supply juries with the requisite standards. Given statutory-imposed standards, the judge could be required to instruct the jury accordingly; the jury would then have to base its sentencing recommendation on these standards. Or the judge could apply these standards in assessing the recommendations of an uninstructed jury and either increase or reduce its recommended sentence accordingly. Under either alternative, the appellate courts would be empowered to refer to these standards in reviewing the trial court sentence. Provision would also have to be made for introducing in evidence such facts about the crime and the criminal as would enable the courts to apply the relevant standards. In a few states (notably California), something like this is now being done during a further proceeding devoted solely to the issue of assessing punishment.[46]

The unanswered question, of course, is precisely what standards the legislatures would be willing to adopt, and whether they would survive the scrutiny of the higher courts. For several years, the American Law Institute has set forth in its Model Penal Code a set of "aggravating" and "mitigating" circumstances intended to guide statutory enactments, and it might be argued that they could serve to provide juries with the standards needed to exercise sentencing discretion in capital cases. The two lists of circumstances are equally long and complex, and constitute a formidable check list for any jury and for the contending counsel. The aggravating circumstances include: the murder was committed by a convict under sentence of imprisonment; the murderer had a prior conviction of a felony of personal violence; the murderer knowingly created a grave risk of death to many persons; the murder was committed in the course of committing another felony or in attempt to avoid arrest, escape custody, or for "pecuniary gain," or was "especially heinous, atrocious, or cruel, manifesting exceptional depravity." The mitigating circumstances include: the murderer had no "significant" history of prior criminality; the murder was committed while the murderer was under "extreme mental or emotional disturbance" or while his "capacity" to appreciate the wrong he was doing was "impaired" by "mental disease or defect or intoxication"; his "youth" at the time of the crime; the murderer acted under duress or the "domination" of another; the defendant was an accomplice in a murder committed by another; the murderer believed his act was justifiable or excusable under the circumstances; the victim was a coparticipant with the defendant in the homicidal act or consented to the act.[47]

If in one or more of these ways standards were to be introduced, they would prevent the procedural defects we have been discussing from becoming the device whereby direct judicial abolition of the death penalty can be secured. So much is clear. Would the adoption of such standards, however, result in *de facto* abolition by encouraging the jury or the judges to find mitigating circumstances in every capital case and therefore to sentence accordingly? Some have argued that this is what we should expect. Others have implied the reverse. "[L]egislative specification of criteria for recommendation of life imprisonment," said the New Jersey Supreme Court, "might prejudice a defendant through the exclusion by omission of a factor relevant in a given case."[48] This echoes the judgment of the Model Penal Code reporter, Herbert Wechsler. "No draftsman can really trust his capacity to enumerate all the possible mitigations that might be perceived, or indeed even all the aggravations, but it is more important on the mitigations."[49] Experience so far with specified standards is inconclusive. In California, and later in Pennsylvania and New York, states that pioneered their own versions of these procedures, the proportion of death sentences does not seem to have been noticeably increased or diminished.[50] This is not surprising, perhaps, since the juries in these states continue to be "death-qualified." Equally significant is the fact that the states that have adopted the two-stage trial have not really used the second proceeding on punishment to utilize sentencing standards. In both New York and California, the jurors are still given "absolute discretion to act according to their judgment and conscience."[51]

De facto abolition aside, there is a serious deficiency in all current practices, such as the two-stage trial and the American Law Institute's sentencing recommendations. Even if the jury were to try to use a set of aggravating and mitigating circumstances such as those discussed above, it is doubtful whether this would really constitute using a sentencing standard. A check list of factors relevant to augmenting or diminishing the severity of a sentence is not really a standard. The jury with no more than such a list is neither equipped nor instructed in how to weigh the evidence thereunder—e.g., whether to give all the several circumstances equal weight, or if they are to weigh disproportionately, to determine which should carry the greater and which the lesser weight. The logic of these aggravating and mitigating circumstances is too vague and arbitrary. Unless precise specification is introduced into the use of these aggravating and mitigating factors, sentences based on them can hardly be said to meet or conform to a standard. For it is perfectly obvious that otherwise, there is nothing to prevent juries from weighing these relevant factors a different way every time; in fact, that is presumably what juries have always done. Merely to make explicit a set of factors relevant to sentencing is not sufficient to bring the sentences actually meted out under any uniform standard at all. It is wholly insufficient to provide for fairness in jury sentencing, which is precisely what introducing these factors for the jury's use is intended to obtain. Whether these further specifications on weighting could be made operational is doubtful. Certainly, nowhere else in the law are such statutory sentencing standards available to the criminal trial jury. Perhaps this shows that the entire quest for genuine sentencing standards (whether for judge or jury) is fruitless—or else still lies far in the future. Yet if this is our conclusion, must we not also conclude that the attempt to impose the death sentence in some but not all cases, despite the long familiarity of the practice, is simply arbitrary, gratuitous, without sufficient reason, and that it constitutes a grave departure from the kind of even-handed protection the penal law under the Fourteenth Amendment ought to provide? Sentencing discretion on these terms, in short, cannot be constitutional so long as death is one of the alternatives.

iii Due Process of Law

Early in 1960, three men in New Jersey were scheduled to be executed a few days after Easter. The New Jersey Supreme Court had already granted appeal and sustained the conviction without dissent. At trial, the defendants had been represented by different attorneys. Now, all counsel considered the case closed. The condemned men were without funds with which to retain counsel and had been without legal assistance for some weeks as they faced their last days before electrocution. Yet not all legal remedies were exhausted. In particular, none of the available federal remedies (*certiorari, habeas corpus*) had been pursued. Volunteer legal counsel unexpectedly intervened, pursued these remedies, and at almost the last minute succeeded in averting the executions.[52] Two years later, one of the convictions was reversed, and as of the winter of 1967-1968, the fate of the other two was still under litigation. Had it not been for a succession of volunteers working on behalf of these defendants, their executions would have taken place eight years ago—and one man improperly convicted would have been legally executed. In this single case, we see illustrated two of the major kinds of questions that raise a challenge of "due process" in capital cases: (1) the denial of "due process" in pursuit of postconviction remedies, and (2) the denial of "due process" in pursuit of postappellate remedies. The following series of cases elaborates in greater detail a more subtle point, (3) the denial of "due process" in securing retrospective application of new judicial legislation. In 1956, the Supreme Court held in *Griffin v. Illinois* that the state must provide indigent convicts in noncapital cases with transcripts and court records necessary to appeal their convictions. "There can be no equal justice," said Justice Black for the majority, "where the kind of trial a man gets depends on the amount of money he has. Destitute defendants must be afforded as adequate appellate review as defendants who have money enough to buy transcripts."[53] Two years later, this holding was given retrospective application to a convict who had already been sentenced (and, in that sense, whose case had already been "decided") over twenty years earlier. The convict in this instance was most fortunate: although convicted of murder, he had not been sentenced to death, so he lived to see the protections originally denied to him eventually, and retroactively, provided.[54] Similarly, in 1962, in *Douglas v. California,* the Supreme Court held that appellate counsel must be appointed for indigents convicted of noncapital crimes if the state provides appeal as of right. Two years later this decision was given "absolute retrospective application" in a Kansas case involving a burglary conviction dating from 1960.[55] These cases show the kinds of remedies recently made available to prisoners fortunate enough to be alive to make use of them. They indicate the very real sense in which there is little "finality" in any state criminal conviction, so long as the defendant is alive to press points of "due process" and other federal constitutional protections on his own behalf, and alive to benefit from new rulings originally granted to other convicts but retroactively applicable to him as well.

Not all cases as influential on the law as *Griffin* and *Douglas* have had comparable benefit for capital defendants. In 1932, in one of the most important early holdings affecting state criminal procedures, the famous "Scottsboro Boys" case (*Powell v. Alabama*), the Supreme Court reversed a multiple conviction of rape and voided the ensuing death sentences because the defendants had been denied proper counsel prior to and during trial. The court asserted: "[I]n a capital case, where the defendant is unable to employ counsel, and is incapable adequately of making his own defense because of ignorance, feeble mindedness, illiteracy, or the like, it is the duty of the court, whether requested or not, to assign counsel for him as a necessary requisite of due process of law...."[56] No retrospective application of this decision has been recorded. One can only hope that no convict, who had been convicted without adequate trial counsel, was languishing under sentence of death in 1932 and was later executed because no one sought retrospective application of the ruling in the *Powell* case. Nearly thirty years later, in another case, *Hamilton v. Alabama*, the Court held that the right to counsel in capital cases extends to the accused's arraignment before a judge wherever arraignment is a critical stage in the proceedings. In this instance, retrospective application has been recorded in two cases to men under sentence of death but fortunately not yet executed.[57]

We can therefore understand why attorney Norman Dorsen, an ACLU spokesman, has argued that

the death penalty operates to limit post-appellate review in the class of cases where it is needed most. For example, when the Supreme Court retroactively applied the holding in *Griffin v. Illinois* ... the ones who could never take advantage of this constitutional rule were those who had been executed .... A second example derives from the fact that a defendant in a capital case has no right to the assignment of counsel after his appeal. The failure of states to assign counsel during the post-appellate stage of a capital case frequently precludes indigent prisoners under sentence of death from pursuing those remedies available to prisoners convicted of less serious crimes.[58]

Another important area of post-appellate review, and one that affects persons under sentence of death more than any others, involves the determination of sanity prior to execution. The law has traditionally held that it is a necessary condition of execution that the convict be sane at the time. Explanations of this practice vary (and, one might add, do not wholly convince). At a minimum, it involves the belief that it is nothing but judicial murder to execute a person when he cannot understand what is happening to him or why. Except where there are specific statutory devices to provide otherwise, recent holdings of the Supreme Court leave to "the mere say-so of the warden of a state prison, according to such procedure as he chooses to pursue,"[59] the initiation of investigation to ascertain the sanity of a condemned man in his custody. The prisoner has traditionally had no right to commence a sanity proceeding. Given prolonged detention under sentence of death, many men completely break down. Every prison warden who has kept custody of men awaiting execution knows of such cases.[60] Is it "due process" at this stage of the criminal proceedings to tie the hands of the person who has the greatest interest in securing his rights, and delegate their protection to a prison administrator? The late Justice Felix Frankfurter, long an outspoken opponent of capital punishment (and an equally outspoken defender of judicial restraint in nullifying legislative enactments), did not think so and condemned it in these words:

There can hardly be a comparable situation under our constitutional scheme of things in which an interest so great, that an insane man not be executed, is given such flimsy procedural protection, and where one asserting a claim is denied the rudimentary right of having his side submitted to the one who sits in judgment.[61]

Do these lines of argument, and the cases cited here to illustrate them, show that capital punishment constitutes denial of "due process" in the sense of denying the person under death sentence the right to full pursuit of postconviction, postappellate, and retroactive remedies? In cases where the penalty has been carried out, and where postconviction proceedings would prove the conviction improper, capital punishment denies the fundamental remedy that is still available to those in prison: release and in some cases exoneration and indemnification. Very incomplete records indicate that there is, on the average, one case every other year in the United States involving someone who was convicted of a capital crime but not executed and who either vindicates his innocence and is freed or at least establishes the unfairness of his conviction.[62] If the availability of a remedy is the test of the presence of a right, then capital punishment as it is actually administered has been steadily in violation of offenders' rights.

Yet to many this argument will surely be unpersuasive. Despite the sharp decline in executions since 1962, the number of persons under sentence of death each year has steadily increased; today, the number is over 400. This decline in executions and the corresponding increase in persons under death sentence has resulted primarily from the authorization of federal courts to hold hearings on federal issues arising in state criminal proceedings whether or not these issues had been previously litigated in the state courts.[63] A decade of this appellate procedure, plus the growing availability of volunteer appellate counsel for the indigent death sentence convict, has assured all persons under death sentence of ample postconviction review. The length of time men now spend under death sentence attests to their relentless pursuit of these remedies. In 1960, Caryl Chessman was executed in California after spending a record eleven years and ten months under sentence of death. Today, there are prisoners who have already exceeded that record by more than two years; there is every reason to expect that during the next decade, unless the death penalty is abolished or radical procedural reforms are introduced, it will be commonplace for persons to spend between five and ten years under death sentence before final disposition of their cases. The average time spent under sentence of death has leaped from sixteen months in 1960 to nearly *four years* in 1965; these statistics, moreover, do not include time served under death sentence by the many persons who were not finally executed. Given the availability of federal remedies and their actual widespread use by condemned convicts, the argument that the death penalty is nevertheless an unconstitutional denial of "due process" in postconviction and postappellate proceedings is not so convincing. The death penalty may be unwise, and it may be unnecessary, but that is not to say that it involves an unconstitutional denial of "due process." At least, one should expect to hear the courts reply in this fashion if and when this argument is first presented to them.

There are at least two things to be said in surrebuttal. First, not all death sentence prisoners, especially not all the indigent, have in fact secured all available postsentencing remedies. It is not a sufficiently consoling argument that some have and that others will. Very few states even now *require* appellate review as of right for every death sentence conviction. No statutes or court decisions *require* any federal court to review any state court felony convictions or death sentences. Very few states pay for a public defender or an assigned counsel to direct such appeals where such appeals are not guaranteed as a matter of right. What this shows, of course, is the general inadequacy of state postconviction remedies. These deficiencies yield not merely deplorable but fatal results for one class of convict only: those sentenced to death. Second, postconviction remedies are constantly being scrutinized by the courts, and further reform from this quarter can be expected. This means that despite all the progress forced on the states by the federal courts in the last few years, there are persons now under prison sentence whose convictions, although not at the moment open to attack by retrospective application of recent procedural reforms, will almost certainly benefit from procedural improvements yet to come. This advantage will be denied for certain only to one class of convict: those who have already been executed.

This, then, is the argument for extending "due process" to attack capital punishment for its denial of postconviction remedies. If it were to persuade a court, then—unlike the procedural arguments reviewed so far—there would appear to be *no conceivable* mode of administering the death penalty so as to conform to the new requirements. The only way to meet the challenge of denial of "due process" from the retroactive unavailability of new remedies is to impose only those punishments that permit the convict to reopen the "finality" of the judgment against him. But this is because it is clearly incompatible with capital punishment for any person for any crime in any jurisdiction; a wholly procedural or collateral attack is presented that goes to the complete and final abolition of the death penalty.

The very power of this argument, of course, may prove to be its weakness. To date, the majority of the Supreme Court (contrary to the express wishes of Justices Black and Douglas) has followed an uneven path in retroactive application of holdings that radically affect the finality of state criminal proceedings. In *Johnson v. New Jersey*,[64] the Court specifically denied retrospective application of its important decisions in *Escobedo v. Illinois* and *Miranda v. Arizona* to prisoners under sentence of death whose convictions antedated those holdings by some four years. If, as the Court expressed itself in another recent case, "the Constitution neither prohibits nor requires retrospective effect,"[65] it is doubtful that the Court would accept the proposed argument. Thus, the very conclusiveness of this collateral attack on capital punishment may bar the Court from acknowledging the argument in the first place.

iv Cruel and Unusual Punishment

Early in this century a disbursing officer of the Coast Guard stationed in the Philippines was charged with falsifying a public document in order to conceal diversion into his own pockets of some 616 pesos in public funds. He was convicted and sentenced to not more than fifteen years of *cadena temporal*, 4000 pesos fine, and court costs. The judgment and sentence were affirmed by the Supreme Court of the Islands. On direct appeal to the Supreme Court, he charged that his sentence was a "cruel and unusual punishment," in violation of both the Island and the federal constitutions. *Cadena temporal,* an inheritance from the Spanish occupation, was defined by a Philippine statute to consist of: from twelve to twenty years imprisonment, at "hard and painful" labor, while perpetually chained at the ankle and wrists, plus loss of all civil rights and subjection to surveillance upon release for the rest of one's natural life. After careful and lengthy discussion of the gross disproportion between the severity of the punishment and the gravity of the offense, the excessive harshness of the punishment when compared with that meted out for such a crime in other jurisdictions, the assault upon human dignity of the mode of punishment (the Court said, "No circumstance of degradation is omitted"), and the unity and inseparability of the punishments in the authorizing statute, the Court concluded that "the fault is in the law" and ordered the conviction reversed. This 1910 decision in *Weems v. United States*[66] was the first Supreme Court interpretation of the "cruel and unusual punishment" clause of the Eighth Amendment, the first case in which it reversed a conviction under that interpretation, and the first case in which the Court struck down a statutory mode of punishment as unconstitutional. The decision was far from unanimous; three justices did not participate, and Justice Holmes was one of the two dissenters.

Not for another fifty years did the Court again strike down a statute on the ground that it violated this clause of the Constitution. Then, in 1958, the Court in *Trop v. Dulles* invalidated a section of the Nationality Act of 1940, on the strength of which a dishonorably discharged Army veteran had been held to have forfeited his citizenship for wartime desertion. The Court argued that such a statute, whether or not designed and enforced with punitive intent, constituted "the total destruction of the individual's status in organized society," and denied him "the right to have rights" and concluded that "the Eighth Amendment forbids this to be done."[67]

Four years later, in *Robinson v. California*, the Court was confronted with a conviction under a California statute making "addiction" to narcotics a misdemeanor punishable by ninety days to one year in the county jail. The court held that the statute made criminal a person's condition or status, apart from any overt act or attempt to use narcotics, when, moreover, the condition of addiction was itself an "illness." Accordingly, the statute was invalidated on the ground that it "inflicts a cruel and unusual punishment in violation of the Eighth and Fourteenth Amendments."[68]

Apart from a few relatively insignificant holdings, this is the extent to which the courts to date, both state and federal, have used the constitutional prohibition against "cruel and unusual punishment" to strike down legislation. One might infer from this short history either that American penal practices throughout the past century have been singularly humane, or that this clause of the Constitution has become no more than an empty remonstrance against ancient horrors, common in seventeenth and eighteenth century England, when violent aggravations accompanied hanging for every felony, and almost every crime was a felony. Against the latter is the reliance upon this provision in two cases within the last decade. Against the former looms the continued existence of capital punishment itself.

Before attempting to frame an argument against the death penalty on the ground that it is "cruel and unusual," we should canvas the initial difficulties and possibilities. When we speak of a punishment as "cruel and unusual," any of five different faults might be in question. One may argue that a punishment is "cruel and unusual" because of (1) the *circumstances* surrounding its administration, (2) the *mode* of its infliction, (3) the *crime* for which it is imposed, (4) the *criminal* upon whom it is inflicted, or simply because of (5) its inherent *nature*. Thus, death after ten years under sentence of death, death by crucifixion, death for auto theft, and death for a seven-year-old—in each case, the penalty might be characterized as "cruel and unusual." These five possible grounds for a ruling of unconstitutional cruelty and unusualness are not likely to be equally productive. The decided cases so far plainly show that the Eighth Amendment has been interpreted mainly as a bar to cruelties that arise under (2). Direct assault upon the death penalty either under (3) or—the primary concern—(5) has so far failed to reach the Supreme Court. Before examining these three possibilities more closely, however, something must be said about the other two, (4) and (1).

The courts have never drawn a line to protect juveniles as such from the reach of death sentences or of felony convictions carrying the death penalty on grounds of the unconstitutional cruelty and unusualness of such sentences. They have not even been ready to strain every effort to secure reversal of death penalty convictions of a juvenile, though there have been some distinguished exceptions.[69]

Perhaps less surprising has been the courts' unwillingness to throw out a death sentence on the ground that the attendant delay in executing it has caused the petitioner agony and suffering amounting to a violation of the Eighth Amendment. In his novel, *The Idiot*, Dostoyevsky argued through the person of Prince Myshkin that "[t]o kill for murder is a punishment incomparably more terrible than murder by brigands," because in the former, "[t]here is the sentence, and the whole awful torture lies in the fact that there is certainly no escape, and there is no torture in the world more terrible."[70] The same objection was argued in certain recent cases[71] and also earlier by Caryl Chessman after he had spent almost twelve years under death sentence. The courts, at least in his case, were quite unmoved by his plea: "I do not see how we can offer life . . . as a prize for one who can stall the processes for a given number of years . . ."[72] One is likely to conclude that this line of attack on the death penalty is bound to remain unproductive, even if at some future time the courts may be drawn into agreeing with Prince Myshkin and grant a reversal or otherwise nullify the death sentence in a particularly frightful case. The variety of human responses to detention prior to execution, the uneven lengths of time actually so served, the difficulties in establishing these kinds of facts for the courts, and the knowledge that the delay in execution of a death sentence is usually owing to initiatives undertaken by the convict and not to administrative ineptitude, are bound to discourage this approach.

Alarm over the growing delay in final disposition of capital cases has been expressed for some time. The problem is far worse today than ever before. In 1960, the median period served under sentence of death prior to execution was sixteen months. By 1965, this time had lengthened to 44.5 months. It was with specific reference to the "spectacle of men living on death row for years while their lawyers pursue appellate and collateral remedies" that led the President's Commission on Law Enforcement and Administration of Justice to conclude its discussion of the death penalty with these words:

All members of the Commission agree that the present situation in the administration of the death penalty in many States is intolerable . . . . When a State finds that it cannot administer the penalty . . . with fair and expeditious procedures or that the death penalty is being imposed but not carried into effect, the penalty should be abandoned.[73]

The fundamental obstacle to possibilities (2) and (3) is a steady line of holdings in state and federal courts. Attempted train robbery (New Mexico), assault with a deadly weapon by a life term prisoner (California), and attempted rape (Virginia) are crimes for which, during this century, capital punishment has been upheld as not being "cruel and unusual" under the respective state constitutions. A similar long series of cases sustains each of the presently used modes of execution. In 1878 the Supreme Court held that Utah's optional method of inflicting death by firing squad or hanging is not "cruel and unusual" under the federal constitution; in 1890 the courts upheld the new practice in New York of electrocution under both the state and federal constitutions. Beginning with Nevada in 1923, execution by lethal gas has been upheld in every state where it has been challenged. So was hanging. The Supreme Court in 1947 even upheld Louisiana in its second attempt to electrocute Willie Francis after the first attempt had unexpectedly failed even though Francis had received an enormous jolt of electric current. The Court reasoned: "The fact that an unforeseeable accident prevented the prompt consummation of the sentence cannot, it seems to us, add an element of cruelty to a subsequent execution."[74] A minority of four justices urged, but to no avail, that "death by installments" cannot be anything but cruel and unusual. Twenty years before the *Weems* case, the Court observed that "the punishment of death is not cruel, within the meaning of that word as used in the Constitution. It implies ... something inhuman and barbarous, something more than the mere extinguishment of life."[75] The latest word from the Court (even though expressed in passing in a footnote twenty years ago) is hardly more encouraging: "The death penalty has been employed throughout our history, and, in a day when it is still widely accepted, it cannot be said to violate the constitutional concept of cruelty."[76] In short, not a single death penalty statute, not a single statutorily imposed mode of execution, not a single attempted execution has ever been held by any court to be "cruel and unusual punishment" under any state or federal constitution. Nothing less than a mighty counterthrust would appear to be required to alter the direction of these decisions.

All these holdings seem to be based on two fundamental considerations. One is that such capital penal statutes, modes of inflicting death, and attempted executions as have prevailed in this century in the United States are not unconstitutional under the Eighth Amendment because however cruel and unusual they may now be, they are *not more* "cruel" and *not more* "unusual" than those that prevailed in England and the Colonies two or three hundred years ago. An unbroken line of interpreters has held that it was the original understanding and intent of the framers of the Eighth Amendment (and of all those who incorporated like phrases into the early state constitutions) to proscribe as "cruel and unusual" *only* such modes of execution as compound the simple infliction of death with added cruelties or indignities. The constitutional standard of cruelty and unusualness, therefore, has not only been uniformly rooted in the past; it has been confined solely to measuring the *way* in which the punishment of death is inflicted. Hence the courts have said that burning at the stake, crucifixion, breaking on the wheel, punishments that are inhuman and barbarous, torture and the like, and punishments that involve unnecessary pain, the wanton infliction of pain, are all constitutionally prohibited. Thus, on this theory, one must suppose that a wholly painless death inflicted by a pill or an injection could never be a mode of "cruel and unusual" punishment, especially if it were introduced by a legislature (as were electrocution and lethal gas) in the name of humane reform. Similarly, even if the death penalty were imposed by statute for a trifling offense, it is doubtful that it would be "cruel and unusual" according to the "original understanding." Thus, such statutes as currently provide an optional death penalty for desecration of a grave (Georgia), train-wrecking (Wyoming), and the second conviction of an adult for inducing one under 25 years of age to violate narcotics law (Colorado), though none of these crimes necessarily involves a threat to life or limb and all are crimes that for other reasons might well seem undeserving of capital punishment, would not be contrary to the scope of legislative discretion presumed on this theory to be intended by the framers when they drew up the Eighth Amendment.

The other fundamental consideration is the belief by the courts that not they but the legislatures are best fitted to construct a penal code and that they must, therefore, exercise the utmost restraint in meddling with legislative enactments in this area. As one federal court put it some years ago, "The fixing of penalties for crimes is a legislative function. What constitutes an adequate penalty is a matter of legislative judgment and discretion, and the courts will not interfere therewith unless the penalty prescribed is clearly and manifestly cruel and unusual."[77] It is in this spirit that a recent note in the *Harvard Law Review* concluded its discussion of the problem: "In light of these difficulties and the uniform authority sustaining capital punishment, to hold that it is a method of punishment wholly prohibited by the eighth amendment would be to confuse possible legislative desirability with constitutional requirements."[78]

Yet the effect of this line of reasoning is to condemn the Eighth Amendment to dead-letter law in the face of the plausible and literal reading of the "cruel and unusual" clause: what else is capital punishment if not brutally cruel (why else is it conducted in relative secrecy) and spectacularly unusual (roughly, since 1960 one person executed for every 1000 murders)? What else is the source of the belief in its unique powers of deterrence? Surely, we can do better than this. We need not be content to see this clause in the Bill of Rights remain little more than a bulwark against atrocities practically unknown for generations. Despite judicial tradition and learned opinion to the contrary, we can shield the death penalty from attack on grounds of its unconstitutional cruelty only by a wholly anachronistic and unempirical view of the issues or by appeal to an implausibly reactionary notion of legislative experimentation and judicial restraint. To give the "cruel and unusual" punishments clause viability, we need to reassess entirely the logic of cruelty and unusualness as they figure in the Constitution.

Let us begin by looking at the concept of cruelty. The contrast with the concept of pain is instructive. Pain is a bodily sensation (one has a pain, for example, in his arm), or a bodily state or condition (one is in pain). Cruelty is neither a bodily sensation or bodily condition, even though it must rest for its attribution upon a person's having been caused to have some such sensation or to be in some such condition. Nor can we know how cruel something is simply by knowing how much it hurts; it could be quite cruel but not terribly painful. Contrariwise, knowing how much harm something does is relevant to knowing how cruel it is; cruelty is more nearly (though not wholly) a direct function of the harm inflicted. These seem to me to be the fundamental considerations in evaluating the cruelty of a *mode* of punishment. Consider, by way of contrast, the relation of pain and treatment. Treatment cannot be judged as cruel if there is no known alternative and if it is reasonably believed to be effective; its painfulness is in no way diminished by its not being harmful, but its cruelty is. However, if a method of treatment is judged to be cruelly painful, then even it may be on the verge of a moral prohibition—unless, for example, the patient would otherwise die and he has knowingly and voluntarily consented to the painful treatment. Normally, however, this is precisely what is denied when cruelty is imputed to a practice. Saying that something is both cruel and permissible verges on the self-contradictory, as would saying that something is both cruel and harmless. Roughly, therefore, we may say this: whereas the painfulness of things varies with our sensory experience, the cruelty of things varies mainly according to some standard of the permissible, which is to say, according to some principle of moral judgment. Any honest attempt to fathom the meaning of "cruel" must admit this. So the problem in the end is to determine nothing less than the morality of capital punishments.

Before facing that issue directly, we must pause to consider the conjunction, "and," in the phrase "cruel and unusual." In this context, "and" simply does not express the conjunction of two independent properties of a punishment, *cruelty* and *unusualness*. Though this may be the natural way to read the clause, there is no evidence that the courts have ever done so or that they should. Yet "cruel and unusual" is not a mere pleonasm either. A decade ago, Chief Justice Earl Warren commented on the logic of these words in this way:"[T]he Court simply examines the particular punishment involved in the light of the basic prohibition against inhuman treatment, without regard to any subtleties of meaning that might be latent in the word 'unusual.' "[79] Hence, most recent commentators have maintained that "unusual" has meaning only as a modifier of "cruel"—that its function is essentially adverbial.[80] "Cruel and unusual punishment," one is entitled to conclude, really means "unusually severe punishment." This reading is important for two reasons. First, that this kind of punishment was quite common (and therefore not "unusual") two hundred years ago cannot bar the courts from deciding that capital punishment is "cruel and unusual." If "unusual" had reference only to historic practice contemporaneous with the adoption of the amendment, the conjunctive use of "and" in this context would create an insurmountable obstacle to any argument such as mine. Second, if "unusual" in this context means "unusually severe," then the issue of cruelty turns on whether it is unnecessary, unreasonable, excessive, inhumane, or otherwise unjustifiable. All such terms have implicit reference to some *standard* in light of which necessity and excess is to be determined. The entire interpretation of the clause, then, rests upon identification of this standard.

Although the standard itself has remained tacit, there has occasionally been explicit recognition that one exists. The standard is not static. In commenting on this clause in the Constitution in 1958, the Supreme Court stated: "It must draw its meaning from the evolving standards of decency that mark the progress of a maturing society."[81] This amplifies the thought of the Court in the *Weems* case, where it was wisely observed: "Time works changes, brings into existence new conditions and purposes. Therefore a principle to be vital must be capable of wider application than the mischief which gave it birth. This is peculiarly true of constitutions."[82] What are these acknowledged but unstated "evolving standards of decency"? So far as they affect the issue in question, we can infer their nature from the intention of the framers in excluding as "cruel and unusual" *all* aggravations attendant upon the death penalty, for example, drawing and quartering, disemboweling, burning at the stake. Why, we must ask, were such practices implicitly prohibited even though death by hanging was not? Why was flogging, for instance, not constitutionally prohibited?[83] Surely, there is only one reason: death and flogging were reasonably believed to be *necessary* and *justifiable* given the nature of the offenses for which they were imposed, the available alternative punishments, and the legitimate purpose of a system of legal punishment. To put it another way, hanging and disemboweling may both have been terribly painful and may have provoked horror among humane observers, but only the latter was considered "cruel and unusual" because only it could be recognized as unnecessary given the considerations by which permissible modes of punishment were to be judged.

In 1789, when the Eighth Amendment was adopted (even as in earlier centuries, when "cruel and unusual punishments" were first prohibited in England), only two types of punishment were available to cope with serious offenses: death (with or without aggravations) and banishment, or "transportation," to the Colonies or some other remote and relatively uninhabited region. Imprisonment, as something more than a mode of temporary detention prior to trial or as punishment for a minor offense, was entirely unknown at the time anywhere in Europe or America.[84] How could anyone in 1790 sensibly have demanded that the "evolving standards of decency" require there and then imprisonment rather than death for felons? There were no prisons, no trained custodial and administrative officers, no parole system, no statutes to authorize creating any of these, no public disposition to obtain them—in short, none of the attitudes, facilities, and personnel obviously necessary to run a system of long-term incarceration. Today, of course, banishment is no alternative at all. Instead, imprisonment is an entirely commonplace practice and an effective alternative to banishment and death for every serious criminal. However inhumane and brutal imprisonment may be (and there is no doubt that in practice it often is), involuntary incarceration under close supervision may still be a *necessary* "cruelty" in most cases involving the commission of violent crimes. The undeniably greater severity of death as a punishment over imprisonment is, *ceteris paribus*, sufficient by itself to establish its greater cruelty.

In the face of these facts, there are only two ways in which the death penalty can be untouched by the current state of "the evolving standards of decency." One is if death is not, *ceteris paribus*, more severe and cruel than imprisonment. The other is if despite its admitted severity and cruelty it is nevertheless necessary. Implausible as the first claim may seem, it cannot be wholly ignored. It is a sobering reminder that the most influential abolitionist of his time, Cesare Beccaria (1738-1794), favored "a life sentence of servitude, in place of death penalty" because the former "has in it what suffices to deter any determined spirit."[85] Although I know of no abolitionists today who believe that life imprisonment is more cruel than death and who argue against the death penalty for this reason, there are some who do believe this and partly for this reason cannot oppose the death penalty on humanitarian grounds.[86] Still, those who agree with Beccaria on this point today do so primarily by supposing tacitly that the alternative to the death penalty *must* be literal life imprisonment, imposed by statute, and subject to no remission, pardon, or review. This is, however, neither the intended, the necessary, nor the actually practiced alternative.

The second claim can be true only if the legitimate purposes of punishment are not equally well served by imprisonment. Everything depends on what these purposes are. Although some of the state courts have attempted to define them, the Supreme Court has yet to speak with directness and finality on this issue. But what could these purposes be other than incapacitation, deterrence, and rehabilitation—"deterrence, isolation and rehabilitation," as Justice Goldberg recently put it[87]—some one or a combination of them? As for rehabilitation, much in the actual practice of imprisonment may defeat this goal, but at least the two are not necessarily inconsistent with each other, whereas the death penalty obviously precludes any attempt at rehabilitation. On the other hand, imprisonment is not as perfectly incapacitating as is death. Measured, therefore, by these two purposes alone, the death penalty yields a slight though perhaps not decisive edge in favor of imprisonment. The relative deterrent efficacy of the two punishments, consequently, is the decisive factor. But the absence of any superior deterrent efficacy of death over imprisonment is one of the touchstones in the entire controversy over capital punishment, and this fact constitutes the final link in the present argument against it. Here, it will suffice to cite the *Report of the President's Commission on Law Enforcement and Administration of Justice*. Although the Commission did not come out squarely in favor of abolition, its appraisal of the evidence on the crucial issue of deterrence was unambiguous:

It is impossible to say with certainty whether capital punishment significantly reduces the incidence of heinous crimes. The most complete study on the subject, based on a comparison of homicide rates in capital and noncapital jurisdictions, concluded that there is no discernible correlation between the availability of the death penalty and the homicide rate. This study also revealed that there was no significant difference between the two kinds of States in the safety of policemen. Another study of 27 States indicated that the availability of the death sentence had no effect on the rate of assaults and murders of prison guards.[88]

What can one conclude except that the "cruelties" of capital punishment are unnecessary, and that the pain it directly and indirectly inflicts is to that extent unjustified? The indignity and indecency it involves, not only through the mutilation of the condemned man's body but simply by its very nature—capital punishment is the only governmental practice whereby the standing threat of a violent death is addressed to the citizenry—is inhumane cruelty. The utter inappropriateness of execution to the legitimate purpose of punishment establishes it as unnecessarily cruel. Perhaps nothing so well signifies how the "evolving standards of decency" have caught up with the death penalty than the comment quoted earlier from the Supreme Court only a decade ago, alleging that the death penalty still enjoyed "wide acceptance." No one could say this now and claim to speak for the present generation. And as the court recognized, the matter of "acceptance" is relevant to the issue of cruelty. The death penalty is indecent and inhumane and to that extent cruel if decent and humane men say it is; and today they do.

I conclude that the death penalty under criminal law in this country for any crime—not only for crimes against property, crimes committed by minors, but for all crimes whatsoever—is condemned as excessively, unnecessarily, unusually cruel. Legislative discretion in fixing statutory punishments should no longer be allowed to include the death penalty as the upper bound of the constitutionally permissible.

Convinced as I am by the argument just presented, I hasten to point out two considerations that count against it. First, even if it is correct in its form, it relies on nonexistent evidence regarding the deterrent ineffectiveness of capital punishment for crimes other than murder. There is today no statistical or other evidence of any sort that tends to show that the death penalty as a deterrent, e.g., for rape, is any more effective than is imprisonment. Evidence of this sort exists only for the crime of first degree murder. One may be entitled to be confident about what the evidence would show, as I have been here, but not because one has any of it already in hand. In the absence of such evidence, courts are unlikely to use the argument presented here to reverse any capital statutes for crimes other than murder.

Second, and far more significant, in formulating the concepts of cruelty and unusual cruelty, I have made reference to the relative gravity of the crime and to the proportion or disproportion of the punishment as one factor relevant to establishing its cruelty. However, if severity in a punishment disproportionate to the gravity of the crime is a *necessary* condition of unconstitutional cruelty, then it would be all but impossible to argue to the unconstitutional cruelty of the death penalty for *murder*. To be sure, this condition would allow all other crimes to be freed from the death penalty (provided the necessary premises were properly supported with evidence). But 95 percent of all death sentences in this country have been for murder, and it is the death penalty for this crime that will always be the primary object of attack. In the *Weems* case, where the issue of proportionality was first raised, the court's position is unclear. It rightly said: "[I]t is a precept of justice that punishment for crime should be graduated and proportioned to offense."[89] But is disproportionately excessive punishment a necessary or a sufficient condition of unconstitutional cruelty? In the *Rudolph* case, where three justices raised doubts about the proportionality of the death penalty for rape under the Eighth Amendment, this passage from *Weems* was quoted but without any disambiguation. One commentator has argued that it is anachronistic to construe the Constitution as requiring that the punishment in any sense "fit" the crime.[90] One possible solution is to accept the language in *Weems* so that disproportionate excess of punishment to crime is *only a sufficient* condition of unconstitutional cruelty, not a necessary condition; neither the Constitution nor the "precepts of justice" impose the more stringent requirement.

There is but one remaining hurdle: judicial restraint. Why should any court step in to overrule the legislative will in this matter of penology? The brief but, I think, adequate reply is that the Supreme Court is charged, by the Eighth Amendment, to *judge* whether a given punishment is "cruel and unusual," and it cannot escape this responsibility. The occasional *obiter dicta* of earlier years on behalf of the death penalty are hardly sufficient today. They are not even squarely in point, since in no case to date has the Court been faced directly with the issue of capital punishment as such and its alleged unusual cruelty. Furthermore, after decades of relative restraint on any number of issues touching basic rights expressly and by implication guaranteed to all under the Bill of Rights and the Constitution, the courts have in recent years acted to restore what legislatures, administrative agencies, and other arms of executive power have ignored or denied. The evidence in the present argument against the death penalty is in principle no worse than the evidence that has sufficed to move the Court on these other issues. Legislatures (including the Congress) that refuse to look at or to accept the evidence accumulated over a generation against capital punishment and that instead tacitly yield to the collective wish for vengeance and violent solutions to the problem of crime should not be able to count any longer upon the indulgence of a people whose Constitution expressly prohibits "cruel and unusual punishment."

The easiest and most obvious way for the courts to proceed to invoke the foregoing argument might be to insist that capital punishment for some classes of offenders (e.g., juveniles)—in those states where adolescents are not protected by stringent juvenile delinquency statutes—is "cruel and unusual"; and to do the same for persons sentenced to death for some classes of crimes (e.g., crimes against property). The difficulty in both cases is that it is unlikely for a jury to bring in a death sentence against a juvenile or for a property offense that is not subject to reversal on some ground less novel than violation of the Eighth Amendment. This is the dilemma of finding a death penalty case suitable for appeal, which when appealed presents no plausible reason for reversal except that of "cruel and unusual punishment." Only with such a case could the Supreme Court effectively attack the death penalty using the strategy discussed above.

v The Right to Life

If the Eighth Amendment has so far served mainly to mark off historic cruelties rather than to protect against chronic excesses, the Ninth Amendment had all but been forgotten except by school children studying civics—until June 1965, when the Supreme Court decided *Griswold v. Connecticut*. In that case, the Court rules that the state anti-birth control statute was an unconstitutional invasion of the right of marital privacy. This right, though not specified in the Bill of Rights, was nevertheless among those rights "retained by the people," to which the Ninth Amendment alludes. The *Griswold* case is the first in which these "retained rights" served as the ground for a Supreme Court decision.[91] Commentators have said that the Ninth Amendment is a general recognition of inherent or natural rights,[92] and it is a neglected quarter from which any number of individual rights not otherwise spelled out may yet receive constitutional protection. Hitherto, the main source for expanding the catalogue of individual rights beyond those explicitly listed in the Constitution has been the "due process" and "equal protection" clauses of the Fifth and Fourteenth Amendments. The list of new rights obtained by constitutional interpretation of the doctrine of "retained rights", after lying dormant for generations, is not likely to burgeon overnight. The delphic elusiveness of the constitutional language and the vagueness of the leading (and all but solitary) ruling in *Griswold* provide excellent reasons for the courts to proceed slowly and with great caution. When, therefore, one considers a possible Ninth Amendment argument against the death penalty, one all but crosses the boundary of possible constitutional interpretation and enters upon wholly speculative territory.

If one studies individual rights explicitly asserted in the Constitution and then reviews the "fundamental," "natural," or "human" rights familiar to students of political and social thought, surely the most obvious omission from the Constitution is the historic *right to life*. The appeal to this right was commonplace in theorists such as Hobbes, Locke, Rousseau, and Paine, and equally familiar in the American pamphlet literature of the eighteenth century prior to the Declaration of Independence.[93] Nor can one forget its prominence in the Declaration itself: "[A]ll men are created equal . . . endowed by their Creator with certain unalienable Rights . . . among these are Life, Liberty and the pursuit of Happiness." Constitutional lawyers and the courts are equally silent on the legal status in today's law of the Declaration. What is plain is that in the two hundred years since the Declaration was written, nothing has been said by the Supreme Court about any "right to life" in the course of interpreting the Constitution, and the phrase itself appears in its decisions only in passing.

Yet if one had such a right rooted in the Constitution—and it is hard to see how colonists could have had it in 1776 and citizens have lost it after 1791—it would almost certainly have to emerge through interpretation of the "retained rights" clause. Even so, could it be viewed as consistent with the imposition (state or federal) of death penalties for crimes under the peacetime criminal code? Some may think so, for any of several reasons. Some would reduce the right to life to make it indistinguishable from the guarantees of "due process," however implausible on its face this may be. Others are prepared to see it transformed into a bundle of "welfare" or "social" rights, as in the discussions sponsored from its inception by UNESCO. Most would want to argue, as Locke and his successors did, that any right to life that a person has is forfeited by a crime that violates this right in another. Even if these theories can be avoided, it is unlikely that the right to life, any more than the rights explicitly cited in the Constitution, would be accorded status as an "absolute" right, in the sense that state action under *no* circumstances could justifiably abridge it. Still, appeal to the right to life may have irresistible attraction for anyone conscious of our political and constitutional history and convinced of the folly of capital punishment.

Is it really conceivable, however, that the courts would consider an argument to the effect that the death penalty is inconsistent with a tacit constitutional right to life, and yet reject an argument to the effect that the death penalty is inconsistent with the explicit constitutional prohibition of cruel and unusual punishment? I find an affirmative answer implausible. It is possible that the weight of history might in the end absolutely bar the courts from relying on the Eighth Amendment alone to overthrow the death penalty, and this might seem to make a Ninth Amendment argument somewhat more attractive. The same difficulty, however, arises when one appeals to the historic "fundamental" and "natural" right to life: it was expressly advocated by avowed defenders of capital punishment, such as Locke and Blackstone, without any sense of inconsistency whatever.[94]

One thing is clear. The general layout of the argument developed in Section V, in which the indecency and unnecessary cruelty of the death penalty, as well as its relative inferiority to imprisonment in meeting the legitimate aims of punishment, are the crucial premises, would have to be transferred more or less intact for use in a Ninth Amendment attack on the death penalty. Perhaps what this invites is a consolidation of argument against the death penalty, marshaling reasons from both its unusual cruelty and its putative violation of a fundamental human right.

vi A Mandate for Judicial Repeal

A close student of the workings of the Supreme Court has observed that "the capital case receives more attention than any other class of cases coming before the Court."[95] One can only view this fact with a curious mixture of pride and dismay; but there is no sign of relief so long as the death penalty remains on the statutes. It has been my purpose in this essay to review all the major forms that argument might take against the constitutionality of capital punishment as such, and to urge that the time is ripe for appellate courts to attack the laws that make capital cases possible. One cannot predict whether the courts will accept one or another of the lines of reasoning sketched out here. The arguments all have interest and relevance, though they are of uneven merit. Further empirical research is needed at several crucial points if even the most favorable argument is to succeed. It is urgent that sociologists and criminologists conduct this research, since there is no doubt any longer that the courts will be presented with arguments essentially like those we have reviewed here; yet the arguments are not likely to prevail so long as the relevant evidence is missing. There is also reason, unfortunately, to expect that the state legislatures (and Congress) will continue to be sluggish in discharging their responsibility to bring our penal codes into conformity with the "evolving standards of decency." The courts cannot hope to escape their heavy responsibility. It is time for them to secure as a constitutional bulwark for civilized life what other branches of government have so far failed to provide: abolition of the death penalty for all crimes.[96]

3 Deterrence and the Death Penalty

Ernest van den Haag's recent article, "On Deterrence and the Death Penalty,"[1] raises a number of points of that mixed character (i.e., empirical-and-conceptual-and-normative) that typifies most actual reasoning in social and political controversy but that (except when its purely formal aspects are in question) tends to be ignored by philosophers. I pass by any number of tempting points in his critique to focus in detail only on those that affect his account of what he says in the major topic, namely, the argument for retaining or abolishing the death penalty as that issue turns on the question of *deterrence*.

On this topic, van den Haag's main contentions seem to be these five: (1) Abolitionists of a utilitarian persuasion "claim that capital punishment is useless because it does not deter others." (2) There are some classes of criminals and some circumstances in which "the death penalty is the only possible deterrent." (3) As things currently stand, "deterrence [namely, of criminal homicide by the death penalty] has not been demonstrated statistically"; but it is mistaken to think that "non-deterrence" has been demonstrated statistically. (4) The death penalty is to be favored over imprisonment, because "the added severity of the death penalty adds to deterrence, or may do so." (5) "Since it seems more important to spare victims than to spare murderers, the burden of proving that the greater severity inherent in irrevocability adds nothing to deterrence lies on those who oppose capital punishment."

Against these contentions I propose to argue as follows: regarding (1), utilitarian abolitionists do not argue as van den Haag claims, and they would be in error if they did; his assertion in (2), that situations exist in which the death penalty is the only possible deterrent, is misleading and, in the interesting cases, is empirically insignificant; concerning (3), the heart of the dispute, van den Haag is correct in affirming that deterrence has not been determined statistically, but he is incorrect in denying that nondeterrence has been demonstrated statistically; his suggestion, (4), that the added severity of the death penalty contributes to its deterrent function, is unempirical and one-sided as well; finally, his contention regarding the burden of proof, (5), which he would impose entirely upon abolitionists, is a dodge and is based on a muddled analysis.

The reason for pursuing in some detail what at first might appear to be mere polemical controversy is not that van den Haag's essay is so persuasive or likely to be of unusual influence. The reason is that the issues he raises, even though they are familiar, have not been nearly adequately discussed, despite a dozen

45

state, congressional, and foreign government investigations into capital punishment in recent years. In Massachusetts, for example, several persons under sentence of death have been granted stays of execution pending the final report of a special legislative commission to investigate the death penalty. The exclusive mandate of this commission is to study the question of deterrence.[2] Its provisional conclusions, published late in 1968, though not in the vein of van den Haag's views, are liable to the kind of criticism he makes. This suggests that his reasoning may be representative of many who have tried to understand the arguments and research studies brought forward by those who would abolish the death penalty, and therefore that his errors are worth exposure and correction once and for all.

1. The claim van den Haag professes to find "most persuasive," namely, "capital punishment is useless because it does not deter others," is strange, and it is strange that he finds it so persuasive. Anyone who makes this claim must assume that only deterrent efficacy is relevant to assessing the utility of a punishment. In a footnote, van den Haag implicitly concedes that deterrence may not be the only utilitarian consideration, when he asserts that whatever our penal "theory" may tell us, "deterrence is . . . the *main actual* function of legal punishment if we disregard non-utilitarian ones" (italics added). But he does not pursue this qualification. It may be conceded that if 'the main actual function' means the main intended or professed function of a punishment for those responsible for instituting it, deterrence is probably the main function of punishment. His definition of deterrence, however, remains vulnerable. According to van den Haag, it is "a preconscious, general response to a severe but not necessarily specifically and explicitly apprehended or calculated threat."

This definition of deterrence has two merits and at least one fatal defect. First, it preserves the idea that "a law can have no deterrent effect upon a potential criminal if he is unaware of its existence."[3] Surely, this is a truism necessary to the establishment of a definition of "deterrence." Second, by emphasizing threats, it avoids the errors in defining deterrence as "the preventive effect which actual or theoretical punishment of offenders has upon potential offenders."[4] On such a definition, one could not distinguish between the *deterrent* effect of the death penalty and its more inclusive *preventive* effects. Obviously, an executed criminal is prevented from further crimes, but not by having been deterred from them.[5]

Only rarely will the preventive and the deterrent effects of a given punishment be equivalent. Van den Haag's definition, however, falls before a similar objection upon consideration of the general, though by no means universal, desire of persons to avoid capture and punishment for the crimes they commit. Some criminologists have thought this desire to be the primary outcome of the threat of severe punishments. If so, then the outcome can result whether or not the deterrent function succeeds. Yet such a desire to avoid punishment is embraced by van den Haag's rubric of "general response" and therefore could count as evidence for the deterrent efficacy of a punishment! Since van den Haag's conception of deterrence does not discriminate between such fundamentally different types of "general response" to the threat of punishment, it is too ill-formulated as a definition to be of any serious use.

Among the ideas to be incorporated into any definition of deterrence are a pair of truisms: if someone has been deterred, then he doesn't commit the crime; and conversely, if someone does commit a crime, then he hasn't been deterred. Likewise, the key notion in deterrence is prevention by threat of punishment.

Accordingly, let us say (definition 1) that a given punishment (P) is a *deterrent* for a given person (A) with respect to a given crime (C) at a given time (t) if and only if A does not commit C at t because he believes he runs some risk of P if he commits C, and A prefers, *ceteris paribus*, not to suffer P for committing C. This definition does not presuppose that P really is the punishment for C (a person could be deterred through a mistaken belief); it does not presuppose that A runs a high risk of incurring P (the degree of risk could be zero); or that A consciously thinks of P prior to t (the sort of theory needed to account for the operation of A's beliefs and preferences on his conduct is left open). Nor does it presuppose that anyone ever suffers P (P could be a "perfect" deterrent), nor that only P could have deterred A from C (some sanction less severe than P might have worked as well). Finally, it does not presuppose that because P deters A at t from C, therefore P would deter A at any other time or anyone else at t. The definition ensures that we cannot argue erroneously from the absence of instances of C to the conclusion that P has succeeded as a deterrent: the definition contains conditions that prevent this. But the definition does allow us to argue from occurrences of C to the conclusion that P has failed on each such occasion as a deterrent. Further, the definition prevents the commission of the more subtle converse error of arguing from the fact that A has not been deterred by P to the conclusion that A will (or must have) commit(ted) C. Both these errors arise from supposing that "the educative, moralizing and habituative effects of punishment",[6] which serve to prevent the bulk of the public from committing crime, are euphemisms for "deterrence" or operate by the same mechanisms that deterrence does.

Definition 1 suggests a general functional analogue appropriate to express scientific measurements of *differential deterrent efficacy* of a given punishment for a given crime with respect to a given population. Let us say (definition 2), that a given punishment, P, deters a given population, H, from a crime, C, to the degree, D, that the members of H do not commit C because they believe that they run some risk of P if they commit C and, *ceteris paribus*, they prefer not to suffer P for committing C. If $D = 0$, then P has completely failed as a deterrent; whereas if $D = 1$, P has proved to be a perfect deterrent. Given this definition and the appropriate empirical results for various values of P, C, and H, it should be possible to establish on inductive grounds the relative effectiveness of a given punishment (the value of D) as a deterrent.

Definition 2 in turn suggests the following corollary for assertions of relative superior deterrent efficacy of one punishment over another. A given punishment, P_1 is a superior deterrent to another punishment, P_2, with respect to some crime, C, and some population, H, if and only if: if the members of H believe that they are liable to P_1 upon committing C, then they commit C to the degree D_1; whereas if the members of H believe that they are liable to P_2 upon committing C, they commit C to the degree D_2, and $D_1 < D_2$. This formulation plainly allows that P_1 may be a more effective deterrent than P_2 for C_1 and yet less effective as a deterrent than P_2 for a different crime C_2 (with H constant), and so forth, for other possibilities. When speaking about deterrence in the pages that follow, I presuppose these definitions and this corollary. For the present, it is sufficient to notice that they have, at least, the virtue of eliminating the vagueness of van den Haag's definition complained of earlier.[7]

Even if van den Haag's notion of deterrence did not need to be reformulated to accommodate these improvements, we would still be left with a decisive objection to his claim. Neither classic nor contemporary utilitarians have argued for or against the death penalty *solely* on the ground of deterrence, nor would their ethical theory entitle them to do so. One measure of the nondeterrent utility of the death penalty derives from its elimination (through death of a known criminal) of future possible crimes from that source; another arises from the elimination of the criminal's probable adverse influence upon others to emulate his ways; another may lie in the lower budgetary outlays of tax moneys needed to finance a system of capital punishment as opposed to long-term imprisonment. There are still further consequences apart from deterrence, which the scrupulous utilitarian must weigh, along with the three I have mentioned. Therefore, it is incorrect to think that if it could be demonstrated that the death penalty is not a deterrent, then we would be entitled to infer, on utilitarian assumptions, that "the death penalty is useless" and therefore ought to be abolished. The problem for the utilitarian is to make commensurable such diverse social utilities as those measured by deterrent efficacy, administrative costs, etc., and then to determine which penal policy in fact maximizes utility. Finally, inspection of sample arguments actually used by abolitionists[8] will show that van den Haag has attacked a straw man: there are few if any contemporary abolitionists (and van den Haag names none) who argue solely from professedly utilitarian assumptions, and it is doubtful whether there are any nonutilitarians who would abolish the death penalty solely on grounds of its deterrent inefficacy.

2. Governments faced by incipient rebellion or threatened by a coup d'état may well conclude, as van den Haag insists they should, that rebels (as well as traitors and spies) can be deterred, if at all, only by the threat of death, since "swift

victory" of the revolution "will invalidate [the deterrent efficacy] of a prison sentence."[9] This does not yet tell us how important it is that such deterrence be provided, any more than the fact that a threat of expulsion is the severest deterrent available to university authorities tells them whether they ought to insist on expelling campus rebels. Also, such severe penalties might have the opposite effect of inducing martyrdom, of provoking attempts to overthrow the government to secure a kind of political sainthood. Van den Haag recognizes this possibility, but claims in a footnote that it "hardly impair[s] the force of the argument." Well, from a logical point of view it impairs it considerably; from an empirical point of view, since we are without any reliable facts or hypotheses on politics in such extreme situations, the entire controversy remains quite speculative.

The one important class of criminals deterrable only by the death penalty, if at all, consists, according to van den Haag, of those already under "life" sentence or guilty of a crime punishable by "life." In a trivial sense, he is correct; a person already suffering a given punishment, P, for a given crime, C_1, could not be expected to be deterred by anticipating the reinfliction of P were he to commit C_2. For if the anticipation of P did not deter him from committing C_1, how could the anticipation of P deter him from committing C_2, given that he is already experiencing P? This generalization seems to apply whenever P = "life" imprisonment. Actually, the truth is a bit more complex, because in practice (as van den Haag concedes, again in a footnote) so-called "life" imprisonment always has its aggravations (e.g., solitary confinement) and its mitigations (parole eligibility). These make it logically possible to deter a person already convicted of criminal homicide and serving "life" imprisonment from committing another such crime. I admit that the aggravations available are not in practice likely to provide much added deterrent effect; but exactly how likely or unlikely this effect is remains a matter for empirical investigation, not idle guesswork. Van den Haag's seeming truism, therefore, relies for its plausibility on the false assumption that "life" imprisonment is a uniform punishment not open to further deterrence-relevant aggravations and mitigations.

Empirically, the objection to his point is that persons already serving a "life" sentence do not in general constitute a source of genuine alarm to custodial personnel. Being already incarcerated and integrated into the reward structure of prison life, they do not seem to need the deterrent controls allegedly necessary for other prisoners and the general public.[10] There are exceptions to this generalization, but there is no known way of identifying them in advance and their number has proved to be small. It would be irrational, therefore, to design a penal policy (as several states have)[11] that invokes the death penalty in the apparent hope of deterring such convicted offenders from further criminal homicide. Van den Haag cites no evidence that such policies accomplish their alleged purpose, and I know of none. As for the real question that van den Haag's argument raises—is there any class of actual or potential criminals for which the death penalty exerts a marginally superior deterrent effect over every less severe alternative?—we have no evidence at all, one way or the other. Until this proposition, or some corollary, is actually tested and confirmed, there is no reason to indulge van den Haag in his speculations.

3. It is not clear why van den Haag is so eager to discuss whether there is evidence that the death penalty is a deterrent, or whether—as he thinks—there is no evidence that it is not a deterrent. For the issue over abolishing the death penalty, as all serious students of the subject have known for decades, is not whether (1) *the death penalty is a deterrent*, but whether (2) *the death penalty is a superior deterrent to "life" imprisonment*, and consequently the evidential dispute is also not over (1) but only over (2). As I have argued elsewhere,[12] abolitionists have reason to contest (1) only if they are against *all* punitive alternatives to the death penalty. Since few abolitionists (and none cited by van den Haag) take this extreme view and are reconciled to a punitive alternative of "life" imprisonment, we may concentrate on (2) here. We should notice in passing, however, that if it were demonstrated that (1) were false, there would be no need for abolitionists to go on to marshal evidence against (2), since the truth of (1) is a presupposition of the truth of (2). While it is true that some abolitionists may be faulted for writing as if the falsity of (1) followed from the falsity of (2), this is not a complaint van den Haag makes nor is it an error on which the abolitionist argument against the death penalty depends. Similar considerations inveigh against certain prodeath penalty arguments. Proponents must do more than establish (1), they must also provide evidence in favor of (2); and they cannot infer from evidence which establishes (1) that (2) is true or even probable [unless, of course, that evidence would establish (2) independently]. These considerations show how important it is to distinguish (1) and (2) and the questions of evidence that each raises. Van den Haag never directly discusses (2), except when he observes in passing that "the question is not only whether the death penalty deters but whether it deters more than alternatives." Since he explicitly argues only over the evidential status of (1), it is unclear whether he chose to ignore (2), or whether he thinks that his arguments regarding the evidence for (1) also have consequences for (2). Perhaps van den Haag thinks that if there is no evidence disconfirming (1), then there can be no evidence disconfirming (2); or perhaps he thinks that none of the evidence disconfirming (2) also disconfirms (1). (If he thinks either, he is wrong.) Or perhaps he is careless, conceding on the one hand that (2) is important to the issue of abolition of the death penalty, only to slide back into a discussion exclusively about (1).

Van den Haag writes as if his chief contentions were these two: first, we must not confuse (*a*) the assertion that there is no evidence that (1), with (*b*) the assertion that there is evidence that not-(1) [i.e., evidence that (1) is false]; and second, abolitionists have asserted (*b*) whereas all they are entitled to assert is (*a*).[13] I wish to proceed on the assumption that since (1) is not chiefly at issue, neither is (*a*) nor (*b*) (though I grant, as anyone must, that the distinction between these propositions is legitimate and important). What is chiefly at issue, even though van den Haag's discussion obscures the point, is whether abolitionists must content themselves with asserting that there is no evidence against (2), or whether they may go further and assert that there is evidence that not-(2). I shall argue that abolitionists may make the stronger, latter, assertion.

In order to see the issue fairly, it is necessary to see how (2) has so far been submitted to empirical test. First of all, the issue has been confined to the death penalty for criminal homicide; consequently, it is not (2) but a subsidiary proposition which critics of the death penalty have tested, (2*a*) *the death penalty is a superior deterrent to "life" imprisonment for the crime of criminal homicide*. The falsification of (2*a*) does not entail the falsity of (2); the death penalty could still be a superior deterrent to "life" imprisonment for the crime of burglary, etc. However, the disconfirmation of (2*a*) is obviously a partial disconfirmation of (2). Second, (2*a*) has been tested only indirectly. No one has devised a way to count or estimate directly the number of persons in a given population who have been deterred from criminal homicide by fear of the penalty. The difficulties in doing so are plain enough. For instance, it would be possible to infer from the countable numbers who have not been deterred (because they did commit a given crime) that everyone else in the population was deterred, but only on the assumption that the only reason a person did not commit a given crime is because he was deterred. Unfortunately for this argument (though happily enough otherwise) this assumption is almost certainly false. Other ways that one might devise to test (2*a*) directly have proved equally unfeasible. Yet it would be absurd to insist that there can be no *evidence* for or against (2*a*) unless it is *direct* evidence for or against it. Because van den Haag nowhere indicated what he thinks would count as evidence, direct or indirect, for or against (1), much less (2), his insistence upon the distinction between (*a*) and (*b*) and his rebuke to abolitionists is in danger of implicitly relying upon just this absurdity.

How, then, has the indirect argument over (2*a*) proceeded? During the past generation, at least eight different hypotheses have been formulated, as corollaries of (2*a*), as follows:[14]

i. use of the death penalty ought to cause a decrease in the subsequent rate of criminal homicide;
ii. use of the death penalty should not lead to an increase in the subsequent rate of criminal homicide;
iii. death-penalty jurisdictions should have a lower annual rate of criminal homicide than abolition jurisdictions;
iv. jurisdictions that abolished the death penalty should show an increased annual rate of criminal homicide after abolition;
v. jurisdictions that reintroduced the death penalty should show a decreased annual rate of criminal homicide after reintroduction;

vi. given two contiguous jurisdictions differing chiefly in that one has the death penalty and the other does not, the latter should show a higher annual rate of criminal homicide;
vii. police officers on duty should suffer a higher annual rate of criminal assault and homicide in abolition jurisdictions than in death penalty jurisdictions;
viii. prisoners and prison personnel should suffer a higher annual rate of criminal assault and homicide from life term prisoners in abolition jurisdictions than in death penalty jurisdictions.

It could be objected to these eight hypotheses that they are, as a set, insufficient to settle the question posed by $(2a)$ no matter what the evidence for them may be [i.e., that falsity of (i)-(viii) does not entail falsity of $(2a)$]. Or it could be argued that each of (i)-(viii) has been inadequately tested or insufficiently (dis)confirmed so as to establish any (dis)confirmation of $(2a)$, even though it is conceded that if these hypotheses were highly (dis)confirmed they would (dis)confirm $(2a)$. Van den Haag's line of attack is not entirely clear with respect to these two alternatives. It looks as if he ought to take the former line of criticism in its most extreme version. How else could he argue his chief point, that the research used by abolitionists has so far failed to produce *any* evidence against (1)—he presumably means (2) or $(2a)$? Only if (i)-(viii) were *irrelevant* to $(2a)$ could it be fairly concluded from the evidential disconfirmation of (i)-(viii) that there is still no disconfirmation of $(2a)$. And this is van den Haag's central contention. The other ways to construe his reasoning are simply too implausible to be considered: he cannot think that the evidence is indifferent to or *confirms* (i)-(viii); nor can he think that there has been no *attempt* at all to disconfirm $(2a)$; nor can he think that the evidence which disconfirms (i)-(viii) is not therewith also evidence that confirms the negations of (i)-(viii). If any of these three was true, it would be a good reason for saying that there is "no evidence" against $(2a)$; but each is patently false. If one inspects (i)-(viii) and $(2a)$, it is difficult to see how one could argue that (dis)confirmation of the former does not constitute (dis)confirmation of the latter, even if it might be argued that verification of the former does not constitute verification of the latter. I think, therefore, that there is nothing to be gained by pursuing further this first line of attack.

Elsewhere, it looks as though van den Haag takes the other alternative of criticism, albeit rather crudely, as when he argues [against (vi), I suppose, though he nowhere formulated (i)-(viii)] that "the similar areas are not similar enough." As to why, for example, the rates of criminal homicide in Michigan and in Illinois from 1920 to 1960 are not relevant because the states aren't "similar enough," he does not try to explain. But his criticism does tacitly concede that if the jurisdictions *were* "similar enough," then it would be logically possible to argue from the evidence against (vi) to the disconfirmation of $(2a)$. And this seems to be in keeping with the nature of the case; it is this second line of attack that needs closer examination.

Van den Haag's own position and objections apart, what is likely to strike the neutral observer who studies the ways in which (i)-(viii) have been tested and declared disconfirmed is that their disconfirmation, and, *a fortiori*, the disconfirmation of (2*a*), is imperfect for two related reasons. First, all the tests rely upon *unproved empirical assumptions*; second, it is not known whether there is any *statistical significance* to the results of the tests. It is important to make these concessions, and abolitionists and other disbelievers in the deterrent efficacy of the death penalty have not always done so.

It is not possible here to review all the evidence and to reach a judgment on the epistemic status of (i)-(viii). But it is possible and desirable to illustrate how the two qualifications cited above must be understood, and then to assess their effect on the status of (2*a*). The absence of statistical significance may be illustrated by reference to hypothesis (vii). According to the published studies, the annual rate of assaults upon on-duty policemen in abolition jurisdictions is lower than in death penalty jurisdictions (i.e., a rate of 1.2 attacks per 100,000 population in the former as opposed to 1.3 per 100,000 in the latter). But is this difference statistically significant or not? The studies do not answer this question because the data were not submitted to tests of statistical significance. Nor is there any way, to my knowledge, that these data could be subjected to any such tests. This is, of course, no reason to suppose that the evidence is really not evidence after all, or that though it is evidence against (vii), it is not evidence against (2*a*). Statistical significance is, after all, only a measure of the strength of evidence, not a *sine qua non* of evidential status.

The qualification concerning unproved assumptions is more important, and is worth examining somewhat more fully (though, again, only illustratively). Consider hypothesis (iii). Are we entitled to infer that (iii) is disconfirmed because in fact a study of the annual homicide rates (as measured by vital statistics showing cause of death) unquestionably indicates that the rate in all abolition states is consistently lower than in all death penalty states? To make this inference we must assume that (A_1) homicides as measured by vital statistics are in a generally constant ratio to criminal homicides; (A_2) the years for which the evidence has been gathered are representative and not atypical; (A_3) however much fluctuations in the homicide rate owe to other factors, there is a nonnegligible proportion that is a function of the penalty; and (A_4) the deterrent effect of a penalty is not significantly weakened by its infrequent imposition. There are, of course, other assumptions, but these are central and sufficiently representative here. Assumption A_1 is effectively unmeasurable because the concept of a criminal homicide is the concept of a homicide that *deserves* to be criminally prosecuted. Nevertheless, A_1 has been accepted by criminologists for over a generation.[15] A_2 is confirmable, on the other hand, and bit by bit, a year at a time, is apparently being confirmed. Assumption A_3 is rather more interesting. To the degree to which it is admitted or insisted that factors other than the severity of the penalty affect the rate of homicide, A_3 becomes increasingly dubious; but at the same time testing (2*a*) by (iii) becomes increasingly unimportant. The urgency of testing (2*a*) rests upon the assumption that it is the deterrent efficacy of penalties that is the chief factor in the rate of crimes, and it is absurd to hold that assumption and at the same time doubt A_3. On the other hand, A_4 is almost certainly false (and has been believed so by Bentham and other social theorists for nearly two hundred years). The falsity of A_4, however, is not of fatal harm to the disconfirmation of (iii) because it is not known how infrequently a severe penalty such as death or life imprisonment needs to be imposed in order to reach its maximum deterrent efficacy. Such information as we do have leads one to doubt that for the general population the frequency with which the death sentence is imposed makes any significant difference to the rate of criminal homicide.

I suggest that these four assumptions and the way in which they bear upon interpretation and evaluation of the evidence against (iii), and therefore the disconfirmation of (2*a*), are typical of what one finds as one examines the work of criminologists as it relates to the other corollaries of (2*a*). Is it reasonable, in the light of these considerations, to infer that we have no evidence against (i)-(viii), or that although we do have evidence against (i)-(viii), we have none against (2*a*)? I do not think so. Short of unidentified and probably unobtainable "crucial experiments," we shall never be able to marshal evidence for (2*a*) or for (i)-(viii), except by means of certain additional assumptions such as A_1-A_4. To reason otherwise is to rely on nothing more than that it is logically possible to grant the evidence against (i)-(viii) and yet deny that (2*a*) is false; or it is to insist that the assumptions that the inference relies upon are not plausible assumptions at all (or though plausible are themselves false or disconfirmed) and that no other assumptions can be brought forward that will both be immune to objections and still preserve the linkage between the evidence and the corollaries and (2*a*). The danger now is that one will repudiate assumptions such as A_1-A_4 to guarantee the failure of efforts to disconfirm (2*a*) via disconfirmation of (i)-(viii); or else that one will place the standards of evidence too high before one accepts the disconfirmation. In either case one has begun to engage in the familiar but discreditable practice of "protecting the hypothesis" by making it, in effect, immune to any kind of disconfirmation.

In sum, then, the abolitionist's argument regarding deterrence has the following structure: an empirical proposition not directly testable, (2), has a significant corollary, (2*a*), which in turn suggests a number of subordinate corollaries, (i)-(viii), each of which is testable with varying degrees of indirectness. Each of (i)-(viii) has been tested. To accept the results as evidence disconfirming (i)-(viii) and as therefore disconfirming (2*a*), it is necessary to make certain assumptions, of which A_1-A_4 are typical. These assumptions in turn are not all testable, much less directly confirmed; some of them, in their most plausible formulation, may even be false (but not in that formulation necessary to the inference, however). Since this structure of indirect testing, corollary hypotheses, and unproved assumptions is typical of the circumstances that face us when we wish to consider the evidence for or against any complex empirical hypothesis such as (2), I conclude that while (2) has by no means been disproved (whatever that might mean), it is equally clear that (2) has been disconfirmed, rather than confirmed or left untouched by the inductive arguments we have surveyed.

I have attempted to review and appraise the chief "statistical" arguments (as van den Haag calls them) marshaled during the past fifteen years or so in this country by those critical of the death penalty. To assess these arguments more adequately, it is helpful to keep in mind two other considerations. First, most of the criminologists skeptical of (1) are led to this attitude not by the route we have examined—the argument against (2)—but by a general theory of the causation of crimes of personal violence. Given their confidence in that theory, and the evidence for it, they tend not to credit seriously the idea that the death penalty deters (very much), much less the idea that it is a superior deterrent to a severe alternative such as "life" imprisonment (which may not deter very much, either). The interested reader should consult in particular Marvin E. Wolfgang's monograph, *Patterns of Criminal Homicide*, and his reader, *Studies in Homicide*. Second, very little of the empirical research purporting to establish the presence or absence of deterrent efficacy of a given punishment is entirely reliable, because almost no effort has been made to isolate the relevant variables. Surely, it is platitudinously true that *some* persons in *some* situations considering *some* crimes can be deterred from committing them by *some* penalties. To go beyond this, however, and supplant these variables with a series of well-confirmed functional hypotheses about the deterrent effect of current legal sanctions is not possible today.[16]

Even if one cannot argue, as van den Haag does, that there is no evidence against the claim that the death penalty is a better deterrent than life imprisonment, this does not yet settle the reliability of the evidence. Van den Haag could, after all, give up his extreme initial position and retreat to the concession that although there is evidence against the superior deterrent efficacy of the death penalty, still, the evidence is not very good—indeed, not good enough to make reasonable the policy of abolishing the death penalty. The reply, so far as there is one, short of further empirical studies (which undoubtedly are desirable), is twofold: the evidence against (i)-(viii) is uniformly confirmatory; and this evidence is in turn made intelligible by the dominant current sociological theory of the causation of crimes of personal violence. Finally, there do not seem to be any good empirical reasons in favor of keeping the death penalty, as a deterrent or for any other reason, a point to be amplified in the paragraphs that remain.

4. Van den Haag rests considerable weight on the claims that "the added severity of the death penalty adds to deterrence, or may do so"; and that "the generalized threat of the death penalty may be a deterrent, and the more so, the more generally applied." These claims are open to criticism on at least three grounds.

First, as the modal auxiliaries signal, van den Haag has not really committed himself to any affirmative empirical claim, but only to a truism. It is always logically possible, no matter what the evidence, that a given penalty which is *ex hypothesi* more severe than an alternative, may be a better deterrent under some conditions not often realized, and be provably so by evidence not ever detectable. For this reason, there is no possible way to prove that van den Haag's claims are false, no possible preponderance of evidence against his conclusions that must, logically, force him to give them up. One would have hoped those who believe in the deterrent superiority of the death penalty could, at this late date, offer their critics something more persuasive than logical possibilities. As it is, van den Haag's appeal to possible evidence comes perilously close to an argument from ignorance: the possible evidence we might gather is used to offset the actual evidence we have gathered.

Second, van den Haag rightly regards his conclusion above as merely an instance of the general principle that, *ceteris paribus*, "the Greater the Severity the Greater the Deterrence," a "plausible" idea, as he says. Yet the advantage on behalf of the death penalty produced by this principle is a function entirely of the evidence for the principle itself. But we are offered no evidence at all to make this plausible principle into a confirmed hypothesis of contemporary criminological theory and specially relevant to crimes of personal violence. Until we see evidence concerning specific crimes, specific penalties, specific criminal populations, which shows that in general the greater the severity the greater the deterrence, we run the risk of being stupefied by the merely plausible. Besides, without any evidence for this principle we will find ourselves at a complete standoff with the abolitionist who, of course, can play the same game. He has his own equally plausible first principle: *the greater the severity of punishment the greater the brutality provoked throughout society*. When at last, frustrated and exhausted by mere plausibilities, we once again turn to study the evidence, we will find that the current literature on deterrence in criminology does not encourage us to believe in van den Haag's principle.

Third, van den Haag has not given any reason why, in the quest for deterrent efficacy, one should fasten (as he does) on the severity of the punishments in question, rather than, as Bentham long ago counseled, on all the relevant factors, notably the facility, celerity, and reliability with which the punishment can be inflicted. Van den Haag cannot hope to convince anyone who has studied the matter that the death penalty and "life" imprisonment differ only in their severity, and that in all other respects affecting deterrent efficacy they are equivalent; and if he believes this himself it would be interesting to see the evidence that convinced him. The only thing to be said in favor of fastening exclusively upon the question of severity in the appraisal of punishments for their relative deterrent efficacy is that augmenting the severity of a punishment in and of itself usually imposes little if any added direct cost to operate the penal system; it even may be cheaper. This is bound to please the harried taxpayer, and at the same time gratify the demand that government "do something" about crime. Beyond that, emphasizing the severity of punishments as the main (or indeed the sole) variable relevant to deterrent efficacy is unbelievably superficial.

5. Van den Haag's final point concerning where the burden of proof lies is based, he admits, on playing off a certainty (the death of the persons executed) against a risk (that innocent persons, otherwise the would-be victims of those deterrable only by the death penalty, would be killed).[17] This is not as analogous as he seems to think it is to the general nature of gambling, investment, and other risk-taking enterprises. In none of them is death deliberately inflicted, as it is, for instance, when carrot seedlings are weeded out to enable those remaining to grow larger (a eugenic analogy, by the way, which might be more useful to van den Haag's purpose). In none, that is, do we venture a *sacrifice* in the hope of a future net gain; there is only the *risk* of a loss in that hope. Moreover, in gambling ventures we recoup what we risked if we win, whereas in executions we must lose something (the lives of persons executed) no matter if we lose or win (the lives of innocents protected). Van den Haag's attempt to locate the burden of proof by appeal to principles of gambling is a failure.[18]

Far more significantly, van den Haag frames the issue in such a way that the abolitionist has no chance of discharging the burden of proof once he accepts it. For what evidence could be marshaled to prove what van den Haag wants proved, that "the greater severity inherent in irrevocability [of the death penalty] ... adds nothing to deterrence"? The evidence alluded to earlier in this essay does tend to show that this generalization (the negation of van den Haag's own principle) is indeed true, but it does not prove it. I conclude, therefore, that either van den Haag is wrong in his argument that shows the locus of burden of proof to lie on the abolitionist, or one must accept less than proof to discharge this burden (in which case, the very argument van den Haag advances shows that the burden of proof now lies on those who would retain the death penalty).

"Burden of proof" in areas outside judicial precincts where evidentiary questions are at stake tends to be a rhetorical phrase and nothing more. Anyone interested in the truth of a matter will not defer gathering evidence pending a determination of where the burden of proof lies. For those who do think there is a question of burden of proof, as van den Haag does, they should consider this: advocacy of the death penalty is advocacy of a rule of penal law that empowers the state to take human life deliberately and in general to threaten the public with the taking of life. *Ceteris paribus*, one would think anyone favoring such a rule would be ready to offer considerable evidence for its necessity and efficacy. Surely, some showing of necessity, some evidentiary proof, is required to satisfy the skeptical. Exactly when and in what circumstances have the apologists for capital punishment offered evidence to support their contentions? Where is that evidence recorded for us to inspect, comparable to the evidence cited earlier in this essay against the superior deterrent efficacy of the death penalty? Van den Haag conspicuously cited no such evidence, and so it is with all other proponents of the death penalty. The insistence that the burden of proof lies on abolitionists, therefore, is nothing but the rhetorical demand of every defender of the status quo who insists upon evidence from those who would effect change, while reserving throughout the right to dictate criteria and standards of proof and refusing to offer evidence for his own view.[19]

I should have thought that the death penalty was a sufficiently momentous matter and of sufficient controversy that the admittedly imperfect evidence assembled over the past generation by those friendly to abolition would have been countered by evidence tending to support the opposite, retentionist, position. It remains a somewhat sad curiosity that nothing of the sort has happened; no one has ever published research tending to show, however inconclusively, that the death penalty after all is a deterrent, and a superior deterrent to "life" imprisonment.[20] Among scholars, at least, if not among legislators and other politicians, the perennial appeal to burden of proof really ought to give way to offering of proof by those interested enough to argue the issue.[21]

4

The Death Penalty in America: Review and Forecast

The threshold of a new decade is a conventional period for stocktaking, so it is not unfitting that the accomplishments, frustrations, and prospects of the movement to abolish the death penalty in the United States should undergo a review at this time. Let us look first at a dozen of the highlights from the past decade and the trends of rapid change we have experienced.

In the 1960s, six states—Oregon (1964), West Virginia (1965), Vermont (1965), Iowa (1965), New York (1965), and New Mexico (1969)—abolished the death penalty with few or no qualifications. In only one other decade have more states entered the abolition category. That was between 1907 and 1917, when ten states abolished the death penalty for murder; but by 1919, five had reintroduced it.[1]

During the 1960s, only one state, Delaware, reintroduced the death penalty (in 1961) after having abolished it in 1958. Late in 1970, the constitutionality of the hasty legislation that reintroduced it has been challenged in court on quite technical and perhaps insufficient grounds.[2]

During the past decade, the last mandatory death penalties for first degree murder were repealed—in the District of Columbia (1962) and New York (1963)—to be replaced by optional death sentences subject to jury discretion. A dozen other felonies, not all involving criminal homicide, in more than a dozen jurisdictions continue to carry the mandatory death penalty. The crimes for which they are specified, however, rarely occur.[3]

Between 1961 and 1970 several new kinds of crime were made capital offenses by the federal government, notably air piracy (1961) and assassination of the president or vice president (1964). In 1970 Governor Ronald Reagan of California signed into law the death penalty for anyone who explodes a "destructive device" causing great harm or injury to a person.[4]

Whereas the number of persons received annually under death sentence has not significantly changed between 1961 and 1970, the total death sentence population has *tripled* during the decade. It increased from an average of 145 during the 1950s[5] to an average of 325 during the 1960s (see Table 4-1). As of February 1971 it stands at the all-time high of 617 (see Table 4-2).

During the 1960s, hearings were held on the federal death penalty in the House (in 1960) under Congressman Abraham J. Multer, and in the Senate (in 1968) under Senator Philip A. Hart.[6] This was the first time in history that both houses of Congress held such hearings. While they did afford an unprecedented national forum for attack on the death penalty, they did not really compare to

Table 4-1
Executions, Commutations, and Death Sentences in the United States, 1961-1971

Year	Received Under Death Sentence	Total Under Death Sentence[a]	Commutations	Executions
1961	140	219	17	42
1962	103	266	27	47
1963	93	268	16	21
1964	106	298	9	15
1965	86	332	19	7
1966	118	351	17	1
1967	85	415	13	2
1968	102	434	16	0
1969	*	479	*	0
1970	*	525[b]	*	0
1971		620[c]		

Source: *National Prisoner Statistics*, Number 45, tables 1 and 4, "Executions 1930-1968," August 1969, for the years 1961-1969.

[a]As of January 1.

[b]Source: Bureau of Prisons, *National Prisoner Statistics*, as reported by LDF in its brief *amici curiae* in *McGautha v. California*, O.T. 1970, No. 203, p. 15 note 18.

[c]Source: *Newsweek*, 11 January 1971, p. 23.

*No data available as of March 1971.

the forceful parliamentary inquiries on the death penalty conducted in Great Britain (1954) and Canada (1956), which subsequently led to all but complete abolition in both countries for experimental periods beginning in 1965 and 1968, respectively.

During the 1960s, opposition to the death penalty continued to be the policy of almost all major organized church groups in the country, and became the national policy of a number of secular nationwide organizations with professional or political stature. Chief among these were the National Council on Crime and Delinquency (1963), the American Civil Liberties Union (1965), the American Correctional Association (1966), and the NAACP Legal Defense and Educational Fund.

Because of delays in the courts and appeal litigation, the record time spent under death sentence rose during the past decade from eleven years, ten months, seven days (set by Caryl Chessman, executed 2 May 1960 in California) to more than thirteen years in several cases.[7] Over the same period, the *average* time under death sentence *more than doubled*, from 14.4 months to 32.6.[8]

Table 4-2
Persons Under Death Sentence in the United States, 1971

State	Total	Murder	Rape	Other
All states	617	433*	78*	5*
Alabama	28	20	7	1 (robbery)
Arizona	17	17		
Arkansas	0			
California	94	*	0	*
Colorado	7	7		
Connecticut	3	3		
Delaware	3	3		
D.C.	1	1		
Florida	72	49	23	
Georgia	28	19	8	1 (robbery)
Idaho	0			
Illinois	30	30		
Indiana	7	7		
Kansas	1	1		
Kentucky	16	16		
Louisiana	43	27	16	
Maryland	19	15	4	
Massachusetts	15	15		
Mississippi	7	*	*	*
Missouri	11	11		
Montana	0			
Nebraska	2	2		
Nevada	6	6		
New Hampshire	2	2		
New Jersey	22	22		
New York	1	1		
North Carolina	15	13	1	1 (rape/robbery)
Ohio	42	42		
Oklahoma	12	12		
Pennsylvania	27	27		
South Carolina	10	7	3	
South Dakota	0			

Table 4-2 (cont.)

State	Total	Murder	Rape	Other
Tennessee	12	6	6	
Texas	41	31	8	2 (armed robbery)
Utah	4	4		
Virginia	8	6	2	
Washington	11	11		
Wyoming	0			

Source: Citizens Against Legalized Murder, Douglas Lyons, chairman.
*Data are reported as of 8 February and are incomplete as to capital crimes under which death sentence prisoners were convicted.

In 1965 Ramsey Clark, then deputy attorney general of the United States, announced that the office of the attorney general was opposed to the death penalty in the District of Columbia.[9] During the next three years Clark lent the weight of his office to the cause of abolition. In a memorable speech in 1968, during the hearings before Senator Hart's subcommittee, the then Attorney General Clark said, in part:

Society pays a heavy price for the penalty of death it imposes. Our emotions may cry vengeance in the wake of a horrible crime. But reason and experience tell us that killing the criminal will not undo the crime, prevent other crimes, or bring justice to the victim, the criminal, or society. Executions cheapen life. We must cherish life .... The death penalty should be abolished.[10]

In 1967 unprecedented class actions initiated by the LDF attorneys were successful in blocking all executions in Florida, then California, and subsequently, in effect, throughout the nation, pending judicial determination of federal "due process" and "equal protection" issues raised against state death sentences for murder, rape, and other crimes.[11] At the same time, the LDF undertook to provide counsel for all condemned persons anywhere in the United States for whom adequate legal representation could not otherwise be obtained.

The year 1968 was recorded as the first calendar year in American history during which no execution occurred anywhere under American civil law. What many hope will turn out to be the last legal execution in the United States occurred in Colorado on 2 June 1967.[12]

In 1969 the United States Supreme Court for the first time heard argument against the death penalty on the ground that it is unconstitutional under the Eighth Amendment ("cruel and unusual punishment"), in *Boykin v. Alabama*,[13] a case involving not murder or rape, but robbery. The court reversed the conviction, though not on this ground.

Within the last month of 1970 and the first month of 1971, four extraordinary and unprecedented events occurred, and they may prove to be auguries of even more profound changes to come in the months and years immediately ahead:

On 11 December 1970 the United States Court of Appeals for the Fourth Circuit held in the case of *Ralph v. Warden* that the death penalty for rape, when the victim's life was neither taken nor endangered, violates the Eighth Amendment prohibition against cruel and unusual punishment.[14] This is the first judicial determination by an appellate court that any capital statute is in violation of the Eighth Amendment.

On 29 December 1970 Governor Winthrop Rockfeller of Arkansas, although defeated for his bid for reelection in the previous November, commuted the sentence of all fifteen men under sentence of death. "I hope the position I take will have an influence on other Governors," he is quoted as saying.[15] Governor Warren Hearnes of Missouri, chairman of the National Governors Conference, said he was certain the matter would be taken up at the next Governors Conference, slated for 23 February 1971.[16]

On 7 January 1971 the National Commission on Reform of Federal Criminal Laws, under the chairmanship of Edmund G. Brown, former governor of California, released its final report. The Commission recommended abolition of all federal death penalty statutes, a shift from the position it took in the study draft in June 1970.[17] Although the recommendation against the death penalty was not accepted by two of the twelve commissioners, Senators Sam J. Ervin and John L. McClellan,[18] considerable editorial interest and support has been registered across the nation for this particular recommendation.[19]

On 19 January 1971 Attorney General Fred Speaker of Pennsylvania ordered the state's electric chair dismantled and declared that Pennsylvania's death penalty was "unconstitutional and unenforceable." Louis Schwartz, director of the National Commission for Reform of Criminal Laws, commented, "The constitution is the supreme law of the land and the governor and attorney general take an oath to support it. But if in good faith they decided that executions are forbidden by the constitution, I see no way the courts could compel the governor to carry them out."[20] Less than two weeks later, however, J. Shane Creamer, Mr. Speaker's successor as attorney general, rescinded the constitutional ruling. He did let stand the dismantling of the electric chair, and further ordered all death row prisoners to be returned to the general prison population.[21]

Some of these events and trends do not warrant a further elaboration in this necessarily brief survey. Others have been treated elsewhere at adequate length, as the references and citations show. But several are interesting surface phenomena of deeper causes, and they deserve further scrutiny. Still other important patterns and possibilities are not so easily depicted in a memorable event or striking statistic; they, too, require commentary and analysis. Accordingly, I shall devote the remainder of this review and forecast to five topics:

Public Opinion, Deterrence, Miscarriages of Justice, Legislative Reform, and *Constitutional Litigation*. These topics by no means exhaust all the general themes of importance deserving survey, but they are the most prominent and they will have to suffice here. Much of the other information of interest is available through a volume I edited, *The Death Penalty in America.*

Public Opinion. What the American public currently believes about the death penalty must be inferred from two quite different sorts of data at least. One sort has been obtained at the voting booths in four different states during the past decade. In 1964 Oregon abolished all its death penalties by a constitutional referendum; the vote was 455,654 to 302,105. In 1966 the voters of Colorado upheld its death penalty statutes by a vote of 389,707 to 193,245. Then, in 1968, Massachusetts voters, in an advisory referendum, also voted to keep the death penalty, 1,159,348 to 730,649. In Illinois, late in 1970, the electorate approved a new state constitution but defeated an amendment to outlaw capital punishment by 1,110,189 to 607,096.

In no other decade of American history have there been such referenda on this issue, and in three of these four cases, as we see, the public preferred to keep rather than discard capital punishment. A careful study of even one of these campaigns has yet to be published, but from my personal participation in two of them, I would say it is fairly clear that the public will vote against the death penalty only if it has been skillfully persuaded by a well-organized campaign, fully supported by state and local politicians, and not opposed by law enforcement spokesmen or any other major interest group. Only the first of these can be secured by money alone (it is worth noting that to win the 1964 Oregon referendum, four times the money per voter was spent as in Massachusetts in 1968). Otherwise, public campaigns such as this are at the mercy not only of money but also of chance. One brutal slaying a few weeks before the election can destroy months of patient and otherwise effective education. The prospect in this country for abolition at the polls during the 1970s, therefore, is not very great.

Among specialized groups surveyed for their attitudes on the death penalty, the sharp conflict that can emerge is well illustrated by two polls published during November 1969. *Psychology Today* reported that 65 percent of its readers polled were against the death penalty even for the "premeditated murder of a policeman" and 86 percent were against it for "forcible rape."[22] But *Good Housekeeping* declared that its readers supported the death penalty "nearly two to one"; 62.1 percent believed it was "a deterrent to murder and other serious crimes," including kidnapping and political assassination.[23] How scientific either of these polls was it is impossible to judge. What is strongly suggested by these results is that since the more sophisticated and better educated readership tends strongly to oppose the death penalty even for the gravest crimes, there is considerable basis for hope that in the years ahead, as mass higher education continues to expand, we shall see more rather than less opposition to the death penalty and other brutal forms of social control.

Comprehensive public opinion polls of the Gallup and Harris type, as I have reported elsewhere,[24] show that over the years from 1936 to 1966 the American public moved noticeably away from support of capital punishment to a (near or bare) majority in opposition to it. But that majority is shifting and unstable. A recent review of such surveys[25] shows that the latest Gallup Poll (February 1969) puts the American public back exactly where it was a decade earlier: 51 percent of the people are still "for" the death penalty for convicted murderers, and 40 percent against it (in 1960 it was 36 percent).[26] This study confirms the generally accepted view that younger persons tend to oppose the death penalty, that women oppose it more strongly than men, but it disconfirms the view that whereas the better educated oppose it the blue collars and "hard hats" support it. Despite the polls that showed significant support for capital punishment in Canada and in Britain during the 1960s, their parliaments voted significantly in favor of all but complete abolition.[27] Only in a handful of states in America have we seen comparable legislative leadership during the past decade.

With the possible exception of Oregon, therefore, the six states that abolished the death penalty in this country during the past decade probably did so without the support of a majority of the public. Since there is no reason to expect public sentiment to undergo a significant and rapid shift favoring abolition during the present decade, one can nourish hopes for statutory repeal of the death penalty in the immediate years ahead only if significant moral suasion and political skill are brought on behalf of repeal in Congress and state legislatures. The public is almost certainly not going to rise up in collective indignation and demand it.

Deterrence. In October 1968 the Special Commission of the Massachusetts Legislature to Investigate the Effectiveness of Capital Punishment as a Deterrent to Crime rendered its seventeen-page interim report. Although the Commission undertook no research of its own, the majority had no difficulty in reaching the conclusion, expressed in the report's opening sentence, that "the death penalty is not a deterrent to crime." This position had received some national publicity during the previous year, as it was essentially the same conclusion reached by the President's Commission on Law Enforcement and Administration of Justice.[28] A minority of the Massachusetts Commission, six of the fourteen members, however, were dissatisfied with this conclusion. They argued that "because of the lack of enforcement of the death penalty in Massachusetts [no execution since 1947], no one can intelligently determine whether it is a deterrent—it certainly is not an effective deterrent as presently administered...."

I believe these conclusions of the majority and minority in the 1968 Massachusetts Study Commission are typical of where the line of disagreement is drawn at present on the issue of capital punishment as a deterrent. With the precipitous nationwide falling off of executions during the past decade, the argument of the minority will likely become generally heard throughout the nation. Nonopponents of the death penalty (one hesitates to call them "retentionists") will be heard increasingly to argue that since the death penalty is not really used any more (or very much), and since we cannot expect the unenforced statutory provisions of capital punishment to constitute much of a threat, therefore we cannot conclude that the death penalty as such is no deterrent, but only that as presently administered it is not effective as a deterrent.

There is a certain irony, therefore, in the *de facto* trend toward abolition. It further weakens the ability of those who would oppose the death penalty on grounds of its failure as a general deterrent to marshal convincing evidence to establish their case. Skepticism and the appeal to ignorance will remain the last ditch defense for those who, in their heart of hearts, *know* that the death penalty is an effective deterrent and therefore do not want it abolished. Their ultimate argument (as we have heard it expressed so many times) goes like this: "It is easy to number the failures, but we cannot number the successes. No one can ever know how many people have refrained from murder because of the fear of being hanged." As Thorsten Sellin has rightly said, this is a red herring.[29]

It is still somewhat surprising, however, that the past decade has produced no new research on the differential deterrent efficacy of capital punishment—namely, research that would show whether it is more or less or equally (in)effective as imprisonment in deterring capital crimes. Even so, the belief that the death penalty is no deterrent, or (what is more to the point) that it is no better a deterrent than imprisonment, has become a commonplace of contemporary criminology.[30] The earlier well-known research conducted mainly by Sellin during the 1950s, and summarized in his article in *Federal Probation* ten years ago,[31] continues to be the mainstay in the area, and the prospects are not very good for adding to it in any novel or decisive way. At most, perhaps, we can develop (as I have tried to sketch elsewhere)[32] a fuller analysis of the relevant variables in the very concept of deterrence, and a closer fit between the familiar statistical correlations from the research of Sellin and others and a general theory of the causation of crimes of personal violence, their diminution and prevention.

What we should watch for, in the years immediately ahead, is to see whether those in authority who believe the death penalty is a deterrent (provided it is actually enforced) will be successful in their attack upon the procedural safeguards developed during the past two decades. This raises a question that honest believers in the deterrent efficacy of the death penalty seem unwilling to face: how many constitutional rights should criminal defendants be expected to sacrifice so that they can be convicted and executed more swiftly, in order to obtain the deterrent protection it is believed will ensue? The tragedy is that whereas it is easy to identify the rights in question, it will be difficult to point to any gain in security from crime. History has yet to record a single empirical study undertaken by those who defend the death penalty on deterrent grounds. It will be interesting to see whether the forthcoming decade in any way remedies this notable failure.

Miscarriages of Justice. The classic argument that the death penalty must be abolished to avoid executing innocent persons—expressed in the quotation, attributed to the Marquis de Lafayette, "I shall ask for the abolition of the punishment of death until I have the infallibility of human judgment demonstrated to me"[33]—no longer plays the role in debates over the death penalty that it once did. Not that miscarriages of justice in capital cases no longer occur. A far from complete list published since my survey in 1962[34] shows a number of examples that deserve wider publicity. In his testimony before the Senate hearings on abolition of the death penalty, Donal McNamara cited three clear cases (in South Carolina, Florida, and Pennsylvania) where homicide convictions were secured against persons innocent of the crime.[35] Four recent cases, three of them from New York alone, may be mentioned here as additions to the record. In 1966 the manslaughter conviction of Miguel Arroyo was dismissed after Arroyo had spent a year in prison and another man, Jose Velasquez, was arrested for the crime.[36] Isidore Zimmerman spent twenty-four years under arrest and in prison, including three years on Sing Sing's death row, for the murder of a policeman he did not kill.[38] In Texas, Anastacio Vargas spent four years in jail and was on the verge of execution in 1964 when the real murderer confessed.[39]

None of these cases represents the execution of an innocent person, and that is some consolation. But they do show that research into the past and into current events will continue to uncover cases that come closer than one would want to that tragic extreme. No doubt, a vastly greater number of miscarriages of justice go all but unnoticed in connection with crimes that do not carry the death penalty. It is also a false sentimentality to argue that the death penalty ought to be abolished because of the abstract possibility that an innocent person might be executed, when the record fails to disclose that such cases occur. But one may justifiably reply that the social advantages obtained from capital punishment are too elusive to warrant its preservation, given the incontestable record of our failure to convict only the guilty.

Far more significant as a development than the discovery of death sentences of the innocent was the growing documentation during the 1960s of systematic miscarriages of justice in the normal administration of capital crimes. Chief among these demonstrable unfairnesses was the role played by *race* in determining indictments, convictions, sentences, appeals, clemency, and executions. More research needs to be done on the subject, as on all other aspects of racism in America, and especially in the criminal justice system of the several states. Even so, the pattern of discrimination and injustice has begun to receive documentation. Two minor studies appeared during this period and tended to confirm the belief that convicted murderers are more likely to be sentenced to death[40] and less likely to be commuted[41] if they are black than if they are white. The major research effort in this area in recent years has been conducted under the auspices of the LDF and directed by Marvin Wolfgang. To date, only some of the results have been published, notably in support of appellate court cases contesting death penalty convictions for rape.[42] What was carefully studied was whether the race of the criminal and his victim would prove to be correlated at a statistically significant level with type of sentence among convicted rapists. In the case of *Maxwell v. Bishop*, Arkansas data were reported and the analysis showed "conclusively that Negro defendants convicted of rape of a white woman were disproportionately frequently sentenced to death"[43] and "no non-racial variable of which analysis was possible could account for the differential observed."[44] Wolfgang naturally concluded that "Negro defendants who rape white victims have been disproportionately sentenced to death, by reason of race, during the years 1945-1965 in the State of Arkansas."[45]

Sociology is not infrequently accused of laboring to demonstrate the obvious, and this conclusion one might well view in that light. Yet the difference between science and superstition, between verified claims and conventional wisdom, lies in precisely such careful data gathering and statistical analysis as can be found in Wolfgang's studies. So far, the courts before whom this evidence has been laid have turned their backs on the legal argument it was meant to bolster, and in some cases found other reasons to reverse.[46]

What has happened during the past decade, I suggest, is that the attack against the death penalty on grounds of unfairness has shifted away from the classic questions surrounding the innocent (their conviction, sentence, or execution) to a whole host of procedural unfairnesses that exhibit irreversible harm when they involve the death penalty. Racial discrimination is perhaps only the most obvious of these systematic miscarriages of justice. As all of them have been documented with increasing accuracy and publicity and used to raise constitutional questions about capital punishment, I defer further discussion of these issues to a later section of this review.

Legislative Reform. During the 1960s repeal of death penalty statutes was achieved in five states. Only in Oregon was the death penalty lodged in the state constitution. In four—Iowa, West Virginia, Vermont, and New Mexico—it came as a result of direct action by the legislature, in each case with the support (and notably in Vermont and New Mexico, with the active leadership) of the governor. Although the full story has not been told in detail, the general outlines of the way abolition was achieved seem comparable to what happened in Delaware in 1958 (the first state to end the death penalty in forty years; both Hawaii and Alaska, which abolished capital punishment in 1957, did so while they were still territories). The story of Delaware has been told elsewhere in detail and need not be recounted here.[47] Only in New York was the death penalty abolished as a result of a recommendation by a special penal law revision commission. It remains to be seen whether the recommendation from the National Commission on Reform of Federal Criminal Laws (cited earlier) will have a comparable influence on Congress.

No one has kept close watch and marked the progress of the bills filed annually during session of the three dozen state legislatures where the death penalty for murder still prevails. Since the high water mark five years ago, few abolition bills have been near passage. Despite occasional successes, the defeats have been numerous, repeated, and seemingly unavoidable. In Massachusetts, for example, hearings before the Judiciary Committee on abolition bills have been held each spring in the past decade, but those who participate in them (no doubt on both sides of the platform) cannot escape a sense of futile repetition in these annual performances. In Massachusetts, it seems, we can go for a generation without a legal execution in our prisons; we cannot go one day without the death penalty on our statutes. The factors that explain this nationwide legislative apathy are not difficult to identify: (1) police spokesmen still form an organized lobby in favor of death penalties in many states; (2) the diminishing number of executions and the remoteness of death row from the ambit in which politicians prefer to travel make the issue of capital punishment slightly less real each year for the legislature; (3) the readiness of appellate courts to extend stays of execution, to grant reversals of death penalty convictions, and to cooperate with resourceful defense counsel for condemned men, encourages the typical legislator to believe that abolishing the death penalty is no longer his problem because it has become one for the judiciary; (4) the enormous political pressure since 1968 built up behind "law and order candidates" tends to make abolition of the death penalty an unpopular public stance for a politician.

Nevertheless, legislative reform of death penalty laws remains in the 1970s, as it has for decades, the main challenge facing the abolition movement in this country. What is needed is well illustrated by the continuous labors of responsible state legislators, such as Senator Robert K. Holliday of West Virginia. Beginning in 1963, he introduced abolition bills in his State legislature, and after seeing his work succeed in 1965, he has continued to keep a watchful eye on the subject and to use his good offices to secure continuing education among subsequent legislatures.[48] Elsewhere, notably in California, where the abolition issue for a decade has caused continuous controversy and is now caught up in the political struggle between "ins" and "outs," it is very difficult to see how forward progress can be made. The only hope, I believe, lies in those smaller states where a simpler, more rational, less acrimonious political setting prevails, and thus where patient, trusted politicians can exercise leadership on this issue. Then, we can hope the larger states will be encouraged (or even shamed) into following the lead of their neighbors. Even as I say this, however, I cannot wholly suppress a certain skepticism. My own state, Massachusetts, for example, has had the example of abolition in its immediate neighbor, Rhode Island, since 1852. I wish I could believe that the Bay State will learn in the next decade what it has not learned in the past century.

Constitutional Litigation. It has rightly been said more than once that, in this country, a moral controversy tends to become a legal dispute, whereas a legal dispute tends to become an issue of constitutional interpretation. So it is not surprising that during the 1960s the fight to abolish the death penalty—carried on for over a century in legislative halls and gubernatorial chambers around the nation—has become increasingly concentrated in appellate courts, state and federal, at every level. The typical educated person, acquainted with the facts about the actual operation of the death penalty in this country, is bound to wonder how it is possible for the death penalty to continue year after year in the face of constitutional prohibitions of "cruel and unusual punishment" and constitutional protections of "due process of law" and "equal protection of law." It now seems incredible that the first serious scholarly attack on the constitutionality of capital punishment under the Eighth Amendment did not occur until Gerald Gottlieb's pioneering essay in 1961.[49] The first notice of this line of argument by the Supreme Court did not come until 1963, in the dissenting opinion of then Justice Arthur J. Goldberg in *Rudolph v. Albama.*[50] By 1970, the traditionally conservative *Harvard Law Review* carried a lengthy article by former Justice Goldberg and his erstwhile law clerk, Alan M. Dershowitz, developing this line of argument to the fullest degree.[51] As I mentioned earlier, the first attempt to present this argument before the Supreme Court, in the *Boykin* case in 1969, was unsuccessful, despite the fact that this case (a death sentence for simple robbery, unaccompanied by any assault, much less murder) "presented the strongest possible setting for a cruel and unusual punishment holding."[52]

Meanwhile, as I have also previously noted, the LDF attorneys since 1967 have secured nationwide delays in all executions pending resolution of various other constitutional issues they have raised in a host of death penalty cases. The most important of the LDF cases was *Maxwell v. Bishop*, held over for reargument from the 1968 to the 1969 term, and finally decided in June 1970.[53] Maxwell was sentenced to death for rape, but the case raised issues having possible effect upon almost all death penalty statutes and death penalty convictions. Under attack were two almost universal practices in death penalty cases: *standardless sentencing* and *the unitary trial*. The first of these means that juries with discretionary power to award a death or life sentence, subsequent to conviction of a capital crime, operate without any statutory or other standards in arriving at the sentence they mete out. The second means that the defendant is torn between his right of allocution (to address the court on his own behalf) and his right against self-incrimination, cross-examination, and impeachment.

These twin obstacles to fair procedures, it is argued, help us account for the facts that, since 1930, 54 percent of all persons executed and 89 percent of all those executed for rape were black.[54] Clarence Darrow and other founders of the American League to Abolish Capital Punishment in the 1920s made famous the fact that the executed were "the poor, the ignorant, the friendless." In the 1960s, the LDF made it clear that they were black, and that this was no mere accident, either. But the Supreme Court, although it spared Maxwell, did so without making any new ruling of general application.

If *Boykin* and *Maxwell* represent less than perfect success for those trying to use constitutional resources in attacks upon death penalty statutes, two other 1968 cases managed to have a favorable effect. In the first of these, *United States v. Jackson*, the Supreme Court held that the Federal Kidnapping Act contained an unconstitutional death penalty provision.[55] The kidnapping statute provided that a defendant could guarantee that he would avoid a death sentence if he chose to avoid a trial by jury and accept sentencing by a judge; but this, the Court held, was bound "to discourage assertion of the fifth amendment right not to plead guilty and to deter the exercise of the sixth amendment right to demand a jury trial."[56] A subsequent memorandum from the attorney general's office indicated that this decision probably rendered seven of the sixteen federal death penalty statutes unconstitutional.[57]

The second case was *Witherspoon v. Illinois*. In its decision in this case, the Court held that the usual practice of excluding prospective jurors for cause from capital trials because of their conscientious scruples against the death sentence rendered the verdicts of those trial juries constitutionally invalid.[58] The essence of the Court's argument was that the defendant cannot have an impartial jury on the issue of his guilt or innocence when the jury has been drawn with an explicit bias in favor of the death penalty. The background of this line of reasoning is to be found in the research by Walter E. Oberer, then of the University of Texas Law School, beginning in 1961.[59] In the following years his argument received some experimental support that showed that these so-called "scrupled juries" tend in fact to be biased against the defendant on questions such as guilt versus innocence.[60] The immediate result of the *Witherspoon* ruling, even though it was given full retroactivity by the Court, was slight. Even though many cases have been remanded by the courts to determine whether the *Witherspoon* ruling applied, only in a minority of cases have death sentences been vacated on the ground that they violated *Witherspoon*.[61]

As of this writing, the chief cases before the Supreme Court are *McGautha v. California* and *Crampton v. Ohio*, combined for argument in November 1970 and likely to be decided some time in the spring of 1971. They continue questions raised earlier but unsuccessfully in *Maxwell* and attempt to show that the death penalty juries have arbitrary sentencing power in violation of the "equal protection" and "due process" clauses of the Constitution. The argument developed by the petitioners, however, reaches to the situation of all but a few of the hundreds now under death sentence.[62] A reversal in these cases would be potentially so comprehensive that the solicitor general has been invited by the Court to supply a brief *amicus curiae* arguing against all of the claims advanced by the petitioners. (This is perhaps consistent with the reputed support being given to capital punishment by the attorney general's office in the Nixon administration.) The battle lines in 1971, therefore, have been drawn more clearly than before, as the pressure mounts on the Supreme Court to use its powers to end death penalties.

If the Court refuses to overthrow the unitary trial and standardless sentencing in the cases now before it, what lies ahead? Are there further possibilities available whereby on essentially collateral attack (viz., attack on procedure alone) the death penalty might be rejected by the Court because it can be administered only by unconstitutional methods? I have reviewed the possibilities elsewhere.[63] No doubt, inchmeal progress toward abolition has been and will continue to be made by pursuing the procedural gambits reviewed above. As in the *Witherspoon* case (merely the latest of a long line of cases, going back at least as far as the famous "Scottsboro Boys" in the 1930s), the Court can and will, if pressed, introduce administrative reforms in the administration of criminal justice (state as well as federal) and these will make it more difficult to convict and sentence to death anyone of any crime.

As of February 1971 over 100 death penalty cases were pending before the Supreme Court on writ of *certiorari*, in which an enormous range of procedural objections to capital punishment have been raised and will be pursued in the years ahead. But procedural palliatives are rarely sufficient to achieve substantive cures. That is why the frontal assault on capital punishment as "cruel and unusual punishment"—a direct attack on the substance of the penalty, no matter how decently, fairly, and rationally it may be administered—looms as the profound issue of controversy in the 1970s. Indeed, it can be argued that all the judicial reforms in recent years have served only to set in a brighter light the fundamental, inescapable inhumanity of capital punishment. Fairly drawn juries, using rational standards for sentencing, can no doubt be achieved even in capital cases if we really want them. But for what purpose? To see that men are fairly, rationally—and therefore deservedly—sentenced to death and executed? Government lawyers might as well have spent their energies in the 1840s and 1850s attempting to create rational rules and procedures so as to mitigate the brutality, unfairness, and inefficiency of chattel slavery. The very attempt to make such things as slavery and executions fair and rational can only weaken the motives in decent men to preserve these practices at all. The chief legal developments to watch, therefore, are the ways in which legal scholars hammer away at the theme that the death penalty is in irremediable violation of the constitutional prohibition against "cruel and unusual punishment."

Conclusion. As we contemplate the threshold of an epoch without recourse to the death penalty, can abolitionists face the American public and assure them that getting rid of the death penalty, *de jure* as well as *de facto*, is truly reasonable, humane, and safe? Do we really know enough to support our moral, religious, and sentimental convictions? During the past decade, a considerable amount of relevant research has been published, far in excess of that made available in any previous decade. Some of it I have already cited, but some more of it also deserves mention. For instance, we have had published (1) extensive descriptive studies of the death sentence populations in states from every part of the country;[64] (2) records of judicial miscarriages of justice (discussed previously); (3) analyses of juror attitudes toward questions of guilt and sentence (also discussed previously); (4) records of incarceration and parole behavior of convicted murderers;[65] (5) studies in jury sentencing bias in capital cases (discussed previously); (6) an extensive search for implicit bias and/or standards in jury sentencing in murder cases;[66] (7) the practice and the law controlling the exercise of executive clemency;[67] (8) studies of how incarceration affects men awaiting execution on "death row";[68] and (9) a full digest of parole eligibility statutes for life term prisoners.[69] While it is true that little has been added to our knowledge on the controversy over deterrence beyond what was available in 1960 (as I have already explained), we can say that today we have an enormous body of research dealing with every important aspect of the death penalty, and that we have produced evidence for views that hitherto rested upon surmise and hypothesis.

Some years ago, after listening for several hours to "emotional and religious" views expressed in a public hearing, a state legislator in New Jersey asked with exasperation, "Are facts and figures and information available that can be laid on the table and discussed and considered, at least to attempt to evaluate the social effect of abolition of the death penalty?"[70] No one at the hearing or anywhere else had the answers he wanted. That was in 1957. Today, few arguments over the death penalty need to go begging for lack of relevant data.

What is most encouraging is that despite the nationwide preoccupation during the last few years with issues of law and order, anxiety over the rising crime rate, particularly flagrant crimes of personal violence (aircraft piracy, bombings of police stations, widespread use of addictive drugs—all of which have led to proposals for capital punishment), the trend against the death penalty has not been reversed or even significantly stalled. The only possible explanation is the steadily growing disbelief in the uniquely deterrent effect of severe criminal penalties. Interestingly enough, the war in Vietnam may have helped rather than hindered the growing revulsion at officially sanctioned violence—next to war, capital punishment remains the greatest affront to our civilized pretensions.

Abolitionists in the last two years occasionally have been overcome by apocalyptic nightmares of a "bloodbath" of executions in the mid-1970s unless the courts or legislatures or governors do something to cope with the rapidly growing numbers under death sentence. The very success in stalling executions since 1967 has created unprecedented possibilities of mass executions in many states. But a brighter prospect also emerges, as each day extends the moratorium of executions. No governor or court or legislature anywhere in the nation, despite occasional boasts and threats to the contrary, really wants to gain instant and worldwide notoriety as the first to violate the moratorium and resume executions. The pressures, therefore, to reverse death penalty convictions and to commute death sentences steadily increase even as the legislatures continue to evade or to balk at outright appeal. We are witnessing, therefore, a subtle struggle among powerful political forces deployed over a wide arena.

The striking quartet of events in the winter of 1970-1971 mentioned earlier shows precisely the kind of *official* sense of moral urgency that we must have if we are to survive this century in coping with the larger social ills confronting us. It is gratifying to see this moral urgency at last directed toward ending the long and bloody history of legal executions. When courts, governors, attorneys general, and penal reform commissions will openly reject executions, death sentences, and capital statutes despite the predictable grumbling from yahoo constituents, there is considerable hope that capital punishment in this nation will soon pass from desuetude into oblivion.

Addendum. On 3 May 1971, when this article was already in proof, the Supreme Court announced its decision in the *McGautha* and *Crampton* cases. By a vote of six to three, the Court affirmed both convictions, thereby dealing a severe but not wholly unpredicted blow to the aspirations of those who hope to have the federal courts dismantle the capital punishment system in this country. There is not space here to review the reasoning of the Court, of the dissenting Justices, nor to try to forecast whether this decision will lead to the first execution(s) since 1967 or what tactics in further appellate litigation will now unfold. From initial and scattered reports in the news media, it appears that in some states executions are now significantly more likely, whereas in other states the *McGautha* and *Crampton* decisions will have little effect. Two things only are clear. The Supreme Court has brought itself one significant step closer to facing the ultimate constitutional argument: is the death penalty "cruel and unusual punishment"? Meanwhile, the burden on the prison system (with 649 persons under death sentence as of May 1) and on the conscience of all thoughtful persons is noticeably heavier.

5 The Politics of Death

In the immediate aftermath of the bloody Attica prison rebellion, one small news item seems to have escaped public notice. The *New York Times* published the reassuring information that although New York has "officially" abolished the death penalty, it still retains this punishment for such crimes as the Attica rebels were widely (though, according to reliable later reports, falsely) believed to have committed: killing of a prison guard or official by a prisoner under life term imprisonment. The idea behind such provisions in the criminal law is not hard to identify. If a policeman's job is not a happy one, a truth we learned as children from Gilbert and Sullivan, imagine what it must be like to be a guard for long-term prisoners. Since prison policies have long prohibited the possession of weapons by the custodial force, what protection can society offer the keepers from the assaults of the kept? Only the threat of the stiffest possible penalty. On that theory, presumably, the guards at Attica and elsewhere have been able to leave their families each day feeling a little more secure than they would have without the backing of the most extreme sanction. It is society's way of paying its debt of conscience to the prison guards.

That, or something like it, is what we would expect officials to say in defense of capital punishment for prison killings. Ever since Rhode Island abolished the death penalty over a century ago, only to reintroduce it for homicide by life term prisoners, the complete and unqualified abolition of capital punishment has had a steady opposition expressed by those who believe that police and prison guards need the special protection the death penalty provides. Perhaps even more than that, they need the visible proof that society stands behind them in the war on crime and will not hesitate to provide the fullest possible protection for these defenders of law and order.

It may come as something of a shock to learn that research published during recent years shows convincingly that the rate of assaults, fatal or otherwise, in prisons by prisoners bears no correlation whatever to the severity of the punishment for such crimes. Prisoners in death penalty states are as likely, or more likely, to commit such crimes as are convicts in abolition states. The same conclusion has been reached concerning the special protection afforded to the police by the death penalty: actual research on murder and assault rates of police shows that law enforcement officers run no higher risk in abolition states than they do in death penalty jurisdictions. Indeed, criminologists are in uniform agreement that so far as the general safety of society is concerned, the death penalty makes no difference to homicide one way or the other.

So much for the evidence in support of the death penalty on grounds of deterrent efficacy. One suspects a rather different set of beliefs and attitudes really explains the policy of extermination of convicted criminals. Behind the belief in deterrence is an attitude of vengeance. Prison has failed to restrain the violence in these men; if they kill behind bars they deserve no more patience from the rest of us. Their lives are now, once and for all, forfeited to society. They deserve to be executed twice over: first, for the crime that got them a life sentence, and, second, for the homicide in prison. But that is not all. Behind revenge is the sense of helplessness and rage that seizes so many when they learn that convicts have killed guards. "What else are we to do with these savages?" the public asks. In sheer desperation, many are willing to embrace a policy of execution for violence by prisoners. The reports from Attica after the rebellion was put down showed precisely this sentiment among many of the local townspeople whose sons, fathers, and husbands had to reestablish authority over the mass of sullen convicts.

Sober belief in deterrence, suppressed desire for revenge, and a pervading sense of helplessness—this is the triad of motives that accounts for the repressive violence of the prison system in general, for brutal punishments, and especially for the threat of execution directed at dangerous persons inside and outside prisons.

The reality of capital punishment in the United States today, however, tells a very different story. A third of a million persons served time behind bars last year in this country. No one can seriously believe that all and only the worst convicts were those under sentence of death. No rational examination of the facts will allow anyone to believe that executing them will provide complete social defense against violent crime, even if it would reinforce some comforting illusions concerning crime.

Since June 1967, all executions have been stalled, in some cases at the last moment, through concerted action directed from New York by the NAACP Legal Defense and Educational Fund. Their efforts in securing appellate review, especially in federal courts, has resulted in a nationwide *de facto* moratorium. Meanwhile, over 700 persons are now under death sentence in thirty-four different states. Nothing stands between them and a fatal date with the executioner some time in 1972 or 1973 except a favorable outcome of the litigation now before the Supreme Court. More than half of the 700 are black, and all but seven are men. The youngest is a 16-year-old boy in Arkansas convicted of murdering and mutilating a farmer. Most of them are under death sentence for murder; seventy-four in ten southern states are awaiting execution for rape, and sixty-five of them are blacks found guilty of the rape of a white woman.

The interest of the nation's highest judicial tribunal in capital punishment dates from 1932, when, in the notorious "Scottsboro Boys" case, the Court threw out rape convictions on the ground that the defendants had been effectively denied counsel prior to trial. But not until the past few years has the Court been confronted with direct challenges to the imposition of death penalties under state law.

In 1968, near the very end of the Warren Court, two important decisions were handed down. In *Jackson v. United States*,[1] the federal kidnapping statute was declared unconstitutional because it induced a defendant to plead guilty to avoid the risk of the death penalty in a jury trial. This imposed too grave a burden on the naive but sincere defendant who pled not guilty and took his chances of life or death with the jury. The most significant attack on the death penalty in 1968 came in *Witherspoon v. Illinois*.[2] Here, it was held that the usual practice of excluding prospective jurors for cause from capital trials because of their conscientious scruples against the death sentence rendered the verdicts of those juries constitutionally unacceptable. Since this decision was given retroactive application, almost every person on death row was presented with a litigable issue.

During 1970 and 1971, the Court turned back major arguments in *Maxwell v. Bishop*,[3] in *McGautha v. California*,[4] and *Crampton v. Ohio*.[5] In these cases, the practices of "standardless sentencing" and the "unitary trial" were attacked as constitutionally flawed under the Fourteenth Amendment. Against the first practice, it was argued that juries with discretionary power to award a death or a life sentence in fact operated without any statutory or other standards in arriving at the sentence, and in fact were demonstrably subject to whim and prejudice. Against the second, it was objected that the unitary trial impales the defendant on the horns of a dilemma: he waives either his right of allocation, or his rights against self-incrimination, cross-examination, and impeachment. The Court was split in its verdicts, but it decided against the abolitionists.

The result of these decisions has been to place everything in the delicate balance of one final issue: whether the death penalty is unconstitutional under the Eighth Amendment prohibition of "cruel and unusual punishment." It does not take an ardent opponent of capital punishment to suppose that any constitution, such as ours, that officially carries such a prohibition, might eventually find the death penalty too much to tolerate. Nor does it take a shrewd constitutional lawyer to calculate that there must be some plausible explanation why the Bill of Rights could carry this prohibition since 1971 and yet allow the death penalty to continue as a respected bulwark of social defense to the present day.

A harbinger encouraging to abolitionists occurred in 1969, when, in *Ralph v. Warden*, the United States Court of Appeals for the Fourth Circuit held that a Maryland statute that imposed death on a rapist who neither otherwise harmed nor killed his victim was "cruel and unusual" punishment.

In May 1971 the Supreme Court indicated that it would hear arguments on the general question of the death penalty as "cruel and unusual" punishment during the next term, and briefs were filed at the end of the summer. At issue were cases from three states (California, Georgia, Texas) involving four different capital crimes: first degree murder,[6] unintended homicide during burglary (felony murder),[7] aggravated[8] and unaggravated rape.[9] The printed briefs submitted to the Court ran to hundreds of pages. Civil rights, civil liberties, and religious groups, legal aid and correctional associations, psychiatrists, and leading former governors opposed to the death penalty all supplied briefs as *amici curiae*. Oral argument was scheduled for early October, only to be postponed by the sudden resignation of Justices Hugo L. Black and John Marshall Harlan. Finally, with their successors, Lewis F. Powell, Jr., and William H. Rehnquist, duly nominated and appointed, the long-awaited argument was presented to the full bench of Justices on 17 January.

The legal setting in which the oral argument began was affected by two other events. On 6 January, in Los Angeles, Anthony G. Amsterdam of Stanford Law School argued before the California Supreme Court that capital punishment was "cruel and/or unusual" under the state and federal constitutions. In 1968, the California high court, by a vote of four to three, had ruled that the death penalty did not offend these constitutions. But the issue of cruelty and unusualness was not squarely at issue. Now, in *Anderson* and *Miller* cases, it was. Amsterdam, the nation's most experienced advocate before state and federal appellate courts on death penalty questions later expressed a guarded optimism over the outcome in California. If he was correct, it would be the first time in history that a state supreme court had declared any death penalty statute unconstitutional. This would be a significant departure from the usual judicial deference to legislative control over the permissible severity of punishments imposed by statute. With 105 convicts on death row in California, more than in any other state, much was at stake in whether Amsterdam's argument prevailed.

Then, on 17 January the New Jersey Supreme Court announced its decision in *State v. Funicello*.[10] The court declared that New Jersey's first degree murder statute was unconstitutional, and ordered all of the twenty convicts under death sentence to be resentenced to life imprisonment immediately. This unprecedented ruling by the state's highest court grew out of wholly technical considerations and was not based on any judicial revulsion at death penalties *per se*. Yet it illustrates vividly the wide range of legal and constitutional issues set in motion during recent years, mainly by the LDF, any of which can suddenly render a capital conviction or a capital statute null and void.

New Jersey was one of the few states whose principal capital statute seemed to suffer from exactly the same defect as the federal kidnapping statute knocked out in the 1968 *Jackson* ruling. Despite an earlier split verdict of the New Jersey Supreme Court to the contrary, the state attorney general's office filed a brief in the fall of 1971 in the *Funicello* case in support of ruling the state's death penalty statute for murder unconstitutional. With some show of reluctance, the New Jersey Supreme Court has now agreed and overruled itself. Governor William T. Cahill indicated he would not seek to restore the death penalty in a new murder statute drawn consistently with the *Jackson* and *Funicello* requirements. Instead, he would wait for the advice of his own special commission already at work studying the death penalty and until the United States Supreme Court speaks with finality on the constitutionality of capital punishment. Since all the other New Jersey capital statutes suffer from the same flaw that the murder statute was found to contain, the New Jersey Supreme Court's ruling effectively deprived the state of legally imposing the death penalty for any crime whatever. Thus, in New Jersey the burden of future argument over capital punishment has dramatically shifted from the opponents of execution to the proponents. Despite the constant demand for more law and less criminal disorder, no state that has abolished the death penalty during the past decade has so far reintroduced it.

On the same day that the New Jersey Supreme Court struck down that state's capital statutes, Amsterdam and Jack Greenberg, executive director of the LDF, together gave their long-awaited argument before the United States Supreme Court. For four hours the full Court listened to counsel and engaged them in continuous questioning from the bench. The focus of the long debate was Amsterdam's argument in *Aikens v. California*. His one-hundred-page printed brief was a masterpiece of legal, sociological, and historical argument in the highest traditions of constitutional litigation. The essence of his position was simple, original, and persuasive. The Supreme Court, Amsterdam claimed, is not engaged in illegitimate "judicial law-making" when it exercises supervision over state penal codes, to assure that they square with the protections in the Bill of Rights. Nor is the constitutional barrier against "cruel and unusual punishment" forever frozen in its meaning to apply only to those modes of punishment the Founding Fathers could not stomach.

Amsterdam and Greenberg were particularly emphatic that the Court is not to use as its standard of cruelty whatever "shocks the conscience" of the nine justices themselves. There is a more objective standard available. It is to be found by implication in what the state and federal governments *do* by way of actual punishments, not merely by what state legislatures and Congress, trial juries, and police spokesmen *say*.

What does this record show? Clearly, they argued, it shows that in the United States today we are willing to execute none but the social pariahs, that small minority of murderers and rapists who are too poor, too unpopular, too unlike the majority to be sentenced (as is the overwhelmingly large percentage of all offenders) to imprisonment. Capital punishment, at one time a general and regular mode of punishing serious offenders, has for a generation been all but unacceptable. It can exist today on the statute books only because it is used in practice almost not at all, and then only selectively, infrequently, unnecessarily. It follows from this that when it is used it is inevitably excessive and exceptional, and hence "cruel and unusual" in the true meaning of these words.

The several deputy attorneys general from California, Georgia, and Texas who had to reply to the Amsterdam-Greenberg argument were hard put to keep up a coherent rebuttal. Although Justices William Brennan and Lewis Powell seemed content merely to listen hour after hour, their colleagues continually interrupted counsel with questions. Justices William Douglas, Potter Stewart, and Byron White, especially, seemed troubled by many aspects of the cases. The questions they asked often had the lawyers defending the constitutionality of the death penalty under some strain. Perhaps the low point was reached when California's deputy attorney general accused Amsterdam of "regarding himself as some sort of self-appointed guardian of evolving standards of decency," and of asking the Court to "become a superlegislature to enact his own personal view of what the standards should be." This was a travesty of the thrust of Amsterdam's careful plea for objective and contemporary standards of punitive justice under the Constitution.

The Supreme Court is not expected to announce its decision until late in the spring. No one supposes that the Court will be easily persuaded to strike down capital punishment. Nevertheless, as Amsterdam and Greenberg expressed in their written brief, "Like flogging and banishment, capital punishment is condemned by history and will sooner or later be condemned by this Court."

Exactly a month later, in *People v. Anderson*, the California Supreme Court declared the death penalty "cruel or unusual punishment" under the state constitution. The opinion, written by Chief Justice Donald Wright and supported by the Court, with only one dissenter, held: "Capital punishment is unnecessary to any legitimate goal of the state and is incompatible with the dignity of man and the judicial process."[11] The language of California's own constitutional prohibition against "cruel or unusual punishment" and that of the federal constitution are not identical, and there is more than one way to preserve this judicial breakthrough without following it mechanically if the United States Supreme Court wishes.

Nevertheless, this stunning decision by one of the most prestigious state courts should make it just that much more difficult for the nation's highest court to decide otherwise, and the movement toward nationwide abolition on Eighth Amendment grounds may be irresistible.

Since the Attica rebellion, the great hope is that all forms of punishment have suddenly and dramatically been put on the defensive. Viewed against the deep and probing attitudes surfacing all around us, the death penalty may at last be generally recognized for the anachronism it is—a vestigial survivor from an earlier era, inglorious testimony to our incapacity and unwillingness to cope with violent crime except with violent repression.

Once viewed in this light, there need be no difficulty in consigning it to oblivion, to join all those other brutal methods of social control that have outlived every pretense of necessity and usefulness.

6

Challenging the Death Penalty

To appreciate the story that Michael Meltsner tells in his absorbing study, *Cruel and Unusual: The Supreme Court and Capital Punishment*, we have to think back to the status of the death penalty in our society a dozen years ago. In the summer of 1962, some 270 persons in eighteen state jurisdictions were waiting out stays of execution, and each week an average of two more persons entered prison under sentence of death. Nationwide, executions by electrocution, hanging, or lethal gas occurred at the rate of about one a week. Roughly two persons per month would leave "death row" for the general prison regimen because they had been granted executive commutation of sentence, and in an equal number of cases, the appellate courts would intervene and order a new trial. Generally, the death penalty and its constitutionality seemed immune from attack. No statute or court procedure or mode of inflicting the death sentence had ever been declared unconstitutional. No class of offenders had ever been declared constitutionally exempt from the application of a death penalty statute. No death sentence had ever been voided as a violation of due process, equal protection, or on any other ground. About the only way to have the courts nullify a death sentence was to attack the *conviction* of a capital crime itself by a showing of reversible error. In other words, the courts had never provided anything but individually litigated, piecemeal relief.

There were no indications of anything more sweeping or revolutionary in the wind. Efforts to abolish the death penalty through statutory repeal languished. Out of a total of fifty-two civil jurisdictions in the United States competent to impose the death penalty, only five—Alaska, Hawaii, Maine, Minnesota, and Wisconsin—had totally abolished capital punishment for all crimes. Delaware, the state in which the legislature had most recently abolished the death penalty for murder, had reintroduced it in December 1961, less than four years later.[1] In few states was there any realistic prospect for repeal of capital punishment statutes or for significant statutory alterations affecting persons under death sentence, such as provision for automatic review by state appellate courts, or abolishment of various disabilities attendant upon status as a death row prisoner.[2] Even discretionary sentencing in capital cases had yet to be adopted nationwide. As of March 1962, the law in the District of Columbia was changed to include this provision; in New York, however, death was still the mandatory penalty for first degree murder. In Congress, the first hearing in this century on the federal death penalty was held in 1960,[3] but it led to no further legislative action. The office of the attorney general indicated no discontent with the status of the federal death penalty or unwillingness to seek the death penalty in its prosecutions.

Public knowledge of the history and social effects of capital punishment was limited. Social science research was (apart from the deterrence issue) sporadic, inconclusive, and unorganized, and public opposition to capital punishment received almost no financing or direction. National organizations interested in corrections, civil liberties, civil rights, or political reform had not adopted a policy in opposition to capital punishment.[4] Apart from various religious groups,[5] only the American League to Abolish Capital Punishment and its state affiliates were available as a resource for literature, speakers, and public testimony.[6] In only one state, New Jersey, did a volunteer group of lawyers exist solely for the purpose of undertaking appeals of death sentences on behalf of indigent defendants,[7] and the activities of this group were limited by the magnitude of the task and a lack of funds. The most prestigious professional group in the country then studying the issue of capital punishment was the American Law Institute (ALI). Although its advisory committee on the death penalty favored abolition by a wide margin, the membership voted overwhelmingly not to take any policy position. The Model Penal Code itself was drawn up by the ALI to provide two basic models for sentencing in capital crimes. According to one model, the most severe sentence would be life imprisonment. According to the other, which retained the death penalty as an alternative to life imprisonment, a two-stage trial was recommended, with the sentence of death contingent upon findings by the jury that no "mitigating" and some "aggravating" circumstances were present. As for the attitudes of the American public, the 1960 Gallup Poll showed a surprisingly small majority (51 percent) in favor of the death penalty for murder.

It would appear on balance, therefore, that although the death penalty in 1962 had declined both in popularity and in the frequency of its use when compared with earlier decades, it was not quite a moribund institution. Certainly, no one had good reason to think that its days were already numbered.

But a decade later, on 29 June 1972, the United States Supreme Court announced its decision in *Furman v. Georgia* and consolidated cases. In a brief per curiam opinion, the Court ruled that "the imposition and carrying out of the death penalty ... constitutes cruel and unusual punishment in violation of the Eighth and Fourteenth Amendments."[8] On the same day, the Court, citing the authority of *Furman*, reversed summarily death sentences in some 120 other cases from twenty-six states.[9] Of the more than 600 persons then under sentence of death,[10] the ruling in *Furman* would lead to resentencing of all but a few.[11] Although only two of the five Justices argued that the death penalty *per se* was in violation of the Eighth and Fourteenth Amendments,[12] the immediate effect of *Furman* was to overturn the entire prevailing system of capital punishment in this country. A few observers hailed *Furman* as a sign for the future and as a mandate to the nation to rethink its traditional methods of dealing with its most serious and dangerous criminal offenders. Most commentators expressed dismay and bewilderment at the close ruling, at the inability of the majority Justices to join in any one rationale for their decision, and at the resulting uncertainty over the modes of capital punishment that might still be constitutionally imposed. Yet the basic message of *Furman* seemed clear: for the first time in our history, national policy on capital punishment had been set by a branch of the federal government in a direction that favored abolition, and that, short of constitutional amendment, was very likely to be irreversible.

What had happened in the years between 1962 and 1972 to bring about this remarkable transformation? How, in particular, had the issue of capital punishment—not visibly on the implicit agenda of the Supreme Court in 1962, for all the distress of particular Justices when confronted with a capital case—been brought before the federal courts and forced to a resolution favorable to abolition? Michael Meltsner's book provides the narrative background and the judicial and political reflections needed to answer these questions in an intelligible and persuasive way. Although the volume is by no means a history of capital punishment in the United States, not even for the decade prior to 1972, *Cruel and Unusual* is by far the most elaborate, authoritative, and absorbing contribution to that history that anyone has so far provided. Much more needs to be written, of course, and perhaps unbeknownst to any of us the subject has already found its Radzinowicz.[13] Yet, Meltsner's book will remain an indispensable narrative of events, personalities, and issues, and probably the only firsthand account we will ever have.

The story begins in 1961 when Meltsner was employed in New York City as a young staff attorney with the NAACP Legal Defense and Educational Fund, Inc. (LDF); there he promptly learned that many of the LDF's indigent black clients were victims of the death penalty system. The first notable straw in the wind was provided in the fall of 1963 by Justice Arthur J. Goldberg's dissent in *Rudolph v. Alabama*. This led to preliminary discussions in the following months among Meltsner and two young colleagues at the LDF, Frank Heffron and Leroy Clark, to consider ways to exploit this signal.[14] With the LDF's clientele of mainly southern black defendants, the death penalty for rape became a logical initial target for constitutional attack. Accordingly, in 1965, Anthony G. Amsterdam, the Fund's chief legal strategist,[15] decided to launch a major research project into indictments, prosecutions, convictions, and sentences for rape in those states where it was punishable by death. The purpose was to develop empirical evidence to sustain a charge of systematic denial of equal protection and violation of the Fourteenth Amendment. By 1966, the LDF board and its executive director, Jack Greenberg, were ready to take the plunge; they decided to organize "a campaign of test cases" to challenge the constitutionality of the death penalty for all crimes and all defendants. In 1967 the LDF decided to try to obtain a *de facto* national moratorium on executions pending resolution of the constitutional issues.[16] The same year Jack Himmelstein, then a recent graduate of Harvard Law School, was hired to be the "managing attorney" of the campaign,[17] and over the next six years he became the national coordinator for litigation, publicity, and social science research on capital punishment.

The bulk of Meltsner's book consists of a step-by-step explanation of litigation strategy during the subsequent five years in a whole series of cases, chief among which were *Adderly, Maxwell, Boykin, McGautha, Anderson*, and *Furman*. Lawyers experienced in civil rights and constitutional litigation may find Meltsner's patient explanations tedious and superfluous, but students and the general reader should be more grateful. Not since Anthony Lewis's *Gideon's Trumpet* have we had such an educational study of fundamental change in the criminal law.

To some extent, the story of the nine-year campaign is one of losing every major battle except the first and the last. The opening assault, made in Florida in 1967, was in *Adderly v. Wainwright*.[18] *Adderly* provided the novel class action stay of execution for all of Florida's death row prisoners; stays of execution could then be sought elsewhere by referring to the constitutional issues raised in that case. This was a workable strategy, and it gave the LDF attorneys much-needed time to gather facts, prepare briefs, and organize their legal tactics. Thus, the "pileup on death row"[19] was set in motion, as well as the steady increase of persons under sentence of death whose fate turned on the same constitutional issues. The moratorium on executions, Meltsner insists, provided the necessary "threat of crisis" that put the death penalty into the headlines month after month, where the large bold type would catch the judicial eye. Also, the "death-row logjam" showed that "each year the United States went without executions, the more hollow would ring claims that the American people could not do without them."

The first major testing by the LDF of its two basic procedural arguments, against the single-stage capital trial jury and against standardless sentencing, was brought to the Supreme Court in 1969 in *Maxwell v. Bishop*.[20] Whereas the lower federal courts had objected to the elaborate empirical evidence on racial discrimination in the administration of capital punishment presented by sociologist Marvin Wolfgang,[21] the Court passed by this issue. In fact, the Court evaded all the constitutional issues raised, and decided *Maxwell* by referring to an earlier ruling in *Witherspoon v. Illinois*,[22] one of the two important Supreme Court decisions on capital cases between 1963 and 1972 not involving LDF clients but incorporated into its overall strategy.[23] In the next major test, *McGautha v. California*,[24] the LDF attorneys returned to their argument against standardless sentencing and took a beating in one of the last opinions Justice John Marshall Harlan wrote for the Court.

The *McGautha* defeat extinguished all hope of an effective constitutional attack on the death penalty that would rely on procedural grounds alone. As Meltsner remarks:

After six years of litigation (beginning with the early phases of *Maxwell* in 1964 through *McGautha*, decided in May 1971), the Supreme Court had finally and decisively rejected the two mainstays of the moratorium strategy. More importantly, it had refused an invitation to abolish capital punishment piecemeal . . . . Would the Court now grasp the nettle and decide the ultimate question of a state's power to kill?

Only an Eighth Amendment argument against the death penalty, as "cruel and unusual punishment," remained to be tried. The initial version of the argument developed by Amsterdam had already been presented to the court in an *amicus* brief in *Boykin v. Alabama*,[25] but the Court had dodged it by reversing Boykin's conviction on relatively narrow and strategically irrelevant grounds. Then, in December 1970, the Fourth Circuit decision of *Ralph v. Warden*[26] brought the long-awaited breakthrough: at last an appellate court ruled that the death penalty for rape was unconstitutionally cruel and unusual punishment. As Meltsner explains it, however, this ruling was not entirely encouraging because the circuit court's reasoning proceeded on assumptions inapplicable to the wide variety of situations presented by the LDF clients.

The last stage of the campaign, as it turned out, was fought on two fronts, *People v. Anderson* in California and *Furman v. Georgia* in the Supreme Court. *Anderson* represents the first holding by any court that the death penalty *per se* violates constitutional provisions.[27] The California court announced its decision in February 1972, a month after the oral arguments in *Furman*. The opportunity for the *Anderson* case to be decided *before* the Supreme Court's decision in *Furman* was, in 1970, completely unpredicted. It was at least in part a consequence of the retirements of Justices Black and Harlan and the ensuing controversy and delay in filling the vacancies with Nixon administration nominees, a matter to which Meltsner devotes some space. As it turned out, *Anderson* was a correct forecast of the result reached four months later in *Furman*.

Meltsner's book, as I commented earlier, is not a comprehensive history of the struggle over capital punishment during the 1960s. The "primary purpose" of the book, Meltsner says, "is to convey the craft and cunning of the lawyers who orchestrated a stunning legal victory; of the means they employed to right a deeply felt, historic wrong." Despite its emphasis on the central role played by the LDF, it is not a company history nor does it provide a particularly intimate inside look at the nation's most famous public interest law firm. Although much of the book is given over to discussion of the leading cases from *Maxwell* and *Adderly* to *Furman*, Meltsner has not written a scholarly analysis of any of these cases. Even with its focus on the work and personality of Anthony Amsterdam, and its structure built entirely around Meltsner's own career with the LDF, *Cruel and Unusual* is not a personalized essay from either the history-is-biography or the I-was-there schools of journalism.

Meltsner also provides an opportunity for criticism and appraisal of every aspect of the death penalty controversy. A review of *Cruel and Unusual* is an occasion to review as well the entire status of capital punishment in the United States. Tempting as it is to seize this opportunity, I shall resist it. At least one major point, however, deserves some detailed comment.

Meltsner's book culminates, quite properly, in the *Furman* decision. What he writes about that decision, especially about the argument that Amsterdam and his LDF associates constructed in the briefs, is of particular interest. The issue is first introduced in a somewhat hyperbolic remark of Meltsner's when he writes, "[I]n 1969 one man's lonely act of intellection had discovered a clue to unravelling the mystery of the Eighth Amendment." What clue? Which man? What mystery? Unravelled with what result? The man, of course, is Amsterdam, who in December 1968, "went into seculsion to write an LDF *amicus curiae* brief in the *Boykin* case ... [to] tell the Court why ... Boykin's death sentence amounted to cruel and unusual punishment." At that time there was exactly one argument publicly available for study that purported to show that the death penalty for any crime was unconstitutional under the Eighth Amendment: the analysis, already much reprinted by 1968, was by Gerald H. Gottleib, "a Los Angeles antitrust lawyer."[28] Gottlieb's pioneering argument originated as a memorandum for the Southern California Branch of the ACLU in May 1960. Thanks to Gottlieb's initial efforts, the ACLU five years later adopted the position that the death penalty posed crucial constitutional issues.[29]

What are the differences between the Eighth Amendment argument Gottlieb developed in 1960 and Amsterdam's argument eight years later? In one respect, they are exactly alike, in that both seized on the crucial notion, supplied in *Trop v. Dulles*, that the Eighth Amendment embodied "evolving standards of decency." Only under such "standards" could it be plausibly argued that although hanging, electrocution, and other modes of inflicting the death penalty might not have been "cruel and unusual punishments" in 1789, or in 1890, they might be so declared by the Court (as Justice Harry A. Blackmun observed during the hearing on his nomination to the Court) in "1970 or 1980." The obvious importance of the notion of "evolving standards of decency" had already been emphasized by Justice Goldberg's dissent in *Rudolph* some two years after Gottlieb's article was published. In addition, both arguments placed little weight on verbal hairsplitting over the meaning of the key words, "cruel and unusual punishment," but placed great weight on the available empirical evidence showing the effects of the death penalty compared to the alternative of imprisonment. There was, as it turned out, considerably more empirical evidence of this sort available in 1968 than in 1960, and it naturally found its way into Amsterdam's brief.

The true differences between the Gottlieb and Amsterdam arguments lie in that "clue" to which Meltsner alludes. The "mystery" of the Eighth Amendment, simply put, is this: when does a traditionally accepted penal practice that is widely imposed by statute nevertheless violate the constitutional prohibition against "cruel and unusual punishment"? This does not appear to be a question Gottlieb had directly posed for himself. In the absence of the right kind of answer to this question, the Eighth Amendment and the death penalty could not be inconsistent. The clue to the right answer lies in Amsterdam's notion that we must "draw the distinction between what public conscience will allow the law to *say* and what it will allow the law to *do*—between what public decency will permit a penal statute to threaten and what it will allow the law to carry out."[30] Given this clue to the mystery, the argument itself rapidly gathers momentum: (1) our practice, as crime and execution statistics show, is to use the death penalty only upon "unhappy minorities, whose numbers are so few, whose plight so invisible, and whose persons so unpopular, that society can readily bear to see them suffer torments which would not for a moment be acceptable as penalties of general application to the populace";[31] (2) we cannot infer, therefore, from the statutory provision of the death penalty for murder, rape, or burglary that the public conscience does tolerate executions for these crimes; (3) we can infer that these death penalty statutes are preserved in law with no intention of applying them regularly, uniformly, and equally, because society— from the prosecutors with the power of indictment to the chief executives with the power of clemency—would not tolerate a widespread use of such a severe punishment in this day and age; (4) we must also conclude, given the actual facts about the imposition of the death penalty, that anyone who is sentenced to death for murder, rape, or burglary suffers "a cruel and unusual punishment because it affronts contemporary standards of decency, universally felt, that would condemn the use of death as a penalty ... if such a penalty were uniformly, regularly and even-handedly applied either to all ... [those convicted of such a crime] or to any non-arbitrarily selected subclass of ... [them all]."[32] That, with a minimum of paraphrase, is the gist of the argument Amsterdam developed in *Boykin* during 1968-1969. I am ready to agree with Meltsner that it represents a significant and original theory of the Eighth Amendment, a theory that is especially attractive as an assault upon the death penalty.

In the years between *Boykin* and *Furman*, a few other writers attempted to interpret and expand the Eighth Amendment to encompass prohibition of the death penalty.[33] Did those arguments show any influence of reasoning that owes its origin to Amsterdam? (It is important to realize that between writing the *Boykin* brief and the *Furman* brief, Amsterdam himself published, as far as I know, nothing further of his argument, nor did any of the other attorneys working with the LDF.[34]) The short answer is that they do not. The most weighty of these post-*Boykin*, pre-*Furman* arguments was made by Justice Goldberg and his law clerk, Alan M. Dershowitz, in 1970, essentially a much more elaborate and sophisticated version of Gottlieb's original argument a decade earlier. Nothing of the very distinctive line of reasoning originating in *Boykin* can be found there. What is true of Goldberg and Dershowitz is true of the rest of the commentators. Either they were unaware of Amsterdam's argument, they did not understand its novelty, or they did not regard it as the best possible treatment of the issue in question.

What of this argument in the *Furman* brief itself and of the Court's response to it? Did Amsterdam significantly change his line of reasoning from *Boykin* to *Furman*? Did the Court borrow from his written and oral argument? Meltsner does not pose any of these questions directly, although his account does suggest answers—answers, in my opinion, not wholly correct. First of all, Meltsner says nothing at all about the content of the written brief in *Furman*. His narrative with regard to these Eighth Amendment issues moves directly from the submission of the brief in *Boykin* to the organization twenty-seven months later of the briefwriting in *Furman* and then to the oral arguments six months after that, without showing that the essential features of the earlier brief provide the precise and visible structure of the later one. All the steps in *Boykin*, outlined here, are retained in *Furman*. To put it another way, none of the lines of reasoning sketched out by others in the interval between *Boykin* and *Furman* appears to have persuaded Amsterdam to revise his original argument, or even to shift its emphasis. In the oral argument as well, Amsterdam persisted in his theory of the Eighth Amendment and of its application to capital punishment.

When we look for evidence of the impact of this argument upon the Court, Meltsner again deserts us. He reviews very briefly "the approximately 25,000 words written by the concurring Justices" in their nine opinions in *Furman*. Not once does he pause to comment on the degree to which Amsterdam's theory of the Eighth Amendment showed up in the Justices' opinions. Having tried to rivet the reader's attention on Amsterdam's original reasoning in *Boykin*, Meltsner then unaccountably forgets to show the reader whether that reasoning really mattered in *Furman* after all. In fact, from reading Meltsner's summaries of the five concurring and four dissenting opinions in *Furman*, one would be entitled to infer that the Justices were totally indifferent to Amsterdam's carefully wrought theory.

I think Meltsner's silence is not a fair indication of the impact of Amsterdam's theory upon the Court. It is true that the theory was apparently held in such slight regard by the dissenting Justices that none of them bothered to rebut it explicitly. Similarly, three of the concurring opinions in the majority come close to echoing Amsterdam's line of reasoning, but the echo is faint and uncertain. Justices William J. Brennan, Jr., and Byron R. White, however, adopt it almost entirely. Since there is some evidence that the vote of Justice White was the one most avidly courted in the LDF's brief and the oral argument[35] —for without him and Justice Potter Stewart there was no possibility of a majority favorable to abolition—this impact of Amsterdam's reasoning deserves some notice. It is also possible that Justice White's opinion, roughly amounting to the least common denominator of the five majority opinions, will be the one most closely identified in history with the holding in *Furman*, and that by this route,

Amsterdam's theory of the Eighth Amendment will come to shape its future applications and extensions.

Having come this far, we are likely to wonder whether a different theory of the Eighth Amendment might have produced another vote or two to bolster the *Furman* opinion or at least might have led to a more cohesive majority. Meltsner does not consider this question either, though I suspect that his answer, like mine, would be in the negative.

Looking back now, we can see that the LDF's moratorium strategy and the *Furman* decision itself represented a considerable gamble. The risk is that law enforcement agencies will turn more and more to quasi-punitive acts prior to arrest or arraignment, in order to visit upon the most offensive criminals the pent-up rage of society. If this were to happen, we would see a tragic displacement of legalized violence from the arena of the courts to that of the streets. In addition, new fuel would be provided for what is already the most influential and least rebuttable argument for the death penalty: the presumed superiority of its deterrent effect. No sooner was *Furman* decided than President Richard M. Nixon sounded this theme in a press conference,[36] and it continues to be heard on every side. The most troublesome version argues that since we do not know how many murderers, rapists, etc., the death penalty does deter, but only how many it does not deter, we cannot possibly take seriously the evidence of Thorsten Sellin and others, and we cannot safely abolish it. As a spur to further research, this argument has merit. Otherwise, as has been pointed out elsewhere,[37] it is an unsophisticated appeal to ignorance. What we do not know cannot be evidence in any sound argument. Yet the seven-year judicial moratorium on executions has encouraged defenders of the death penalty to argue in this way. One constantly hears the lament, "If only the death penalty had been used during the 1970s, and used more frequently in the 1960s, we'd have had fewer murders and rapes today." It is undeniable that as the death penalty has been used less frequently in recent years, the crime rate, including the rate of crimes of violence, has gone up. This is undoubtedly a coincidence.[38] Nevertheless, judicial abolition of the death penalty in the absence of public clamor for legislative repeal has fed the fires of middle class anxiety as well as racist resentment. Our best hope is that during the next few years, murder and other crimes of personal violence will decline, and the public will get used to the idea that the death penalty simply is no longer available. Meanwhile, the clamor for the death penalty—"the oldest panacea of them all"[39]—is unlikely soon to subside.

Meltsner concludes his book with a rapid survey of events in the first few months after *Furman*, bringing his narrative up to March 1973. In the year between the completion of his manuscript and this writing, the pattern of events he describes has not changed. The death penalty has already been reenacted by statute in more than two dozen states.[40] More than seventy-five persons, half of them black, are under sentence of death. More litigation, ultimately before the

Supreme Court, lies ahead. Thus, even as the story Meltsner had to tell was coming to an end, material for a new chapter in our dealings with the death penalty was being prepared by current events.

Nearly a decade ago I predicted with some trepidation that "by 1970 we may have the first year in our history in which no one is put to death as punishment for crime under civil authority in the United States."[41] When I wrote that, I had heard of the LDF but did not know that they were on the verge of a legal challenge to the national death penalty establishment. Who at that time, outside of the close-knit group of lawyers at the Fund would have guessed that 1967 might be the last year in which "judicial homicide"[42] was allowed? Perhaps I may hazard another prediction: we will not see another execution in this nation in this century. If this prediction is correct, and if it is also correct that this will be a valuable development, then Meltsner's book has shown us whom to thank and why.

7 New Research and Literature Since *Furman*

On 29 June 1972 the United States Supreme Court ruled that "the imposition and carrying out of the death penalty ... constitutes cruel and unusual punishment in violation of the Eighth and Fourteenth Amendments." This decision in *Furman v. Georgia* and related cases was based on the way the death penalty was being administered, with trial judges and juries having unguided discretion to sentence to death or life. More than 600 persons were then under sentence of death in thirty-two states, and the effect of the *Furman* ruling was to insure that virtually all of those 600 would be resentenced to prison. However, the Court's narrow (five to four) majority, the absence of any plurality opinion, and the issues left unresolved guaranteed that the death penalty controversy would continue to vex the nation's criminal justice systems for years to come. Future historians may well be able to show this decision to be the watershed in the nation's long-standing controversy over capital punishment. It was especially noteworthy for the way in which complex and varied social science evidence had been presented in the briefs and arguments by the attorneys on behalf of their death row clients. As the Court's opinions showed, this evidence carried persuasive effect and provided the basic foundation for the decision.

Although many of the data accumulated found their way into the nine separate and diverse opinions written in this case, it was the showing of infrequency, arbitrariness, and discrimination in the administration of the death penalty that held together the five Justices who formed the majority. Justice Douglas observed, "One searches our chronicles in vain for the execution of any member of the affluent strata of this society." Justice Stewart commented that those under sentence of death in the United States were "a capriciously selected random handful." Justice White continued the same objection when he wrote, "There is no meaningful basis for distinguishing the few cases where [the death penalty] ... is imposed from the many cases where it is not." Justices Brennan and Marshall concurred in these findings and also stressed a different objection: "... the threat of death has no greater deterrent effect than the threat of imprisonment" (Brennan); "capital punishment cannot be justified on the basis of its deterrent effect" (Marshall). This is but a sampling from a great wealth of dicta in *Furman* that shows how the social science evidence offered to the Court managed to have a powerful impact upon its reasoning.

Impressive as the ruling in *Furman* was, however, it was clear that it did not directly settle the issue of whether the death penalty has any place in our society. Although eight of the nine Justices indicated a personal opposition to capital punishment, only five—a bare majority—agreed that the death penalty as then administered violated the Constitution, and only two maintained that the death penalty in *any* form would be unconstitutional. Even though the prevailing discretionary use of capital punishment was entirely repudiated, there was room in the *Furman* ruling for new experiments with the death penalty, possibly as a mandatory punishment or possibly as a discretionary punishment with clear statutory guidelines for trial juries to follow. Important though these possibilities were, they had not been placed squarely before the Court in the *Furman* litigation, and in characteristic fashion the Court left them undecided.

Furthermore, although the effect of social scientific evidence upon the Court's thinking was evident, and while all the Court agreed on the relevance of factual evidence to the legal issues, several of the dissenting Justices openly complained of the paucity and insufficiency of evidence. Chief Justice Warren E. Burger was especially outspoken on this issue. "Data of more recent vintage is essential," he wrote at one point. He said of the majority Justices that "they share a willingness to make sweeping factual assertions, unsupported by empirical data...." Quite apart from the question of whether such objections are well founded, they are now part of the record of the Supreme Court's assessment of the data base used to attack the death penalty; and such doubts and objections will not be dissipated of their own accord.

There are several results, then, of the *Furman* decision. It irrevocably abolished the prevailing mode of inflicting the death penalty. It defined the factual issues on which the future of the death penalty would eventually be determined. These issues include the deterrent effect of mandatory death penalties, the acceptability to the public of mandatory executions for whole classes of criminals, and the arbitrary and discriminatory results under nominally mandatory death penalties. On these and other empirical questions, "data of recent vintage" will undoubtedly prove decisive in the months and years immediately ahead, provided they can be properly assembled by imaginative researchers and then marshaled effectively by lawyers experienced in the use of social science data in a legal setting.

In October 1972 the NAACP Legal Defense and Educational Fund (LDF) sponsored a conference in New York and brought together two dozen leading researchers and scholars who had wide familiarity with empirical research on sociological, psychological, demographical, historical, and other questions relating to correction and the administration of criminal justice. At this conference Anthony G. Amsterdam and Jack Himmelstein, the two lawyers chiefly responsible for the anti-death penalty litigation since 1967, made clear the interests of courts in further objective social science research on all aspects of the death penalty. It became evident to all at the conference that the first priority was the systematic exploration of the feasibility of coordinated social science research into the area of capital punishment, which would enlist the participation, so far as possible, of investigators around the nation and from all the relevant disciplines. In February 1973 funding for this investigation was sought and obtained from the Russell Sage Foundation by this writer.

During the spring and summer of 1973, a series of interrelated activities were organized to accomplish this project. One of the major instruments conceived and executed during this period was a series of conferences arranged at several of the leading centers of social science research in criminology and criminal justice to bring together prospective researchers and lawyers informed on the legally relevant issues needing research. These conferences were conducted at the Center for Studies in Criminology and Criminal Justice, University of Pennsylvania; the Center for the Study of Law and Society, University of California, Berkeley; the Center for Research in Criminal Justice, University of Illinois, Chicago Circle; the Department of Criminology, Florida State University; the Center for the Study and Reduction of Violence, UCLA Medical School; and the Center for Criminal Justice, Harvard Law School. More than 100 graduate students, faculty, and other researchers attended these conferences by invitation. Two other conferences were arranged to deal with specific areas in which any further research was known to require extensive prior review and investigation: on deterrence, at Yale Law School, and on survey research, at the Russell Sage Foundation offices in New York.

Meanwhile, in the months after *Furman,* the urgency for undertaking this research was being underlined by political events. In July 1972, at a press conference, President Richard M. Nixon indicated his belief that the death penalty was the appropriate punishment for certain crimes. In November 1972 the voters of California passed Proposition 17 to restore a mandatory death penalty for several crimes and to prevent judicial review of such legislation. In the same month the Gallup Poll reported that 57 percent of the adult public supported the death penalty in some form for various crimes. In December the Florida Legislature, in special session, adopted into law several new death penalty statutes. The National Association of Attorneys General voted a resolution to recommend the mandatory death penalty in certain cases. In January 1973 Attorney General Richard G. Kleindienst informed the press that the Nixon administration intended to ask Congress to pass legislation for mandatory death penalties covering several categories of crimes.[1] Within a year after *Furman,* commissions had been formed in several states to make recommendations on the issue, and bills to restore capital punishment had been introduced in three dozen state legislatures. By midsummer such bills had already been signed into law in twenty states. On the second anniversary of *Furman,* twenty-eight states had new death penalty legislation and more than 100 persons in seventeen states had been sentenced to death under these new laws. Although the *de facto* moratorium on executions continued, it was clear that the nation was still a long way from totally abolishing the death penalty.

Thus, in the immediate aftermath of *Furman,* the resources of the social science community had been explored and organized with respect to kinds of research relevant to the future of the death penalty. Concurrently, in the political arena, statutes had been passed in many jurisdictions to restore the death penalty, framed so as to avoid the thrust of the Supreme Court's decision in *Furman*. This guaranteed a further round of litigation on the constitutionality of capital punishment, as well as debate in the legislatures over the merits of new capital statutes and agonizing appraisals by the chief executives over particular executions.

Three kinds of empirical evidence might have sufficed, had they been available, to stem the public and legislative backlash to *Furman*. One would have been a showing that many of those sentenced for capital crimes in recent years were in fact innocent. Another would have been conclusive evidence that the death penalty is not a deterrent (or not as good a deterrent as imprisonment, or that the use of capital punishment incited more violence than it prevented). The third would have been that all capital offenders are one-time criminals, and can be imprisoned and paroled without danger to others. No evidence to support these extreme hypotheses has been forthcoming, and none is likely. They are mentioned here only to indicate that the brush fire of legislative reimpositions of capital punishment since *Furman* could have been prevented and controlled, if at all, only by social science evidence of a stunning and unprecedented nature. Any new increments in our knowledge about capital punishment less striking and less conclusive than this would be simply swept aside or ignored as they have been in the past in the rush to restore statutory authority to execute murderers and other criminals.

On the other hand, these extreme hypotheses do provide suggestions for a possible research agenda. Miscarriages of justice, deterrence, and the criminal histories of capital offenders had been studied during the 1960s, and the results had proved to be relevant to the decision in *Furman*. Any future legislative and judicial action on capital punishment would no doubt be influenced by further empirical findings on these topics. However, since there was no reason to expect novel empirical findings in regard to any of these matters, and since they were essentially unrelated issues, they could not form the nucleus of any actual research agenda, nor could they be relied upon to give it structure and coherence. Another approach was needed.

Conceived in the abstract, one might suppose that the ideal research agenda on the death penalty in the post-*Furman* era would be governed by four major considerations. First, one would distinguish the empirically untestable from the empirically testable issues affecting the administration and effects of capital punishment, and attend only to the latter set of propositions. One of the difficulties in the constitutional argument culminating in *Furman* was to determine which hypotheses relevant to the prohibition of "cruel and unusual punishment" really were empirically testable and which were not. A study of the briefs and of previous arguments by others on the Eighth Amendment issues[2] shows that none of the empirical evidence available to the courts for interpretation was systematically undertaken by social science investigators with Eighth Amendment issues in mind. Instead, the attorneys who argued against the constitutionality of the death penalty were required to adapt the available empirical evidence as best they could. Odd as it may seem, in 1970 there was little or nothing in print to guide empirically oriented lawyers as to what issues were at stake in Eighth Amendment arguments over capital (or any other mode of) punishment.[3]

Second, one would distinguish between the empirical hypotheses related to the forms of capital punishment that the Supreme Court in *Furman* had specifically rejected, and those empirical hypotheses that concerned aspects of the death penalty that the Court left unresolved in *Furman*. It was empirical issues of the latter sort that were most in need of attention from social science investigators, since the holding in *Furman* was not likely to be reversed. Two major topics on which future research should focus were quickly identified. One had to do with actual or likely administration of "mandatory" death penalties. Such statutes had prevailed throughout the nation a century ago, and the dozen or so that survived were not invalidated by *Furman*. New death penalty legislation, therefore, was very likely to take this form. The other had to do with actual or likely administration of death penalty statutes with "guided discretion," whereby after conviction for a capital crime, the defendant's sentence to death or to life would depend on whether the court found, respectively, any "aggravating" or "mitigating" circumstances. In 1972 no capital statutes of this sort existed, and the ruling in *Furman* suggested they might be acceptable to the Supreme Court. Short of a constitutional amendment to overturn the holding in *Furman*—an unlikely eventuality—any new empirical research project that was to have maximum policy relevance would have to be addressed to the death penalty administered in one of these two ways.

Third, one would want to distinguish those empirical issues on which new information might be obtained by research and that probably would not influence either legislatures or courts from those that might yield hypotheses relevant to the inquiries of such groups. Again, one would set aside the former group of issues as undeserving of the scarce time and money available.

Finally, one would attempt to choose from among the latter set those empirically testable hypotheses about capital punishment that, because of their relation to other issues in social science, criminology, and the administration of criminal justice, would be likely to arouse the curiosity of competent investigators and command the attention of funding sources.

These four considerations provided the essential guidelines for constructing the ideal research agenda on capital punishment in the post-*Furman* era. There was, however, a basic problem in hoping to undertake a research agenda guided by such criteria. They would isolate issues and hypotheses that had no likelihood of being transformed into research projects and then implemented without strong central leadership from a research director. Such centrality of direction would be impossible without substantial funding and discretion in its use. Those interested in initiating a program of relevant social science research on capital punishment recognized these contingencies. By the autumn of 1973, efforts were under way to fund a capital punishment research project with a three-to-five-year duration and an annual budget of $150,000. The bid for these funds during 1973-1974 failed.

This was to some extent anticipated; and from the onset smaller research eggs were placed in several different baskets, in the hope they would hatch separately. An ever-present imponderable was the rate at which the new death penalty cases would reach the Supreme Court. Any new social science evidence was better than none; and if the ideal research agenda could be implemented only with the availability of unprecedentedly large sums of money, then it was vital that projects not in need of funding (however low on the priority list) be initiated anyway, lest the new round of appellate litigation be forced to get under way without any support from post-*Furman* empirical research.

All these factors were constantly weighed during 1973, and the result at midyear was shown in a report submitted to the Russell Sage Foundation.[4] That report contained seven proposed research projects by as many different teams of researchers.[5] By the end of that summer, the list of potential investigations had increased to twenty-five. At that time it was still hoped that all these separate projects would in due course be winnowed, supplemented, and integrated in one large overall research project with central management and funding.

While it is true that each of these twenty-five projects was to some extent guided by the fourfold set of criteria outlined above, it is also true that, taken as a whole, they formed an ad hoc set and would yield rather less than the ideally relevant results. Yet these twenty-five projects did represent the genuine interests and competencies of interested researchers in a wide range of social science fields. In that sense they did constitute a genuine measure of the prospects for death penalty research during the mid-1970s. What these hypotheses and issues may have lacked as an agenda for research when measured by ideal criteria, they probably did possess if measured by the practical realities of the academic marketplace. It must be added, however, that most of these projects, and probably all of the dozen or so most valuable, were doomed to remain paper dreams until funding was sought and found in each individual case.

It is hardly surprising that one year after *Furman,* none of the substantial research from this ad hoc agenda was under way, except for the few projects that required no special fund-raising efforts. Two years after *Furman* many of the original projects had been shelved indefinitely for lack of funding. (Fortunately, other research projects had meanwhile been identified, and interested investigators were undertaking the preliminary development of research proposals for them.) Of the original twenty-five research proposals identified in

1973, only two had been funded by mid-1974. One was the project undertaken by a group of social psychologists working at Stanford University to develop a new survey research instrument sensitive to the post-*Furman* legislative options. During the winter of 1973-1974, the Russell Sage Foundation supported the development of the project and its administration to a California sample.[6] The second was a project directed out of the University of Pennsylvania to study the effects of sentencing in three jurisdictions (District of Columbia, Massachusetts, New York) before and after the shift from mandatory to discretionary death sentencing. This project was funded by the Ford Foundation on the second anniversary of *Furman*; the research will test whether "mandatory" death penalties really eliminate discretion or arbitrariness, or only shift it from the sentencing phase to earlier stages in the judicial process—for instance, by allowing the prosecutor to plea-bargain or by encouraging the jury to convict for a lesser offense.[7]

Early in 1974, following a symposium on capital punishment at the annual meeting of the American Orthopsychiatric Association, the decision was made to devote an issue of the *American Journal of Orthopsychiatry* to some of the new social science research results on the death penalty. Several new projects, including some that required special funding, were set in motion by the prospect of this special journal issue.

The July 1975 issue of *Orthopsychiatry* contained eight essays by a dozen social scientists reporting this new research—in many instances on previously uninvestigated aspects of the death penalty controversy. Richard Gelles and Murray Straus, in "Family Experience and Public Support of the Death Penalty," show how attitudes favorable to lethal punishment are fostered by certain child-rearing practices in some American families. Lawrence Kohlberg and Donald Elfenbein describe "The Development of Moral Opinions About Capital Punishment," drawing on Kohlberg's longitudinal studies of moral attitudes, and on his well-known criteria for stages of moral development. George Solomon and Bernard Diamond each report case histories that add further confirmation to the murder-as-suicide phenomenon which capital punishment helps foster. Scattered throughout the scholarly journals since *Furman*, of course, are many noteworthy contributions, but the essays in *Orthopsychiatry* are particularly outstanding and should have a considerable impact.[8]

Earlier in 1975 the Supreme Court had been briefed and had heard oral argument in its first post-*Furman* death penalty case, *Fowler v. North Carolina*. In the more than three years since *Furman*, a small shelf of books and government reports on the history and practice of capital punishment had appeared. What do these materials have to teach us about the death penalty that was unknown or unfamiliar to us before *Furman* was decided?

Prior to *Furman*, much of the best information on capital punishment in America was contained in the reports of several state legislative study commissions. One might have thought that with several dozen states contemplating new death penalty legislation, a series of well-financed investigations into relevant factual issues would have been mounted by legislative study commissions. The contrary seems to be true. The only exception is the report prepared by the special study commission in Pennsylvania.[9] It is of interest to social scientists because of the seven staff reports it contains, some of which undertake research in new areas and most of which address themselves to aspects of the issue of mandatory death sentencing.[10] At no time in our history, however, have we had federal government investigations of the death penalty comparable to those conducted in England and in Canada by parliamentary commissions. Still, three documents of note have emerged from Congress in the past three years. In the spring of 1972 the House Judiciary Subcommittee No. 3, chaired by Robert W. Kastenmeier, held hearings on several bills to suspend or abolish the federal death penalty. These hearings, published under the title, "Capital Punishment," did not appear until after the decision in *Furman* was announced.

The other two documents emerged from the Senate Judiciary Committee. "Imposition of Capital Punishment," published in 1973, was the hearing record before Senator John L. McClellan's Subcommittee on Criminal Laws and Procedures on the Administration's notorious S.1 and related bills to reintroduce a federal death penalty. In opening the hearings Senator McClellan forecast the tone of most of the testimony when he said, "It is clear that the decision in *Furman* is creating havoc in legal systems throughout the country." With a few notable exceptions, the witnesses called by the Chairman put into the record various assurances that, indeed, *Furman* must be circumvented if the nation is not to sink still deeper into a morass of murder, rape, and other violent crimes. The second Senate document appeared early in 1974 and constitutes the report of the Judiciary Committee in favor of S. 1401, the substitute bill for the death penalty provisions of S. 1. (When last heard from, the bill was buried in Kastenmeier's subcommittee in the House, having easily passed in the Senate.) Half this report is devoted to explaining why the majority of the Subcommittee was so enthusiastic over the intricate path it had carved to cope with the prohibitions of *Furman* without actually flouting them. The other half, written primarily by Senator Philip A. Hart, the Senate's most articulate opponent of the death penalty, shows precisely why the majority failed in its effort. His masterful dissection of S. 1401 confirms the judgment that it is beyond human capability to draw up a statute that will provide the death penalty for only the worst murderers, that will be imposed without procedural unfairness, and that will yield effective deterrence.

Perhaps the most widely used book among the new publications is the collection of essays edited by James A. McCafferty, *Capital Punishment*. This book had the misfortune to be published shortly before the *Furman* decision without any indication of that watershed victory. It consists of reprints from journals, public hearings, and other sources; it does not purport to add to the scientific, legal, or historical knowledge already generated by the death penalty controversy. The picture of capital punishment presented in McCafferty's anthology is of a dying and indefensible penal institution, largely discredited in Europe and vestigial in the rest of the world. The chief value of the book is that it makes some of the data and arguments on which the *Furman* decision is based more accessible to general audiences.

The law reviews have so far provided little more than technical criticism of the *Furman* decision, and the case still awaits a thorough evaluation. Two useful books help us to understand this landmark decision in other ways; the more recent is *Cruel and Unusual: The Supreme Court and Capital Punishment* by Michael Meltsner, examined at length in the previous chapter. The other is Burton H. Wolfe's *Pileup on Death Row*. It appeared a few months before Meltsner's and lacks the latter's inside legal perspective. Wolfe is a California journalist, and his account concentrates on the fight against the death penalty as seen from the Golden State. Today it is easy to forget that it was the Caryl Chessman case in California in the late 1950s, more than any other criminal case in the past generation, that stirred the national debate over capital punishment. Not many people realize that the policy position in opposition to the death penalty adopted in 1965 by the ACLU was inspired in 1960 by its Southern California affiliate—or that the first court in the world to declare the death penalty unconstitutional *per se* was the California State Supreme Court in *People v. Anderson*. That ruling was announced a few months before the United States Supreme Court reached its considerably less sweeping ruling in *Furman*. If one were to approach the current national death penalty controversy by studying the political and legal struggle in one state, one could hardly do better than to focus on California. Wolfe's book has other virtues. It is written in a breezy style that is accessible and absorbing. It also provides the less informed reader with some background on older death penalty cases, beginning with the granddaddy of them all: *Powell v. Alabama*, the "Scottsboro Boys" case in the early 1930s. This helps the reader to see the *Furman* ruling of 1972 as a decision continuous with rulings of the Court going back forty years.

By far the most eloquent new volume on the death penalty is *Capital Punishment: The Inevitability of Caprice and Mistake* by Charles L. Black, Jr., of Yale Law School. Black argues brilliantly that the many state legislatures that have reinstated the death penalty since *Furman* have not succeeded in drafting statutes that circumvent the faults *Furman* condemned. In *Furman*, the Court cited the "capriciously random" fashion in which trial juries decided who was to be sentenced to death and who was to be sentenced to life. The Court's attention was focused on those features of sentencing that most obviously accounted for these "random" results. The rest of the criminal justice system, beginning with the prosecutorial decision to indict and culminating in the gubernatorial decision to withhold clemency, was not even discussed in *Furman*. After a quick tour through the entire system as it actually functions in capital cases, Black asserts that "standardless discretion, as well as mistake-proneness ... permeates the whole series of choices that have to be made on the way from street to gallows." He is at his most convincing when he subjects the new death penalty statutes in Texas and Georgia to close examination. These statutes, typical of post-*Furman* enactments, "do not effectively restrict the discretion of juries by any real standards. They never will. No society is going to kill everybody who meets certain preset verbal requirements, put on the statute books without awareness or coverage of the infinity of special factors the real world can produce." The result is that the two kinds of death penalty statutes enacted since *Furman*—so-called "mandatory" death statutes for murder, rape, etc., and "guided discretion" statutes that require the trial courts to impose a death sentence under "aggravating" conditions and to withhold it under "mitigating" ones—demonstrably suffer from the same faults as did the older, nonmandatory, unguided discretion statutes nullified in *Furman*. Black's superb book was timed perfectly; it anticipated the main issues argued in *Fowler*. Its argument is elegant and cogent. No other work states so well the contemporary, post-*Furman* case against the death penalty. In the years to come, informed readers will favorably compare this slender volume with that other famous modern tract, *Reflections on the Guillotine*, written nearly twenty years ago by the Nobel Prize essayist, Albert Camus. Like Camus, Black attacked judicial murder with uncommon lucidity and passion.

Of all the books to appear between *Furman* and *Fowler*, the one that most expands our knowledge of the death penalty is *Executions in America* by William J. Bowers, a research sociologist at Northeastern University. Beginning with the special issue of *The Annals*, "Murder and the Penalty of Death," edited by Thorsten Sellin in 1952, social scientists have accumulated an impressive array of empirical studies on all aspects of the death penalty. Bowers's volume is the latest, in some ways the most ambitious, and certainly the most thorough undertaking in this vein. The most prominent new information it supplies is a complete listing by name, race, date, and jurisdiction, of every execution in the United States conducted under state authority between 1864 and 1967. This record of 5707 executions was originally compiled by Professor Negley Teeters and his assistant William Zibulka; both are now deceased. It was a labor of dedicated, if slightly eccentric, zeal. The most original chapters in the volume are those in which Bowers uses these data to test the deterrent effects of the shift from mandatory to discretionary death penalties earlier in this century and of the nationwide moratorium on executions since 1967. Bowers's chief conclusion is that "... there is no evidence ... that the moratorium on executions ... contributed to increasing the level of homicide in this country, nor that the mandatory application of the death penalty had any greater deterrent effectiveness than its discretionary use. The evidence is remarkably consistent."[11]

Bowers's volume also contains the most extensive scientific and legal bibliography on capital punishment ever prepared, based on the research of Douglas Lyons, the staff person directing the ACLU's national campaign against the death penalty. With the Teeters-Zibulka execution inventory, the Lyons bibliography, and Bowers's own thorough index, *Executions in America* is one of the few books on the death penalty that belongs in the working library of every lawyer, social scientist, and lobbyist who needs comprehensive, recent, and reliable information on the subject.

About the time *Furman* was decided, the Canadian Solicitor General's office published a special report, *A Study of the Deterrent Effect of Capital Punishment With Special Reference to Canada* by Ezzat Fattah. (Bowers reprints a few pages of an earlier draft of some of Fattah's chief conclusions.) Twenty years ago Canada created a parliamentary commission to investigate the death penalty, and some of the best research on the subject was initiated by this commission and published in its proceedings. Fattah's position on deterrence is stated in his summation: "Nothing emerges from the study of trends in violent crimes in Canada that would support or even suggest the proposition that the suspension of capital punishment has caused an increase in the homicide rate." What Fattah's study shows to be true in Canada is confirmed by the work of Sellin, Bowers, and others in this country.

The literature on capital punishment in the United States does not, of course, consist only of works by lawyers, social scientists, and scholarly critics. It includes the more personal narratives written by governors (Michael DiSalle, who employed convicted murderers as housemen when he occupied the governor's mansion in Ohio), wardens (Clinton Duffy), prison chaplains (Byron Eshelman), executioners (Robert Elliott), and death row convicts (Caryl Chessman, executed in 1960, and Edgar Smith, released in 1971 after fourteen years under a death sentence). Two years ago an obscure publishing house in Texas brought out a volume in this genre, *Eyewitness: I Saw 189 Men Die in the Electric Chair* by Don Reid, a newspaperman. Reid covered nearly 200 executions in Texas between 1938 and 1962. His account has an intimacy and directness that helps to bring the whole subject into personal focus.

Probably the most widely read single volume on the death penalty published in this century is Arthur Koestler's *Reflections on Hanging.* Its effect on me when I read it in 1957 was galvanic. Half a century ago, there were books whose authors may have lacked Koestler's literary skill and personal animus (he had been condemned to death before a firing squad during the Spanish Civil War), but which were nevertheless an invaluable spur to abolition. One of these historic volumes, originally published in 1924 and now available in reprint, is *Man's Judgment of Death* by Lewis E. Lawes. At that time warden of New York's famed Sing Sing Prison, Lawes was also one of the founders of the American League to Abolish Capital Punishment. Along with the essays of Clarence Darrow, another founder of the League, Lawes's book set the tone for public opposition to capital punishment among reform-minded Americans of that generation. His day-to-day experience managing one of the nation's biggest and toughest prisons gave an authority to his views that undoubtedly encouraged many people to oppose legal hangings and electrocutions. Lawes's discussion has a quaint, Coolidge-era flavor; still, it is surprising how little has changed in our thinking on crime and punishment in the fifty years since he wrote.

The other vintage volume recently reprinted is Roy Calvert's *Capital Punishment in the Twentieth Century*, originally published in 1927. The new reprint is based on a 1936 revision. The volume is actually two books, for it also contains *The Death Penalty Inquiry*, Calvert's review of the evidence placed before the Select Committee on Capital Punishment in England in 1930. This committee, created by Parliament, conducted the first serious examination of capital punishment by any government in this century, and was the predecessor of the more famous Royal Commission of 1949-1953. Like Lawes's book, Calvert's is not likely now to be of much interest to most readers. In its day, however, it was an indispensable reference book on the worldwide status of capital punishment and a compendium of the best reasoning for the abolitionist position.

Most of what even the new books on capital punishment have to teach us cannot properly be called decisive or novel. And what *is* new in this literature is cumulative and continuous with what has gone before. The exact relationship between social science research and public policy formation by legislatures and courts remains something of a mystery. This is true whether the policy is formed by the legislature or the courts, and whether it is determined at the state or the federal level. It is undeniable that the general skepticism toward capital punishment, not to mention the categorical hostility toward it among many, is largely a result of the social science research on the history, the law, and the effects of executions in this country. But the public pulse, as measured by all the opinion polls of the past few years, indicates that the American people still want the death penalty, and that all the evidence and arguments against it, both in the new and in the old literature, have not significantly changed this attitude. The battle may take more time than most of us thought. As we saw earlier, the Supreme Court's momentous decision in *Furman v. Georgia* showed that the nation's highest tribunal would not only take judicial notice of the results of social science research on this issue, but even ask for more. There is every reason to believe that this will continue to be true in the future. The relevance, therefore, of policy-oriented social science research on the unanswered questions regarding capital punishment is incontestable. In due course, history will show whether the social science community prosecutes with vigor the empirical studies necessary to increase our knowledge of this subject, and whether our governments will respond to that knowledge.

8 Are Mandatory Capital Statutes Unconstitutional?

On 21 April during the final week of oral argument in the 1975 term, the United States Supreme Court for the first time in three years listened to oral argument on capital punishment. In 1973, Jesse T. Fowler had been convicted of first degree murder and sentenced to death, as required by the mandatory death penalty law then in effect in North Carolina. At issue in the case was not only Fowler's fate and that of fifty other persons under death sentence in North Carolina, but a larger national question. Would the Supreme Court, after an interval of three years, undertake to expand further its controversial ruling against the death penalty in *Furman v. Georgia*? Or, instead, would the Court yield to other pressures and begin to narrow and whittle it away?

In June 1972 the Court ruled in *Furman* that "the imposition and carrying out of the death penalty ... constitutes cruel and unusual punishment in violation of the Eighth and Fourteenth Amendments." The Court's reasoning was based on the "freakish" and "selective," "capriciously random" fashion with which the death penalty was actually imposed. The Court did not, however, summarily rule unconstitutional all possible death penalty provisions. It confined itself exclusively to the laws and procedures for inflicting capital punishment where the courts had "unfettered discretion" to bring in a sentence of death or of life. Chief Justice Warren E. Burger noted in his dissent that "if state legislatures and the Congress wish to maintain the availability of capital punishment, significant statutory changes will have to be made." The Fowler case presents the Court with one of the two major forms of capital punishment left untouched by the *Furman* ruling: statutes that make "mandatory" the imposition of the death penalty once an accused has been convicted of a "capital" crime, such as first degree murder.

In the three years since *Furman*, several developments have taken place that are likely to affect the decision of the Supreme Court in the Fowler case.

Even though executions have occurred since *Furman*, thirty-one states have enacted new death penalty legislation, in which capital punishment has been authorized either as the "mandatory" penalty for certain crimes, or as a penalty that the jury may impose under "guided discretion" from statutory standards that attempt to define which "capital crimes" truly deserve death and which deserve imprisonment.[1]

Over two hundred persons are now under sentence of death in twenty states. Their race and sex breakdown reveals that more than half are black (Jesse Fowler among them), and all but two are men.[2] These characteristics, so typical

103

of death row convicts in earlier years, remain unchanged under the new post-*Furman* capital statutes. New evidence shows that in the South, the death penalty for rape has been unquestionably discriminatory against blacks.[3]

Public opinion polls continue to show general support for the death penalty by roughly a two to one margin. But there is no survey research evidence to show that the public is acutely discontent with the cessation of executions since 1967. Studies about to be published suggest that much of the public support for the death penalty rests on fear of violent crime and on the desire for retribution regardless of any alleged deterrent effect of capital punishment.[4]

There has also been one unanticipated and troubling development. New evidence, derived from a highly technical econometric analysis, purports to show that the death penalty is a more effective deterrent than imprisonment. This striking news first reached the general public through an article, "Does Punishment Deter Crime?" by Gordon Tullock published during 1974 in the journal, *The Public Interest*. The written briefs in the Fowler case filed by both sides made it appear that the deterrence issue and this new research would be hotly contested during the oral argument before the Court. Interestingly enough, this did not come to pass, for reasons to be explained in the following paragraphs.

In argument before the Supreme Court, Fowler was represented, as was Furman three years earlier, by the NAACP Legal Defense and Educational Fund. For nearly a decade, in a series of death penalty cases, the Fund has drawn on the prodigious talents of Stanford University law professor Anthony G. Amsterdam. By dint of his unparalleled efforts and skill, Amsterdam has in a few short years transformed the death penalty controversy from one of inconclusive legislative lobbying and desperate last-minute pleas for executive clemency into one of sober and rigorous judicial interpretation of the Bill of Rights. The knowledge that Amsterdam would once again be arguing against the death penalty brought a packed gallery of observers and correspondents to the Supreme Court to hear him confront his adversaries and respond to questions from the nine Justices.

Amsterdam's opening half hour of oral argument highlighted the major contention of his written brief filed earlier in January: the system of criminal procedure used in North Carolina not only allowed, but encouraged, "arbitrary" and "selective" use of the death penalty and was, therefore, in violation of the Constitution. As Amsterdam proceeded to explain, from the moment that a North Carolina solicitor appeared before a grand jury to seek an indictment of criminal homicide to the final decision of the governor to extend or withhold clemency, discretionary legal power and unreviewable authority was at work. Such powers, however traditional and even appropriate for the criminal justice system in general, have fatal and irreversible effects where the death penalty is involved.

The problem was perfectly illustrated by Amsterdam when he pointed out that between January 1973 and April 1974 there were seventeen capital indictments in Wake County, N.C., in which the defendant "plea bargained" into a conviction for lesser offense. Yet if one examined the facts in all these cases, it would be impossible to explain why Jesse Fowler should have been indicted and convicted of first degree murder and thus automatically sentenced to die in Wake County during those months when none of these others was.

It is possible that the Supreme Court could accept Amsterdam's objections to North Carolina's procedure in death penalty cases, but still rule in favor of Fowler on narrow, relatively technical grounds and thereby side-step the large issues in the case. Even if it does, however, these larger issues will have to be faced eventually, probably as soon as the next term of the Court, because there are other death penalty cases from states other than North Carolina that raise all the general issues Amsterdam raised on Fowler's behalf. No doubt for this reason, and because he could not afford to let this opportunity slip by, Amsterdam addressed himself exclusively to the large issues raised by "mandatory" death sentences and not to possible narrow grounds for a reversal peculiar to Fowler's situation. If the Court chooses to rule against Fowler, and does not do so on the narrowest of grounds, then the states will have a clear-cut instruction in how to circumvent the *Furman* ruling.

If, however, a majority of the Court can be persuaded to accept Amsterdam's reasoning, this year the *Furman* ruling could be extended in a significant though natural way. As noted earlier, three years ago in *Furman* the emphasis was on the way judicial discretion in death *sentencing* resulted in manifest and gross arbitrariness, at least where the death penalty was involved.

In the Fowler case Amsterdam argued that the same kind of arbitrary results issues even where the chief cause of former trouble was ostensibly eliminated by so-called "mandatory" death penalty laws. Left untouched by the *Furman* ruling and these new statutes was all that vast reservoir of discretion in the system that begins with the prosecutor's discretion in bringing charges and culminates in the governor's discretion to commute a death sentence.

As Yale Law School's Charles L. Black, Jr., expressed it in his recent book, *Capital Punishment: The Inevitability of Caprice and Mistake,* "in one way or another, the official choices—by prosecutors, judges, juries, and governors—that divide those who are to die from those who are to live are on the whole not made, and cannot be made, under standards that are consistently meaningful and clear, but ... they are often made, and in the foreseeable future will continue to be made under no standards at all or under pseudostandards without discoverable meaning."[5] The point is that so-called "mandatory" statutes of whatever kind are not self-enforcing and self-administering. Like every instrument expressive of the legislative will, they depend for their effect upon the decisions of other persons who actually administer the system in each particular case. The abstract legislative decree of a death penalty to all and only persons convicted of certain crimes has no meaning whatever apart from the decisions and judgments of others. As Amsterdam pointed out more than once in his oral argument, "legislators are not fools." They know that their statutory enactments will never be given rigid and literal application by prosecutors, grand juries, trial courts, and chief executives. Instead, so-called "mandatory" statutes only mask the discretion in the system. All this is true with a special force where the death penalty is involved. Our history shows that, a century ago, mandatory death penalties interfered with the discretion that society wanted for capital crimes. Today, as Amsterdam insisted to the Court, the only way that the death penalty can continue to exist in our society is if it is *not* administered rigidly, uniformly, and without regard to sex, race, and social class. "Mandatory" statutes change none of the social dynamics involved, hence they cannot affect the results of who goes to death row and who does not.

Amsterdam's attempt to use the Fowler case to consolidate and widen the *Furman* ruling may have been the factor that provoked the Justice Department to file a brief *amicus curiae* in support of North Carolina's effort to execute Jesse Fowler. Three years ago, the Justice Department did not file a brief in support of either side in the controversy that culminated in the *Furman* ruling. This time the Justice Department asserted a federal interest in the proceedings and filed a brief in support of state's argument. (Why the Justice Department stayed silent three years ago is an interesting matter for speculation. Now, with a new attorney general, Edward H. Levi, and a solicitor general, Robert H. Bork, both of whom have expressed public though qualified support for the death penalty, it is hardly surprising that the Justice Department chose to intervene.) The department's position, however, is at odds with that of its ally, North Carolina. In his oral argument before the Court, the solicitor general emphasized more than once that the Justice Department does not favor mandatory death penalties for any crimes, and that it does believe legislatures, not appellate courts, should decree the procedures and punishments for violent crimes. But North Carolina judged Fowler's crime under a mandatory death penalty law, and it was North Carolina's highest court, *not* its legislature, that decreed this law.

This oddity arose in the following way. When confronted with the *Furman* ruling, North Carolina's Supreme Court decided that the state trial courts could conform to *Furman* by sentencing all convicted first degree murderers to death. In other states (except Delaware), the courts reasoned that the effect of *Furman* was to nullify their death penalty statutes until such time as the state legislature enacted new statutes in conformity with the apparent requirements of *Furman*. When this deviant practice of the North Carolina trial courts was challenged, the state supreme court ruled, in *State v. Waddell*[6] decided a year ago January, that the effect of *Furman* was merely to nullify the *mercy* provision of the North Carolina death penalty statutes. In this way, the North Carolina state Supreme Court created mandatory death penalties without any statutory revisions or enactments by the state legislature. It was under this kind of law that Jesse Fowler was tried and sentenced to die, and it was this authority of the North

Carolina courts that Jean A. Benoy, deputy attorney general of the state, defended before the United States Supreme Court.

The Department of Justice, therefore, had little choice. Either it had to sit by, silently, and let the LDF attack all "mandatory" death penalties in its effort to get a reversal of Fowler's death sentence, or else the department had to join with North Carolina and seek such common ground as it could find, however thin and unstable it might be. Because the department chose the latter course, the Supreme Court was confronted with the anomaly of North Carolina defending state court-made mandatory death penalty laws, and the Department of Justice attacking federal court-voided mandatory death penalty laws.

The disparity between actual practice in North Carolina and the Justice Department's professed policy preferences merely highlights the dilemma of those who seriously believe that there remain constitutionally permissible forms of capital punishment, if only the right combination of words and phrases can be found in which to formulate them. Justice Potter Stewart's questions from the bench addressed to Solicitor General Bork opened up precisely this dilemma, to the obvious discomfiture of Bork. Amsterdam and his associates could not have wished for a more effective public display of this dilemma than that produced by Justice Stewart's sharp questioning.

For those few among the hundreds listening to the oral argument who had previously studied the written briefs, there was one major surprise. The solicitor general's brief, filed last February, gave prominent mention to one startling claim: the death penalty really was, despite decades of prior evidence and argument to the contrary, a measurably effective deterrent. In the words of the brief, "the most recent study of the deterrent efficacy of the death penalty has tentatively concluded that when capital punishment was actually used ... the death penalty ... may have deterred approximately eight murders for each execution actually carried out."[7] Given the importance attached to the issue of deterrence, especially by some of the Justices who voted with the majority in the *Furman* case, this new though "tentative" result was bound to make a stir. In the media during the days prior to the oral argument in Fowler, understandably more attention was given to this question than to all the others.

At the onset of his oral argument, the solicitor general said he was sure that the Justices would want to reconsider their ruling in *Furman* because of the several "empirical judgments" on which it rested. These judgments, Bork declared, may have seemed true in 1972, but now, in 1975, they were known to be false. To those primed by knowledge of the themes in his written brief, this could only be the preface to an emphatic stress on the new deterrence research. Fifteen minutes later Bork rested his case. Not one word had been mentioned about deterrence. No sign had been given that deterrence was in any way an issue in the Fowler case. As for Amsterdam, in his fifteen-minute rebuttal that followed immediately, he, too, passed over the entire issue in silence.

This was simply incredible! Ninety minutes of oral argument on the death penalty in the Supreme Court, and not *one word* about deterrence by either side! How could this be? What had happened between the filing of the Justice Department's *amicus curiae* brief and the oral presentation of its case? How could the deterrence issue, traditionally the most important single consideration for both sides in the death penalty controversy, have been forgotten?

The explanation may lie in the written reply brief filed five days earlier by Amsterdam and his associates. In that document they subjected this "recent study of the deterrent efficacy of the death penalty" to minute scrutiny, and utterly demolished it.[8] This was not an easy job, for the evidence that confronted them was derived from a technical study that was far more penetrating and sophisticated than anything ever published in earlier years by other social scientists.

This new research, prepared (but so far unpublished)[9] by Isaac Ehrlich of the University of Chicago, argued, in effect, that leaving everything else constant during the years since 1930, merely altering the frequency with which the death penalty was used would have altered the number of murders: the more executions, the fewer murders; the fewer executions, the more murders. Ehrlich's research results thus appeared to confirm common sense: the greater the severity of punishment, the greater the deterrence. No wonder the Justice Department fell all over itself to trot out his news before the Supreme Court at the very first opportunity.

There are many difficulties with Ehrlich's argument. One is the way in which his research relied on other things not changing. Between 1930 and 1965, massive social, legal, economic, and political changes have taken place in this country. They were either inadequately measured or totally neglected by his formulae and his data. Close study of his assumptions and methods reveal point after point where implausible and even in some cases plainly erroneous assertions of fact played a crucial role in developing his conclusions. To cite but one instance, Ehrlich's evidence of the deterrent effect of the death penalty rests almost entirely upon the fact that between 1960 and 1965, at the tail end of the period he studied, executions dwindled almost to zero. If one cuts off that five-year period from the total period studied, the deterrent effect completely vanishes. Curiously enough, however, during those very years (1960-1965), while the crime rate nationally rose very steeply in all major offense categories, it went up the most slowly for murder. As for the modern heyday of executions, the mid-1930s, Ehrlich's techniques, if they show anything at all, show that executions cause a *rise*, not a decline in the murder rate.[10]

Thus, despite the initial appearance of elegance and rigor, the "new" social science research on the deterrent efficacy of the death penalty does not yield any reliable inferences at all. And it leaves pretty much intact the accumulated research by a generation of sociologists to the contrary—no evidence of any special or unique deterrent effect from capital punishment.

One can only assume that when the solicitor general read this critique in the

LDF's reply brief, he and his advisors hastily and reluctantly concluded the solitary buttress on which they leaned so heavily was, after all, just another weak reed. In any case, at the last minute they chose not to lean on it any further. The Department of Justice's omission of any mention of the deterrence issue cannot have been lost on the nine Justices, though with what effect remains to be seen. For the moment, this total reversal of form by the solicitor general must go down as a major tactical victory for the LDF.

Beclouding the resolution of the Fowler case is the state of Justice William O. Douglas's failing health. Newspaper photographs the next day showed him wan and aged in a wheelchair, on his way back to hospital for further treatment. In the courtroom, during the oral argument, he was silent throughout. It is a testimony to how significant he regards the Fowler case that he appeared on the bench at all. He was wheeled in for the opening of Amsterdam's argument and he left ninety minutes later, as soon as the Chief Justice called the next case. Should his health fail to such a degree that he could participate no further in the Fowler case, this could have a decisive effect. Since Justice Douglas has been such a visible and unswerving opponent of the death penalty, his participation in deciding the fate of Jesse Fowler is critical. Three years ago, *Furman v. Georgia* was decided by a five to four majority. Without the vote of Justice Douglas, *Fowler v. North Carolina* could well fail to be decided in a fashion favorable to abolition by even that slender margin.[11]

9 New Life for the Death Penalty

Four years ago, when the Supreme Court announced its decision in *Furman v. Georgia*, opponents of the death penalty were cheered to find a majority on the Court willing to strike down death penalty statutes as unconstitutionally "cruel and unusual." Not only did this spare the lives of more than 600 condemned persons; it also put the Court on record for the first time with a holding that the Constitution was not indifferent to the practice of capital punishment. True, the *Furman* decision did not strike down all possible forms of capital punishment legislation. It left untouched mandatory death penalty laws that leave the court no sentencing discretion for a person convicted of a capital crime; in 1972, a few such laws still remained in force around the country. The *Furman* ruling also indicated that discretionary death penalty laws with a two-stage trial, in which the court first settles the issue of guilt and then in a second hearing consults a list of "aggravated" and "mitigating" circumstances to arrive at a sentence of death or of life, might not be unconstitutional. Nevertheless, the prevailing mood of four years ago in abolitionist circles occasionally verged on the euphoric.

However, encouraged by various spokesmen for the Nixon administration, including the president himself, the national backlash against judicially imposed abolition was immediate. As of this past spring, thirty-five states had enacted new death penalty laws, nearly 500 persons were again under sentence of death (Table 9-1), and the Supreme Court was weighing the constitutionality of these new statutes in cases on appeal from five states. The solicitor general, Robert H. Bork, in his role as *amicus curiae* in support of the death penalty, urged the Court to overturn its *Furman* ruling. He argued on several grounds, including a claim that the major factual assumptions under which the Court ruled against the death penalty had been shown, in the intervening four years, to be false. Public opinion, he said, now favored capital punishment; new evidence showed that executions were a deterrent to murder. Anthony G. Amsterdam and the NAACP Legal Defense and Educational Fund (LDF), counsel for most of the death penalty petitioners, asked the Court to strike down once and for all all death penalties, mandatory or discretionary, with or without statutory guidelines for sentencing. Their chief argument was that these differences in procedure were "cosmetic"; they only masked the arbitrary and discriminatory infliction of capital punishment. Probably neither side expected the Court to adopt such extreme solutions as overruling *Furman* or repudiation of all death penalties. But if the Court would not accept either of these extremes, how would it resolve the mixed legacy of *Furman*?

Table 9-1
Persons Under Sentence of Death by State, Sex, Race, and Crime, 1976

State	M	F	W	B	M-A	N-A	Unknown	M	R	Other	Total
Alabama	1			1				1			1
Arizona	13		8	4	1			13			13
Arkansas	3		2	1				3			3
California	39	1	9	10	4		17	40			40
Colorado	1		1					1			1
Delaware	4		3				1	4			4
Florida	62		32	30				61	1(1)		62
Georgia	28	1	11	18				26[a]	3[a](1)	1[b]	29
Idaho	1							1			1
Indiana	7		4	3				7			7
Kentucky	3						3	3			3
Louisiana	33		5	28				19	14(1)		33
Maryland	1			1				1			1
Mississippi	15		1	14				15			15
Montana	2		1	1				2			2
Nebraska	3		2	1				3			3
Nevada	1		1					1			1
New Mexico	7		4		2	1		7			7
New York	1			1				1			1
N. Carolina	102	4	29	72		5		89	17(3)		106
Ohio	31	2	11	21			1	33			33
Oklahoma	30	1	16	13		2		31			31
Pennsylvania	5			2			3	5			5
Rhode Island	1			1				1			1
S. Carolina	11		3	3			5	11			11
Tennessee	8		4	2			2	8			8
Texas	33		12	13	5		3	33			33
Utah	5			2			3	5			5
Virginia	3			3				3			3
Wyoming	4		2	2				4			4
Total	458	9	161	247	12	8	39	433[a]	35[a](6)	1[b]	467

Source: NAACP Legal Defense and Educational Fund, release of 29 March 1976.
Numbers in parentheses indicate whites included in total.

[a]Includes one person convicted and sentenced to death for murder and for rape.
[b]Kidnapping.

Speculation came to an abrupt end on 2 July when the Court announced its decision in five cases, of which two—*Gregg v. Georgia*[1] and *Woodson v. North Carolina*[2] —will be much discussed. Certainly the most important was the Court's ruling in *Gregg v. Georgia*. By a majority of seven to two, the Court (with only Justices William J. Brennan, Jr. and Thurgood Marshall dissenting) said that "the punishment of death does not invariably violate the Constitution." Writing for the Court in a plurality opinion joined by Justices Lewis F. Powell, Jr. and John Paul Stevens, Justice Potter Stewart argued that the Court cannot compel a legislature "to select the least severe penalty" appropriate to grave crimes. Nor can it be maintained, Stewart insisted, that "death is disproportional in relation to the crime" of murder. "It is an extreme sanction, suitable to the most extreme of crimes." Therefore, since life imprisonment is not required by the Constitution as the punishment suitable for the gravest of crimes, and since death is not prohibited, the punishment of death is permissible, provided the sentencing jury in a capital case has its discretion "suitably directed and limited so as to minimize the risk of wholly arbitrary and capricious action." After scrutiny of the post-*Furman* Georgia death penalty statute for murder under which Gregg was convicted and sentenced, the Court concluded that it insured the required "direction" and "limitations" and thus was not unconstitutional.

The distinctive features of the Georgia law on which the Supreme Court rested its favorable judgment were several: a two-stage capital trial, the second part of which was devoted solely to the issue of sentencing; statutory provision for the jury to consider aggravating and mitigating circumstances in order to channel its assessment of facts pertinent to its choice of punishment; a written ("special") verdict by the court as to its findings relevant to the sentence it imposed; automatic review by the state supreme court of both the legal and factual issues decided by the jury as they relate to sentencing.

In two of the other death penalty cases decided the same day, *Proffitt v. Florida*,[3] and *Jurek v. Texas*,[4] death penalty statutes for murder in Florida and Texas were upheld on the strength of the holding in *Gregg*. The fact that the Florida and Texas procedures differed considerably from those of Georgia's did not perturb the majority of the Court. The similarities in "directing" and "limiting" the jury's discretion, the Court majority implied, were more important than the differences.

The common denominator that emerges from the Court's rulings in *Gregg, Jurek*, and *Proffitt* is that capital punishment is not unconstitutional as long as the statutes under which it is imposed provide, in one way or another, for (1) opportunity to put before the court information about the defendant to assist it in reaching the sentencing decision, (2) special emphasis on any mitigating factors that affect the defendant's blameworthiness, (3) common standards to guide trial courts in death sentence cases, and (4) review of every death sentence by a state appellate court.

In a footnote to his *Gregg* opinion, Justice Stewart noted that the constitutionality of the Georgia death penalty statutes for murder is not to be taken as implying that the death penalty for a crime that "does not result in the death of any human being—such as rape, burglary and armed robbery" is also constitutional. As of this writing, the Court has under consideration for appeal three cases involving the death penalty for rape. It is likely the Court will decide to hear argument in these cases after October, and probable that it will declare the death penalty for these crimes unconstitutionally "cruel and unusual." If so, the harshness of the *Gregg* decision regarding the punishment of murder is not likely to spread to embrace the punishment of lesser crimes.

In its decisions in the other two death penalty cases, the Court moved in a direction somewhat at odds with its rulings in *Gregg, Proffitt,* and *Jurek.* In *Woodson v. North Carolina,* a five to four majority of the Court declared that the mandatory death penalty for first degree murder enacted by the North Carolina legislature in 1974 was unconstitutionally cruel and unusual. Again, in a plurality opinion for the Court, Justice Stewart argued that in this day and age mandatory death penalties fly in the face of the "evolving standards of decency" the Court has long acknowledged as central to the determination of what is "cruel unusual punishment." During the previous century, mandatory death penalties were rejected as "unduly harsh and unworkably rigid" in favor of discretionary sentencing. Thus, their current reintroduction constitutes an unworkable throwback to the past.

The trouble with such penalties, argued Stewart, is that they treat all persons convicted of a given offense "not as uniquely individual human beings, but as members of a faceless, undifferentiated mass to be subjected to the blind infliction of the penalty of death." Instead, what is needed—consistent with the requirements imposed four years ago in *Furman*—are "objective standards to guide, regularize, and make rationally reviewable the process for imposing a sentence of death."

In the last of its death penalty cases, *Roberts v. Louisiana,*[5] the Court invoked its ruling in *Woodson* to set aside as unconstitutionally cruel and unusual Louisiana's mandatory death penalty for murder. Thus, thanks to the rulings in *Woodson* and *Roberts,* at least 170 condemned persons in these two states should have their death sentences voided, and in the months ahead they will be returned to lower courts for resentencing to imprisonment.

There is only one explicit qualification to the Court's condemnation of mandatory death penalties in *Woodson* and *Roberts.* The Court noted that the constitutionality of mandatory death penalties for life term prisoners convicted of murder or aggravated assault had not been presented in the cases on appeal and therefore was not settled by the *Woodson* ruling. It is worth noting that Governor Jimmy Carter said in a recent press interview that, although he now was generally opposed to the death penalty, the one exception he still would favor was for "lifers" who commit a second murder while in prison.

The chief effect of the rulings in the two leading cases, *Gregg* and *Woodson,* is that the Supreme Court has reaffirmed and clarified its *Furman* ruling, thereby meeting the most persistent demand of its critics during the last four years. The plurality opinion in *Gregg* by Justices Stewart, Powell, and Stevens emphasized that the *Furman* decision is valid constitutional law. This effectively lays to rest any possibility that the Burger Court will overturn the *Furman* ruling. In the gloom spread by the *Gregg* decision, it is important not to lose sight of this solid confirmation of *Furman*. Of the two possibilities left open by *Furman*—mandatory and "guided discretion" statutes—only the latter now remains. The states, as well as Congress, now have much clearer guidance as to the sort of capital statutes they can constitutionally enact. The puzzle set by the *Furman* Court has now been solved by the *Gregg* Court. The national posture on the death penalty, so far as its "cruelty and unusualness" is concerned, is stabilized. During the next year or so, one can expect, several legislatures will enact statutes patterned after those upheld in Georgia, Florida, and Texas.

What other effects are the *Gregg* and *Woodson* rulings likely to have? It now seems improbable that the Supreme Court will again in this century rule forcefully and directly against capital punishment on any constitutional ground. During the past decade, the strongest untested argument available to abolitionists—that the death penalty is *per se* "cruel and unusual punishment," no matter for what crime and no matter how administered—has been rejected by a large majority of the Court. Only two Justices, Brennan and Marshall, have embraced the abolitionists' preferred interpretation of the Eighth Amendment. Both Justices Stewart and Byron R. White, who were part of the slender five-man majority in *Furman* four years ago, backed off from the unconstitutional *per se* interpretation sought by the LDF in *Gregg*. Justice White even refused to join Justice Stewart in the *Woodson* majority to condemn mandatory death sentences. (Justices Powell and Stevens, with Justices Stewart, Brennan, and Marshall, constituted the five to four majority in *Woodson* and *Roberts*.) With such a substantial portion of the Court thus turning its back on judicial abolition by the federal courts, it is unlikely that newer and probably weaker constitutional arguments will prevail where the stronger and more familiar ones have failed. As Jack Greenberg, executive director of the LDF has conceded, "The prospects of a decision in the next few years effecting an across-the-board abolition of the death penalty are now exceedingly dim."[6]

Uppermost in many minds is the fate of the 150 or so death row prisoners in Georgia, Texas, and Florida. What lies ahead for them? Are they likely to face the execution chamber—unused anywhere in the United States since June 1967, in Colorado—and if so, how soon? Generalizations on such a delicate subject are unsafe, but it does appear that not before the end of this year are all legal appeals likely to be exhausted. The *Gregg* ruling, addressed solely to the issue of sentencing, leaves untouched and undecided any issues affecting the conviction in each of these cases. Pending the resolution of the constitutionality of the death sentence itself, none of the substantive issues surrounding the convictions in these 150 cases has been litigated. In many instances, lawyers are confident, reversals will be obtained in state or federal courts.

Unlikely though it might seem, the *Gregg* ruling may have some hidden advantages for defense lawyers with capital cases. By insisting that the trial courts and state appellate courts scrutinize carefully the characteristics of a convicted murderer prior to issuing a death sentence, it becomes possible to litigate issues hitherto not easily presented to courts. Since many of the Georgia, Florida and Texas death sentences were imposed after only the most perfunctory appraisal of mitigating circumstances, a virgin field of argument is now opened up for defense lawyers to explore in future cases. Thus, although *Gregg* thoroughly squelched some abolitionist hopes, it opened up new possibilities that with imaginative and resourceful litigation may avoid or nullify many death sentences. A good illustration of how this can work is to be seen in the concept of "Team Defense," unveiled recently by lawyers working with the Southern Poverty Law Center.[7] Their idea is to organize expert testimony for the defense so that the second, or penalty, phase of the trial becomes a forum that in effect puts the death penalty itself on trial. By saturating the court with information about the actual workings of the death penalty, so far as eyewitness testimony and social science evidence can provide it, the belief is that many, even if not all, juries will refuse to bring in a death sentence. This offers new hope in cases where the defendant's guilt is beyond doubt.

How will *Gregg* and *Woodson* affect the death penalty in other states? Aside from steering legislatures toward guided discretion statutes and the two-stage trial in capital cases, the *Gregg* ruling probably will be applied directly to uphold capital statutes in several other states. The Arizona, Arkansas, Colorado, and Ohio death statutes seem fundamentally like those upheld in Georgia, Florida, and Texas. Thus, another four dozen death row prisoners are likely to lose their appeals to the Supreme Court for the same reason that Gregg lost his. Perhaps as early as next year this may culminate in pressures on several governors to commute death sentences wholesale.

One of the galling features of the *Gregg*, *Proffitt*, and *Jurek* decisions is the way the Court reacted, or rather failed to react, to the social science research published in the years since *Furman*. With perhaps one exception, the Court passed it by without significant acknowledgment, discussion, or rebuttal. This was especially conspicuous in the *Gregg* ruling. Both in the written briefs and in the oral argument, LDF arguments had labored to show that such evidence as was available to qualified observers pointed unmistakably to the conclusion that the post-*Furman* death statutes achieved little or no change from the pre-*Furman* statutes, with their unbridled discretion and arbitrary and discriminatory impact. Justice Stewart's opinion in *Gregg* magisterially ignored this evidence, even as it rejected the contention in question.

Similarly, the Court indicated that it was impressed by public opinion surveys (which in recent years report that the American public favors the death penalty by a margin of roughly two to one), despite the superficiality of these findings as shown by critical social scientists.[8] Only Justice Marshall, in dissent, noted that public opinion is relevant to interpreting the Constitution only when it is "informed" opinion. On the deterrence question, the *Gregg* Court did pause to note that, despite a heated debate for the past few years, the empirical evidence is "simply . . . inconclusive." Nevertheless the Court immediately added (without a scintilla of evidence cited in support) that "the death penalty undoubtedly is a significant deterrent" in some cases: murder for hire and murder by a life term prisoner. For social scientists and jurists who had expected that this round of death penalty cases would find the Supreme Court resting its decision, at least in part, on the results of careful and relevant empirical investigations, the *Gregg* decision can be viewed only as a bitter disappointment. Four years ago, in his dissent in *Furman*, Chief Justice Warren E. Burger complained of the "paucity" of evidence relied on by the majority ruling in favor of abolition. This year's ruling in *Gregg* rests on even less.

It may be possible to read *Gregg* and its companion cases in a narrower way, as providing only the judgment that the new Georgia capital statute and its counterparts in other states have merely a veneer of constitutionality. Justice Stewart in his plurality opinion wrote, "On their face these procedures seem to satisfy the concerns of *Furman*. No longer should there be 'no meaningful basis for distinguishing the few cases in which [the death penalty] is imposed from the many cases in which it is not.' " On this interpretation, *Gregg* leaves open to future litigation the question whether in fact these statutes, as actually administered, attain a genuine, functional constitutionality as well. The apparent unwillingness of the *Gregg* court to take seriously the empirical evidence put before it from two years of experience under the new statutes is not an encouraging sign.

However, it is not so much from a scientific as from a moral point of view that the rulings in *Gregg*, *Proffitt*, and *Jurek* are unconvincing. It is troubling to see the plurality in *Gregg*, under Justice Stewart's leadership, invoke the constitutional legitimacy of retribution in punishment and of the death penalty as an instrument of just retribution. The Justices seem to overlook the fundamental fact that punishment, by its very nature, is retributive, as Justice Thurgood Marshall noted in his dissent. This is so because punishments are designed to pay back to offenders suffering and indignities akin to those the offender unjustly imposed on the innocent victim. Hence, imprisonment for murder, no less than the death penalty, is retributive. The question, of course, is whether it is retributive enough. The *Gregg* plurality writes as if by individuating a death sentence for a particular offender, a trial court serves the retributively just purpose, under the Constitution, of making the most severe sentence (as in *The Mikado*) fit the gravest criminal homicides.

But this line of reasoning is open to the Court only if it is also ready to argue that retributive justice, under the Constitution, is not met when all murderers are sentenced only to imprisonment, as they will be in a state that has abolished (or failed to reenact) the death penalty. The Court, of course, has no intention of advancing any such objection. The result is a dilemma. If, as the *Gregg* Court insists, the Constitution permits the death penalty because of its retributive superiority to lesser punishments for murder, then it is difficult to see why the Court extends constitutional toleration, as it does, to less severe (and, *a fortiori*, less retributive) punishments for this crime. On the other hand, if, as the Court implies, the punishment of imprisonment decreed by a legislature and imposed by a trial court is adequately retributive, it is hard to see how retribution can be trotted out to bolster the added severities unique to the death penalty. The principles of retributive justice simply are not a legitimate basis for construing the constitutional prohibition against "cruel and unusual punishment" in a manner tolerant of the death penalty, unless it is to be made mandatory.

Hidden beneath the veneer of constitutional argument is the plain evidence that the Court has proved itself arbitrary and discriminatory in its defense of the death penalty. Where the *Woodson* decision will eventually free scores of prisoners from execution, the *Gregg* decision may consign hundreds to their deaths.

Where is the rational difference in the crimes and criminals that justifies this line drawn by the Court, upholding death sentences in Georgia but condemning the same sentences across the state line in North Carolina? Why should Gregg, a hitchhiker convicted of robbing and murdering the men who gave him a ride, have his death sentence upheld, when Woodson, convicted of robbing and killing a storekeeper, has his death sentence overturned? Why shouldn't both, or neither, be spared? It is more than ironic that if Woodson had robbed and killed in Georgia, and Gregg in North Carolina, it would be Gregg, not Woodson, who was spared and Woodson, not Gregg, whose death sentence was sustained. Is this evenhanded, rational justice where life and death are at issue?

If, as the Court said in *Woodson*, the death penalty is "qualitatively different" from imprisonment, it is odd that the difference seems to arouse the disapproval of the Court only when it occurs in conjunction with death statutes of mandatory or unlimited discretionary application. Nowhere in its recent decisions does the Court address this issue, and no plausible answer is to be found. No doubt unintentionally, the Court's decisions last month are the perfect proof of the major contention urged by abolitionists during the past decade. In this country, today, it is simply not possible to have a death penalty applied with uniform, predictable, rational impact all across the land. Instead, we can have capital punishment only if it is unpredictable, arbitrary, and infrequent in its application. Retributive justice of this sort is simply not justice at all, because it is inequitable.

Of course, the unconstitutionality of capital punishment has never been the major objection. Until fifteen years ago, save for a few mavericks, no one gave any credence to the possibility of ending the death penalty by judicial interpretation of constitutional law. Legislative repeal and executive commutation of sentence were always the chief focus of abolitionist efforts, despite the discouraging results year after year. Thus, the news of Canada's abolition of capital punishment in a close parliamentary vote in July[9] is a sharp reminder that our national posture on this subject is increasingly at variance with that of our traditional neighbors and allies, and that such progress toward total abolition as we have achieved in recent years has been secured not by executive or legislative leadership but by the judiciary. As in most legislative policies affecting civil liberties and civil rights, there are limits to what even the most enlightened appellate courts can do when left adrift by the other branches of government. On the matter of capital punishment, those limits may have been reached, at least for the moment, in *Gregg* and *Woodson*.

It is difficult to believe that the nine Justices of the Supreme Court can contemplate their decisions in *Gregg, Proffitt*, and *Jurek* with any real satisfaction. They have put aside their personal scruples against the death penalty in the name of federalism, judicial restraint, legislative deference, and retribution. Thus, two days before the nation's Bicentennial, the world is told that, so far as the federal Constitution is concerned, our "natural rights to life, liberty and the pursuit of happiness" yield not a condemnation of, but a permission to, death-inclined legislatures and courts—at least where the punishment of murder is concerned. Some will find this, as I do, disheartening. We had hoped the Court might see the Constitution differently in our time, and say so in accents that would command agreement and respect.

10 Epilogue: A Right to Die by Firing Squad?

The spectacle in Utah of condemned murderer Gary Mark Gilmore pleading to be shot as punishment for his crimes, rather than serve more time behind prison bars (where he spent half his life and eighteen of the past twenty-one years), has thrust capital punishment before us in some of its most troubling aspects. The events leading up to Gilmore's execution on 17 January highlight the dilemmas posed by the death penalty today.

Gilmore's case, given his confession in open court, his intelligence and apparent sanity, and his unwillingness to appeal his conviction or sentence, poses few problems for defenders of capital punishment. They are likely to greet his eagerness to accept death by firing squad "with grace and dignity" (his words), with grim satisfaction and perhaps even grudging respect. They might regret the way Gilmore overnight became a creature of the media (*Newsweek* put him on the cover of its 29 November 1976 issue), because his readiness to die in a blaze of rifle fire could transform him into a kind of hero. Nevertheless, proponents of the death penalty will insist that by willfully taking the life of innocent victims, Gilmore forfeited any right to his own. Especially in Utah, with its Mormon traditions, the biblical doctrine of "a life for a life" epitomizes the seeming justice of executing Gilmore. From a moral point of view, therefore, advocates of capital punishment had no ground for quarreling with Gilmore's wish to die by firing squad.

But for opponents of the death penalty, the Gilmore case poses a cruel dilemma. If they insisted that Gilmore not be executed, where was the fairness in that to the condemned man? Was it not unfeeling of them to protest his execution even though he freely admitted his guilt and declared that, for him (and he should have known), the prospect of life imprisonment was much worse than death? When Gilmore said, as he did in a letter to his mother, "I wish to be dead," was it not unseemly for others to interfere? Did he not have the right to die at the time and under the circumstances of his own choosing? Moreover, was Gilmore not correct when he charged that the attorneys seeking to prevent his execution were not only acting without his authorization, but that they were not "motivated by concern for [his] own welfare"? Was it not true that these lawyers (from the American Civil Liberties Union and the NAACP Legal Defense and Educational Fund) wanted to keep Gilmore alive largely for the benefit of their other clients on death row, thereby seeming to use the very kind of reasoning denounced by opponents of capital punishment when executions are defended on grounds of general deterrence?

If, however, Gilmore was abandoned to his fate before the firing squad, then opponents of the death penalty would have to face some nasty consequences. If they could not prevent Gilmore's execution, then they must tolerate it and to that extent give their tacit approval to some executions, namely, those in which the condemned person expresses a wish to die. This is an inconsistency too obvious to be swallowed. If the death penalty is barbarous, it is no less so on those occasions when a murderer welcomes his own legal execution. Furthermore, as several commentators have pointed out, Gilmore's refusal to pursue an appeal (Utah law does not make appellate review of a death sentence mandatory), in conjunction with his expressed wish to die, made the state of Utah his accomplice in what amounted to a suicide pact. Even if Gilmore waived the legal and constitutional protections afforded his rights, Utah could not act responsibly and be indifferent to whether it was violating them in taking his life. Finally, with what right was Gilmore so indifferent to the adverse impact of his execution upon the plight of the hundreds of others currently under death sentence? His execution might not provoke the "national avalanche of legal slaughter" that one observer has predicted, but it certainly brought to an end the nearly ten-year moratorium on executions. Now it will be just that much easier for executions to become routine.

Thus the first dilemma for opponents of the death penalty. Fortunately, much of it can be dispelled if we look more closely at the considerations that seemed to favor yielding to Gilmore's alleged right to die. For the sake of argument, let us grant that some persons in some situations have a right to die, and that Gilmore's expressed wish to die was sane and sincere. Even so, he was a long way from the paradigm of one who has this right: someone with intractable pain, incurable illness, or severe impairment of faculties. However, let us waive this consideration. It is arguable in any case whether this right is the kind that imposes a duty on everyone else not to interfere. If it does, the Utah authorities may have violated Gilmore's rights by rushing him to the hospital on 16 November after his apparent suicide attempt. Nevertheless, there is considerable reason for supposing that attempts at suicide, including Gilmore's, are *prima facie* evidence of mental disturbance and, therefore, that others have a duty of care to intervene.

So much, then, for Gilmore's alleged right to die. His rights do not exhaust the morally pertinent considerations that his case presents. The most important is that his conduct under death sentence was marked by the same calloused and hostile attitude toward human life that he had already manifested in committing murder. He apparently conspired in a double suicide with his girl friend, Nicole Barrett, an unstable mother of two young children. Not only was the sincerity of his attempt doubtful (doctors were quoted as saying that he knew he could not have died from his overdose of drugs even if he had not received medical attention), she was close to death for several days. Gilmore seems to have been untroubled by his part in all this. But above all else, he was indifferent to the quality and value of *his* own life. From all appearances, and despite his amply attested "sociopathic" personality, Gilmore was not untalented. It was not impossible to imagine him as the source of socially valuable contributions, even if he had been confined to prison. But his posturing and manipulation of a series of lawyers, culminating in his expressed desire to die "with grace and dignity" (the *New York Times* made this their "Quotation for the Day" on 9 November 1976), set an example of the worst sort: an unrepentant and callous self-centered attitude toward human life. The fact that the life was his own, and that he would literally see it brought to a violent end (he requested no blindfold, but was hooded at the execution) in as brutal a fashion as our law permits, only etches all the deeper this unsavory fact. The most one can say on Gilmore's behalf, with apologies to Kant, is that at least he was morally consistent in being willing to have his own life treated with the same violence that he visited on several others.

Even if Gilmore did have the right to take his own life, it would not follow that he had the right to compel the state to take it for him in the name of punishment. It is also ludicrous to suggest, as Thomas Szasz has,[1] that Gilmore and the state of Utah, by virtue of his crime and its laws, in effect entered into a contract that gave Gilmore the right to die and Utah the duty to put him to death. At most, the state has this *privilege* once a person has been found guilty of a capital crime and duly sentenced to death. But it makes no sense to say that somebody has the right to compel somebody else into the exercise of a privilege. The state never has any *duty* to punish anyone with death, not even when it enacts capital statutes and finds persons guilty under them. The governor of Utah could have at any time commuted Gilmore's death sentence as an act of executive clemency, and this would have not have violated any duty toward Gilmore.

Did Gilmore have the right not to resist Utah's efforts to execute him, the right not to seek protection of his rights? I think so; I know of no duty which Gilmore had to resist his lawful execution. However, I also think Gilmore was wrong to acquiesce in his death sentence. If capital punishment is morally wrong, as I believe it is, then it cannot have been right for Gilmore to let himself be its unprotesting victim. Even those of us who insist that suicide is not always wrong would have to admit that suicide can be wrongfully committed, as when it jeopardizes the rights or interests of others who have not consented to it.

So far I have assumed that Gilmore was sane and fully accountable for his criminal conduct. But was he? Was not his death wish itself pathological and to some extent the subtle product of social practices over which he had no control? Dr. John C. Woods, chief of forensic psychiatry at Utah State Hospital, and one of the doctors who certified Gilmore's sanity prior to his trial, has been quoted subsequently as saying that Gilmore "went out of his way to get the death penalty; that's why he pulled two execution-style murders he was bound to be caught for. I think it's a legitimate question, based on this evidence and our knowledge of the individual, to ask if Gilmore would have killed if there was not a death penalty in Utah."[2] Many have noted that Gilmore, imprisoned in Oregon (where the death penalty has been unconstitutional since 1964), took his parole release in Utah, the one place in the nation where blood atonement, in the form of a firing squad, may be used to administer the death penalty for murder.

Twenty years ago, in his study on the death penalty for the American Law Institute, Thorsten Sellin reported some outlandish episodes from earlier centuries in which it appeared "the desire to be executed has caused persons to commit a capital crime."[3] This phenomenon, known now as "suicide by execution," has been discussed in considerable detail by three clinical psychiatrists in their contributions to the volume, *Capital Punishment in the United States*, published in 1976 under the auspices of the American Orthopsychiatric Association. Murder and suicide as symbolically interchangeable acts have a long history in the literature of psychopathology. Suicide by execution, in which murder is the intervening step, is much rarer, but the case histories presented by Louis Jolyon West, George F. Solomon, and Bernard L. Diamond and now available in the volume mentioned above should go a long way toward convincing the skeptical. Diamond could have had Gilmore's case in mind when he wrote that this kind of murderer is engaged in a "terminal act," in which the killer "does not fear death, he longs for death. What he fears is life, with its miseries and desperate conflicts. To such a one, prison is to be feared above all else, for it promises a continuation of the old miseries. . . . Death by execution," Diamond concludes, "fits these psychological needs . . . , and the mere existence of the death penalty . . . encourages these pathological gambles with fate."[4]

The most difficult question has yet to be faced. If Gilmore had no significant right to die and the state no duty to execute him, and if the entire practice of capital punishment is morally objectionable, then what is to be done with the Gilmores of the world? I do not believe that they should be made to rot in prison until hell freezes over, for that would inflict on them in the name of the lesser penalty a kind of retribution no one should suffer. Yet they cannot hope to be paroled once again after only a few more years behind bars. So long as Gilmore persisted in a callous disregard for the value of human life, he would have been a danger to society and the public had the right not to have him inflicted on them soon again.

Here is yet another dilemma for abolitionists. We must somehow fashion a humane and realistic alternative to all these other solutions, one tailored to fit the prisoner's actual situation, the requirements of public safety, and the available resources in punitive and therapeutic institutions. Given our ignorance of how to cope with (I hesitate to say "cure") such persons, I am not optimistic that a truly effective alternative can be found. So long as we insist on retaining capital punishment, however, we weaken the very motive needed to find it. The criminologist, like the surgeon, has no right to bury the human consequences of his ignorance, errors, and mistakes. Our first responsibility to those like Gilmore is to ensure they receive individual justice under a fair system of laws. This cannot be achieved by executing them, even at their request. The death they suffered would be no more dignified, no more excusable or justifiable, than the deaths they caused.

Notes

Introduction

1. Jack Greenberg and Jack Himmelstein, "Varieties of Attack on the Death Penalty," *Crime and Delinquency* 15 (January 1969): 112-120.

2. Actually, his essay was published in essentially the same form in two journals, *Ethics* in 1968 and *The Journal of Criminal Law, Criminology and Police Science* in 1969. I submitted my rejoinder to both journals, too, and each published it.

3. David C. Baldus and James W.L. Cole, "A Comparison of the Work of Thorsten Sellin and Isaac Ehrlich on the Deterrent Effect of Capital Punishment," *Yale Law Journal* 85 (December 1975): 170-186, at p. 185.

4. See Leonard W. Levy, *Against the Law*, New York, Harper and Row, 1974, p. 410; James Q. Wilson, *Thinking About Crime*, New York, Vintage Books, 1977, p. 211; and Ernest van den Haag, *Punishing Criminals*, New York, Basic Books, 1975, p. 200 note.

5. Laughlin McDonald, *Civil Liberties*, June 1974, p. 15.

6. Richard Kluger, *Simple Justice*, New York, Alfred A. Knopf, 1976, pp. 101, 113, 147, 161.

7. Formation of the NCADP has been mentioned in *The Los Angeles Times*, 5 October 1976, pp. 1, 15; *AFSC Quaker Service Bulletin*, Fall 1976, p. 3; Diane Leonetti, "Capital Punishment," *Fellowship*, October 1976, pp. 10-14; Deborah Leavy, "The Return of Legalized Murder?" *WRL News*, January-February 1977, no. 198, pp. 5-6. For the sake of the record, it should be mentioned that the American League to Abolish Capital Punishment effectively ceased to exist well before *Furman* was decided. As a single-issue abolitionist organization, its eventual fate was sealed by the number of multi-issue reform organizations which, during the 1960s, adopted policy positions against the death penalty.

Chapter 1
The Issue of Capital Punishment

1. The President's Commission on Law Enforcement and Administration of Justice, *The Challenge of Crime in a Free Society*, Washington, D.C., U.S. Government Printing Office, 1967, p. 143.

2. I have drawn heavily in the following paragraphs upon information in chapter 2 of my book, *The Death Penalty in America*, New York, Doubleday Anchor, 1964, rev. ed., 1967.

3. R.H. Beattie and J.P. Kennedy, "Aggressive Crime," *The Annals* (March 1966): 84.

4. See "Executions 1930-1965," *National Prisoner Statistics* 39 (June 1966).

5. The President's Commission, *The Challenge of Crime*, p. 143.

6. These statements have been collected and reprinted in Bedau, *The Death Penalty*, pp. 130-135.

7. Quoted in a speech by Senator Philip Hart, 25 July 1966, as printed in *The Congressional Record*, p. 16181.

8. Canadian Ministry of Justice, *Capital Punishment*, Ottawa, Canada, 1965, pp. 22-35. This is the most recent public document on capital punishment and is especially valuable for its summaries of other such documents not readily available. See also Joyce Vialet, "Capital Punishment: Pro and Con Arguments," U.S. Library of Congress Legislative Reference Service, 3 August 1966 (mimeo).

9. Donald H. Partington, "The Incidence of the Death Penalty for Rape in Virginia," *Washington and Lee Law Review* (Spring 1965): 43-75. A very elaborate study of this issue, sponsored by the NAACP Legal Defense and Education Fund, has yet to be published; see the preliminary reports in the *New York Times*, 24 April 1966 and 30 November 1966.

10. Edwin D. Wolf, "Analysis of Jury Sentencing in Capital Cases: New Jersey 1937-1961," *Rutgers Law Review* (Fall 1964): 56-64.

11. See Bedau, *The Death Penalty*, pp. 434-452, for a full account of each case.

12. The President's Commission, *The Challenge of Crime*, p. 143.

13. Thorsten Sellin, *The Death Penalty*, Philadelphia, American Law Institute, 1959; "Capital Punishment," *Federal Probation* (September 1961): 3-11; these and other studies on deterrence are also reprinted in chapter 6 of Bedau, *The Death Penalty*.

14. New Jersey Commission to Study Capital Punishment, *Report*, October 1964, p. 9.

15. See Giles Playfair and Derrick Sington, *The Offenders*, New York, Simon and Schuster, 1957.

16. Bedau, *The Death Penalty*, p. 399.

Chapter 2
The Courts, the Constitution, and Capital Punishment

1. See H. Bedau, ed., *The Death Penalty in America*, New York, Doubleday Anchor, 1964, rev. ed., 1967, p. 231.

2. See Rudolph v. Alabama, 375 U.S. 889 (1963), at p. 891.

3. *Civil Liberties* (June 1965): 2. In the December 1964 issue of *Civil Liberties*, argument for and against such a position was reviewed. Other statements of the Union's position may be found in ACLU Feature Press Service Weekly Bulletin No. 2237, 12 July 1965, and *ACLU Annual Report* 45 (1966): 78-79.

4. See *Civil Liberties* (May 1967): 1; *New York Times*, 7 July 1967, p. 12. See also Note, "Multiparty Federal Habeus Corpus," *Harvard Law Review* 81 (1968): 1482. An interesting account of these efforts, as seen by a sympathetic interviewer, appears in Susan Brownmiller, "Bringing Death Row Into the Courthouse," *The Village Voice* (New York), 1 February 1968, pp. 10, 18.

5. *Oregon Constitution*, art. I, § 37 (approved 21 May 1920 and repealed 3 November 1964). See generally my article, "Capital Punishment in Oregon, 1903-64," *Oregon Law Review* 45 (1965): 1.

6. Save possibly for (D), none of these arguments is fundamentally original with the present author; they have been presented in piecemeal fashion to the courts and to scholarly audiences at least since 1960. It would appear, however, that appellants' argument in Adderly v. Wainwright, 272 F. Supp. 530 (M.D. Fla. 1967), and in Hill v. Nelson, 271 F. Supp. 439 (N.D. Cal. 1967), are the first cases in which all of these arguments, save (D), have been advanced in an attack on the constitutionality of the death penalty.

7. Weems v. United States, 217 U.S. 349, 368-369 (1910) (quoting *Congressional Register*).

8. Black, "The Bill of Rights," *New York University Law Review* 35 (1960): 865, 867.

9. See William J. Brennan, "Extension of the Bill of Rights to the States," *Journal of Urban Law* 44 (1966): 11; and his earlier article "The Bill of Rights and the States," *New York University Law Review* 36 (1961): 761. See also Griswold v. Connecticut, 381 U.S. 479 (1965).

10. *Newark News*, 19 October 1961. For further discussion of his case, see my essay, "The Struggle Over Capital Punishment in New Jersey," in *The Death Penalty*, at p. 387.

11. Walter Oberer, "Jury Selection, The Death Penalty and Fair Trial," *Case & Comment* 71 (July-August 1966): 3 (emphasis added), reprinted from *The Nation* 198, 6 April 1964, at p. 342. See also his earlier article, "Does Disqualification of Jurors for Scruples Against Capital Punishment Constitute Denial of Fair Trial on Issue of Guilt?" *Texas Law Review* 39 (1961): 545.

12. *Civil Liberties* (June 1965): 2.

13. State v. Leland, 190 Ore. 598, 625, 227 P.2d 785, 797 (1951), aff'd, 343 U.S. 790 (1952).

14. Oberer, "Jury Selection," at p. 5.

15. Smith v. Texas, 311 U.S. 128, 130 (1940).

16. Brief for Appellant at 35-36, People v. Ketchel, 63 Cal. 2d 859, 409 P.2d 694, 48 Cal. Rptr. 614 (1966).

17. Oberer, "Jury Selection," at p. 5.

18. *Capital Punishment Quarterly* 1 (July 1964): 1 (Texas Society to Abolish Capital Punishment, Austin).

19. Ibid. See also Cody Wilson, "Impartial Juries?" *The Texas Observer*

(Austin), 27 November 1964, p. 5; and Wilson, "Belief in Capital Punishment and Jury Performance" (unpublished memorandum), reprinted in Appendix to Brief for Appellants at 44, People v. Ketchel, Crim. No. 10905 (Cal. Sup. Ct., filed September 12, 1967).

20. Letter from Walter Oberer to the author, 10 July 1967.

21. Robert Crosson, "An Investigation into Certain Personality Variables Among Capital Trial Jurors," January 1966, at pp. 66, 69 (typescript, Psychology Department, Western Reserve University).

22. Ibid. at pp. 79, 82.

23. The empirical evidence on juror bias has recently been brought up to date, and published separately in Hans Zeisel, *Some Data on Juror Attitudes Towards Capital Punishment* (1968).

24. The Court has declared that it will hear argument on this issue. Witherspoon v. Illinois, 389 U.S. 1035 (1968), granting cert. to 36 Ill. 2d 471, 224 N.E.2d 259 (1967); Bumper v. North Carolina, 389 U.S. 1034 (1968), granting cert. to 270 N.C. 521, 155 S.E.2d 173 (1967).

25. People v. Riser, 47 Cal. 2d 566, 576, 305 P.2d 1, 7, cert. denied, 353 U.S. 930 (1957), quoted approvingly in Commonwealth v. Ladetto, 349 Mass. 237, 246, 207 N.E.2d 536, 542 (1965).

26. Both Iowa and South Dakota several decades ago prohibited death-qualified juries once they abandoned mandatory death penalties in favor of discretionary ones. The courts in these states have allowed the prosecutor to continue to elicit from prospective jurors their views regarding the death penalty for the purpose of helping him to determine upon whom to exercise peremptory challenges. See State v. Lee, 91 Iowa 499, 502-503, 60 N.W. 119, 120-121 (1894); State v. Garrington, 11 S.D. 178, 184, 76 N.W. 326, 327 (1898).

27. Andres v. United States, 333 U.S. 740, 748 (1948). For argument favoring split verdicts in criminal cases, see John V. Ryan, "Less Than Unanimous Jury Verdicts in Criminal Trials," *Journal of Criminal Law, Criminology, and Police Science* 58 (1967): 211.

28. Fay v. New York, 332 U.S. 261, 285 (1947).

29. See the classic discussion by Maynard Shipley, "Does Capital Punishment Prevent Convictions?" *American Law Review* 43 (1909): 321. See also *The Death Penalty* at pp. 29 n.51, 418, 423.

30. In re Waiver of Death Penalty, 45 N.J. 501, 213 A.2d 20 (1965).

31. Ch. 500, [1967] Md. Laws 1106.

32. See Negley Teeters and Charles Zibulka, "Executions under State Authority, January 20, 1864–August 10, 1966," reprinted in William Bowers, ed., *Executions in America* (1964).

33. Harry Kalven and Hans Zeisel, *The American Jury* (1966), p. 449.

One matter deserving some research is whether the growth of jury discretion in capital cases, apparently initiated in Louisiana in 1846, see State v. Lewis, 3 La. Ann. Rep. 398 (1848), and rapidly adopted throughout the South, was not only concurrent with the demise of the infamous "Black Codes," but was designed with the tacit purpose of providing all-white juries with a legal device to accomplish in a new way precisely the same ruthless and systematic discrimination hitherto openly permitted through a dual criminal code.

34. People v. Terry, 61 Cal. 2d 137, 141, 390 P.2d 381, 384, 37 Cal. Rptr. 605, 608, cert. denied, 379 U.S. 866 (1964).

35. People v. Riser, 47 Cal. 2d 566, 575, 305 P.2d 1, 7 (1956), cert. denied, 353 U.S. 930 (1957).

36. Commonwealth v. Neill, 362 Pa. 507, 518, 67 A.2d 276, 281.

37. Giacco v. Pennsylvania, 382 U.S. 399, 405 n.8 (1966).

38. *National Prisoner Statistics Bulletin No. 41*, "Executions 1930-1966." The six jurisdictions (and the number of black rapists executed since 1930) are: District of Columbia (3), Louisiana (17), Mississippi (21), Oklahoma (4), Virginia (21), West Virginia (1).

39. Brief for Appellants, Johnson v. New Jersey, 368 U.S. 145, dismissing appeal from 34 N.J. 212, 168 A.2d 1 (1961). On 6 May 1968 the New Jersey Supreme Court ruled that under the 1947 state constitution, the court had the "inherent" power to modify a sentence, including the death sentence, whether imposed originally by judge or jury; through this ruling it upheld its own interim ruling of September 1967, nullifying the death sentence in two cases. N.Y. Times, 7 May 1968, at 1, col. 7.

40. State v. Johnson, 34 N.J. 212, 230, 168 A.2d 1, 10, cert. denied, 368 U.S. 933 (1961).

41. Edwin Wolf, "Abstract of Analysis of Jury Sentencing in Capital Cases: New Jersey: 1937-1961," *Rutgers Law Review* 19 (1964): 56-64.

42. See my article, "Death Sentences in New Jersey, 1907-1960," *Rutgers Law Review* 19 (1964): 14-15; also Bedau, "Capital Punishment in Oregon," at pp. 19-20; and *New York University Law Review* 39 (1964): 136 *passim*.

43. Wolfgang established his results by the familiar chi-square (χ^2) technique. For a discussion of this technique in legal argument, see Finkelstein, "The Application of Statistical Decision Theory to the Jury Discrimination Cases," *Harvard Law Review* 80 (1966): 338, 366-373.

44. Maxwell v. Bishop, 257 F. Supp. 710, 718-719 (E.D. Ark. 1966), (footnotes omitted).

45. Ibid. at p. 72.

46. *California Penal Code* § 190.1 (Deering 1960).

47. *Model Penal Code* § 210.6(3), (4), (Proposed Official Draft 1962).

48. State v. Johnson, 34 N.J. 212, 230, 168 A.2d 1, 10-11, cert. denied, 368 U.S. 933 (1961).

49. 36 *A.L.I. Proceedings* (1959): 179.

50. See in general Note, "The Two-Trial System in Capital Cases," *New York University Law Review* 39 (1964): 50. On California, see Note, "A Study of the California Penalty Jury in First-Degree-Murder Cases," *Stanford Law Review* 21 (1969): 1297.

51. Bischoff, "Constitutional Law and Civil Rights," *New York Law Review* 35 (1960): 30, 55, 73. We might digress to notice one minor sentencing reform that though in no way touching the matter of standards in sentencing, would if generally adopted be very likely to reduce the number of death sentences issued by the trial courts. Since 1961, Illinois has required that the death penalty be imposed only if the jury explicitly recommends it and if the judge explicitly agrees. See *Illinois Annual Statutes* ch. 38, § 1-7(c) (Smith-Hurd, 1964). Statistics now available show that in all capital cases where judge and jury agree in convicting a given defendant, they go on to agree to impose the death sentence in only 40 percent of these cases; i.e., in nearly two-thirds of all cases where the death penalty could be imposed on a convict, either the judge or the jury would prefer not to do so. H. Kalven and H. Zeisel, *The American Jury*, at p. 436-48 and n.31. Thus, the requirement that both must agree on the death sentence would approach, if not entirely achieve, *de facto* abolition.

52. See my essay "The Struggle over Capital Punishment in New Jersey," in *The Death Penalty*, at pp. 390-395.

53. Griffin v. Illinois, 351 U.S. 12 (1956), at p. 19.

54. See Eskridge v. Washington State Board of Prison Terms and Paroles, 357 U.S. 214 (1958).

55. Smith v. Crouse, 378 U.S. 584 (1964), construed in Donnell v. Swenson, 258 F. Supp. 317, 329-330 (1966).

56. Powell v. Alabama, 287 U.S. 45, 71 (1932).

57. Hamilton v. Alabama, 368 U.S. 52 (1961); White v. Maryland, 373 U.S. 59 (1963); Walton v. Arkansas, 371 U.S. 28 (1962).

58. Norman Dorsen, "In Regard to Capital Punishment," 2 January 1964, at pp. 8-9 (unpublished memorandum to the ACLU Due Process Committee), later published in Dorsen, *Frontiers of Civil Liberties* (1968), at p. 275.

59. Caritativo v. California, 357 U.S. 549, 552 (1958) (Frankfurter, J., dissenting). For discussion see Ralph Slovenko, "And The Penalty Is (Sometimes) Death," *Antioch Review* 24 (1964): 351, 354-55, 362; *cf.* Solesbee v. Balkcom, 339 U.S. 9, 14-32 (1950) (Frankfurter, J. dissenting).

60. An extensive catalogue of cases and expert opinion on the generally deleterious effects of prolonged detention under death sentence has been offered in evidence during 1967 to the California courts, in the *amicus curiae* brief

prepared by Gerald H. Gottlieb and Earl Klein. In re Anderson, Crim. No. 11572 (Cal. Sup. Ct., filed 27 December 1967), and In re Saterfield, Crim. No. 11573 (Cal. Sup. Ct., filed 27 December 1967), both petitions for habeas corpus. For a brief clinical study, see Harvey Bluestone and Carl McGahee, "Reactions to Extreme Stress: Impending Death By Execution," *American Journal of Psychiatry* 119 (1962): 393.

61. Caritativo v. California, 357 U.S. 549, 552-553 (1958) (Frankfurter, J., dissenting).

62. See my essay "Murder, Errors of Justice, and Capital Punishment," in *The Death Penalty*, at p. 434.

63. See Fay v. Noia, 372 U.S. 391 (1963); Townsend v. Sain, 372 U.S. 293 (1963); Brown v. Allen, 344 U.S. 443 (1953).

64. Johnson v. New Jersey, 384 U.S. 719, 729-735 (1966).

65. Linkletter v. Walker, 381 U.S. 618, 629 (1965).

66. Weems v. United States, 217 U.S. 349 (1910).

67. 356 U.S. 86 (1958), (five to four decision) at 101-103.

68. Robinson v. California, 370 U.S. 660, 666 (1962). This case settled the application to the states of the "cruel and unusual punishment" clause of the Eighth Amendment, a point expressly left undecided in Louisiana ex rel. Francis v. Resweber, 329 U.S. 459, 462-465 (1947).

69. See, e.g., Haley v. Ohio, 332 U.S. 596, 600-601 (1948). The concurring opinion of Justice Frankfurter is especially in point. Id. at 603-607. See also "Juveniles and Capital Punishment," in *The Death Penalty* at pp. 52-56.

70. Fyodor Dostoyevsky, *The Idiot* (tr. C. Garnett), New York, The Heritage Press, 1956, p. 24.

71. See, e.g., In re Saterfield, Crim. No. 11573 (Cal. Sup. Ct., filed 27 December 1967); and In re Anderson, Crim. No. 11572 (Cal. Sup. Ct., filed 27 December 1967).

72. Chessman v. Dickson, 275 F.2d 604, 607 (9th Cir. 1960) (Chambers, J.). See also Al Wirin and Paul M. Posner, "A Decade of Appeals," *UCLA Law Review* 8 (1961): 768.

73. *Challenge of Crime in a Free Society* (1967), at p. 143.

74. Louisiana ex rel. Francis v. Resweber, 329 U.S. 459, 464 (1947).

75. In re Kemmler, 136 U.S. 436, 447 (1890).

76. Trop v. Dulles, 356 U.S. 86, 99 (1958).

77. *Bailey v. United States*, 74 F.2d 451, 452-453 (10th Cir. 1934) (footnote omitted).

78. Note, "The Cruel and Unusual Punishment Clause and the Substantive Criminal Law," *Harvard Law Review* 79 (1966): 635, 639.

79. Trop v. Dulles, 356 U.S. 86, 100 n.32 (1958).

80. Note, "The Effectiveness of the Eighth Amendment: An Appraisal of Cruel and Unusual Punishment," *New York University Law Review* 36 (1961): 846, 849-850. Note, "The Cruel and Unusual Punishment Clause," *Harvard Law Review* at p. 638.

81. Trop v. Dulles, 356 U.S. 86, 101 (1958).

82. Weems v. United States, 217 U.S. 349, 373 (1910).

83. State v. Cannon, 190 A.2d 514 (Del. 1963), held that Delaware's statutory imposition of flogging as a punishment is not cruel and unusual under either the state or federal constitution. Five years later, the federal courts concluded that flogging was indeed unconstitutionally cruel and unusual punishment. Jackson v. Bishop, 404 F.2d 571 (1968).

84. Negley Teeters, *The Cradle of the Penitentiary* (1955): pp. 1-5. For a modification of this view see Thorsten Sellin, "A Look at Prison History," *Federal Probation* 31 (1967): 18.

85. Cesare Beccaria, *On Crimes and Punishments* (Paolucci transl., 1963) p. 48.

86. See Jacques Barzun, "In Favor of Capital Punishment," *American Scholar* 31 (1962): 181, 188-191; Sidney Hook, "The Death Sentence," *The New Leader* 44, 3 April 1961, at p. 18. See my reply "Death as a Punishment," in *The Death Penalty*, at pp. 214, 217-20.

87. Rudolph v. Alabama, 375 U.S. 889, 891 (1963), (dissenting opinion). The omission of *retribution* from the list of permissible purposes of punishment may be misleading. It is generally agreed that retribution is definitionally part of punishment as such. It cannot be an objection to any punishment, and *a fortiori* to capital punishment, that it is retributive. But this is not in any way a concession to those who would justify the death penalty for its unique retributive merits ("a life for a life"). It is neither logically necessary nor morally desirable that any punishment be retributive in this sense. See my essay "A Social Philosopher Looks at the Death Penalty," *American Journal of Psychiatry* 123 (1967): 1361.

88. *President's Commission on Law Enforcement and Administration of Justice, The Challenge of Crime in a Free Society* (1967): 143. The research alluded to by the Commission is from *Capital Punishment* (T. Sellin, ed., 1967), pp. 135-160. For a more comprehensive discussion of deterrence, as well as further empirical studies on the issue, see *The Death Penalty*, at pp. 288-332.

89. Weems v. United States, 217 U.S. 349, 367 (1910); Rudolph v. Alabama, 375 U.S. 889, 891 (1963), (dissenting opinion)

90. Herbert L. Packer, "Making the Punishment Fit the Crime," *Harvard Law Review* 77 (1964): 1071.

91. According to "The Supreme Court 1964 Term," *Harvard Law Review* 79 (1965): 56, 163.

92. See Bennett Patterson, *The Forgotten Ninth Amendment* (1955), p. vi; see Note, "Privacy After *Griswold*: Constitutional or Natural Law Right?" *Northwestern University Law Review* 60 (1966): 813, 826. For a general discussion of the Ninth Amendment, see Norman Redlich, "Are There 'Certain Rights... Retained by the People'?" *New York University Law Review* 37 (1962): 787.

93. See 1 *Pamphlets of the American Revolution, 1750-1776* (Bernard Bailyn, ed., 1965).

94. For discussion of the major historical and contemporary issues involved in this "right" see A. Delafield Smith, *The Right to Life* (1955); Norman St. John-Stevas, *The Right to Life* (1964): pp. 80-102; and my essay, "The Right to Life," *The Monist* 54 (October 1968): 550-572.

95. Barrett Prettyman, Jr., *Death and the Supreme Court* (1961), p. 305.

96. On 21-22 March 1968, hearings were held before a subcommittee of the Senate Committee on the Judiciary on S. 1760, filed by Senator Philip A. Hart, to abolish the death penalty for all crimes under federal civil and military law. A National Committee to Abolish the Federal Death Penalty has been formed under the chairmanship of Michael V. DiSalle, with headquarters in Washington, D.C. Senator Hart's initial remarks on behalf of his bill may be found in 113 Cong. Rec. S6686 (daily ed. 11 May 1967), excerpted in *Civil Liberties* (October 1967): 3.

Chapter 3
Deterrence and the Death Penalty

1. *Ethics* 78 (July 1968): 280-288. Van den Haag later published a "revised version" under the same title in *Journal of Criminal Law, Criminology and Police Science* 60 (1969): 141-147.

2. See Massachusetts Laws, chap. 150, Resolves of 1967; "Interim Report of the Special Commission Established to Make an Investigation and Study Relative to the Effectiveness of Capital Punishment as a Deterrent to Crime," mimeographed, Boston, Clerk, Great and General Court, State House, 1968.

3. John C. Ball, "The Deterrence Concept in Criminology and Law," *Journal of Criminal Law, Criminology and Police Science* 46 (1955): 347-354, at p. 351.

4. Ball, "The Deterrence Concept," p. 347.

5. Ball writes that "Capital punishment can be totally effective as a deterrent.... The executed murderer is no longer a threat to society. He has been permanently deterred." Ibid. at p. 353. This is an erroneous conclusion to reach, and when Ball goes on to use it to argue in favor of the deterrent efficacy of the death penalty, it reveals the menace which lies hidden in a faulty definition.

6. Frank Zimring and Gordon Hawkins, "Deterrence and Marginal Groups," *Journal of Research in Crime and Delinquency* 5 (1968): 100-114.

7. Definitions 1 and 2 have been criticized in the recent book by Jack Gibbs, *Crime, Punishment, and Deterrence*, New York, Elsevier, 1975, pp. 29-31. Elsewhere, I hope to respond to his criticisms. Here, I would comment only that he misquotes my definitions, and reads them as if I had used "only if" as the connective between the *definiens* and the *definiendum*.

8. See the several essays reprinted in H.A. Bedau, ed., *The Death Penalty in America*, rev. ed., New York, 1967, chap. 4, and the articles cited therein at pp. 166-170.

9. The same argument has been advanced earlier by Sidney Hook; see the *New York Law Forum* (1961), pp. 278-283, and the revised version of this argument published in Bedau, *Death Penalty in America*, pp. 150-151.

10. See, e.g., Thorsten Sellin, "Prison Homicides," in *Capital Punishment*, ed. Sellin, New York, 1967, pp. 154-160.

11. Rhode Island (1852), North Dakota (1915), New York (1965), Vermont (1965), and New Mexico (1969), have all qualified their abolition of the death penalty in this way; for further details, see Chapter 1, Table 1-4.

12. Bedau, *Death Penalty in America*, pp. 260-261.

13. Van den Haag accuses Sellin, a criminologist "who has made a careful study of the available statistics," of seeming to "think that this lack of evidence for deterrence is evidence for the lack of deterrence," that is, of thinking that (*a*) is (*b*)! In none of Sellin's writings that I have studied (see, for a partial listing, note 14) do I see any evidence that Sellin "thinks" the one "is" the other. What will be found is a certain vacillation in his various published writings, which span the years from 1953 to 1967, between the two ways of putting his conclusions. His most recent statement is unqualifiedly in the (*b*) form (see his *Capital Punishment*, p. 138). Since van den Haag also cited my *Death Penalty in America* (though not in this connection), I might add that there I did distinguish between (*a*) and (*b*) but did not insist, as I do now, that the argument entitles abolitionists to assert (*b*) (see Bedau, *Death Penalty in America*, pp. 264-265). It is perhaps worth noting here some other writers, all criminologists, who have recently stated the same or a stronger conclusion. "Capital punishment does not act as an effective deterrent to murder" (William J. Chambliss, "Types of Deviance and the Effectiveness of Legal Sanctions," *Wisconsin Law Review* (1967): 706); "The capital punishment controversy has produced the most reliable information on the general deterrent effect of a criminal sanction. It now seems established and accepted that ... the death penalty makes no difference to the homicide rate" [Norval Morris and Frank Zimring, "Deterrence and Corrections," *Annals* 381 (January 1969): 143]; "the evidence indicates that it [namely, the death penalty for murder] has no discernible effects in the United States" [Walter C. Reckless, "The Use of the Death Penalty," *Crime and*

Delinquency 15 (January 1969): 52]; "Capital punishment is ineffective in deterring murder" [Eugene Doleschal, "The Deterrent Effect of Legal Punishment," *Information Review on Crime and Delinquency* 1 (June 1969): 7].

14. The relevant research, regarding each of the eight hypotheses in the text, is as follows:

(i) Robert H. Dann, *The Deterrent Effect of Capital Punishment*, Philadelphia, 1935; Leonard H. Savitz, "A Study in Capital Punishment," *Journal of Criminal Law, Criminology and Police Science* 49 (1958): 338-41, reprinted in Bedau, *Death Penalty in America*, pp. 315-332. (ii) William F. Graves, "A Doctor Looks at Capital Punishment," *Medical Arts and Sciences* 10 (1956): 137-141, reprinted in Bedau, *Death Penalty in America*, pp. 322-332, with addenda (1964); (iii) Karl Schuessler, "The Deterrent Influence of the Death Penalty," *Annals* 284 (November 1952): 57; Walter C. Reckless, "The Use of the Death Penalty—a Factual Statement," *Crime and Delinquency* 15 (1969): 52, table 9; (iv) Thorsten Sellin, *The Death Penalty*, Philadelphia, American Law Institute, 1959, pp. 19-24, reprinted in Bedau, *Death Penalty in America*, pp. 274-284; updated in Sellin, *Capital Punishment*, pp. 135-138. (v) Sellin, *The Death Penalty*, pp. 34-38; reprinted in Bedau, *Death Penalty in America*, pp. 339-343. (vi) See works cited in (v). (vii) Canada, *Minutes and Proceedings of Evidence*, Joint Committee of the Senate and House of Commons on Capital Punishment and Corporal Punishment and Lotteries (1955), appendix F, pt. 1, pp. 718-728, "The Death Penalty and Police Safety," reprinted in Bedau, *Death Penalty in America*, pp. 284-301, and in Sellin, *Capital Punishment*, pp. 138-154, with postscript (1967); Canada, "The State Police and the Death Penalty," pp. 729-735, reprinted in Bedau, *Death Penalty in America*, pp. 301-315. (viii) *Massachusetts, Report and Recommendations of the Special Commission... [on] the Death Penalty...* (1958), pp. 21-22, reprinted in Bedau, *Death Penalty in America*, p. 400; Thorsten Sellin, "Prison Homicides," in Sellin, *Capital Punishment*, pp. 154-160.

15. See, for discussion surrounding this point, Bedau, *Death Penalty in America*, pp. 56-74.

16. For a general discussion, see Gibbs, *Crime, Punishment, and Deterrence*; Johannes Andenaes, *Punishment and Deterrence*, Ann Arbor, University of Michigan Press, 1974; and Franklin E. Zimring and Gordon J. Hawkins, *Deterrence: The Legal Threat in Crime Control*, Chicago, Ill., University of Chicago Press, 1973.

17. The same objection has been raised earlier by Joel Feinberg; see his review of Bedau, *Death Penalty in America* in *Ethics* 76 (October 1965): 63.

18. For a further discussion of this argument of van den Haag's, see David A. Conway, "Capital Punishment and Deterrence: Some Considerations in Dialogue Form," *Philosophy & Public Affairs* 3 (Summer 1974): 431-443.

19. For a general discussion which is not inconsistent with the position I

have taken, and which illuminates the logicorhetorical character of the appeal to burden of proof in philosophical argument, see Robert Brown, "The Burden of Proof," *American Philosophical Quarterly* 7 (1970): 74-82.

20. Now, however, see Isaac Ehrlich, "The Deterrent Effect of Capital Punishment: A Question of Life and Death," *American Economic Review* 65 (June 1975): 397-417, and his subsequent reply to his critics, "Deterrence: Evidence and Inference," *Yale Law Journal* 85 (December 1975): 209-226. For extensive criticism of Ehrlich's research, see H.A. Bedau and C.M. Pierce, eds., *Capital Punishment in the United States*, New York, AMS Press, 1976, pp. 359-416. For an attempt to improve on Ehrlich's findings, see James A. Yunker, "Is the Death Penalty a Deterrent to Homicide? Some Time Series Evidence," *Journal of Behavioral Economics* 5 (Summer 1976): 45-81.

21. Van den Haag replied to my essay criticizing him, and I responded to his reply; see *Ethics* 81 (October 1970): 74-76.

Chapter 4
The Death Penalty in America: Review and Forecast

1. See *National Prisoner Statistics*, No. 42, "Executions 1930-1967," table 16, p. 32. The comparable tables in H.A. Bedau, ed., *The Death Penalty in America*, rev. ed., 1967, p. 12 (hereinafter cited as *The Death Penalty*), and in Walter C. Reckless, "The Use of the Death Penalty—A Factual Statement," *Crime and Delinquency* 15 (January 1969): 49, table 6, are at variance and presumably in error. All statements of fact in the text not specifically documented are based on information in the files of the American League to Abolish Capital Punishment.

2. See *Wilmington* (Delaware) *Evening Journal* 4 January 1971, p. 1. Apparently, in overriding the governor's veto of the bill to reintroduce the death penalty, the lower house of the legislature failed to wait the necessary minimum of one day after receiving the measure from the upper house.

3. See *The Death Penalty*, pp. 29, 46-52; cf. Thorsten Sellin, ed., *Capital Punishment*, 1966, pp. 24-25. The Bedau and Sellin tabulations do not agree precisely.

4. *New York Times*, 23 August 1970, p. 58.

5. See *National Prisoner Statistics*, No. 23, "Executions 1959," February 1960.

6. See 86th Congress, Second Session, House of Representatives, *Hearing Before Subcommittee No. 2 of the Committee on the Judiciary*, on H. R. 870, 25 May 1960; and 90th Congress, Second Session, United States Senate, *Hearings Before the Subcommittee of the Judiciary*, on S. 1760, 20, 21 March and 2 July 1968.

7. See *National Prisoner Statistics*, No. 41, "Executions 1930-1966," April 1967, p. 5, and No. 45, "Executions 1930-1968," August 1969, p. 3.

8. Compare, respectively, James McCafferty, "The Death Sentence, 1960," table 6, reprinted in *The Death Penalty*, p. 102, and *National Prisoner Statistics*, No. 45, "Executions 1930-1968," August 1969, pp. 1-2.

9. See the letter from Deputy Attorney General Ramsey Clark of 23 July 1965; portions are quoted in the speech of Senator Philip A. Hart, *Congressional Record* 119 (25 July 1966) at p. 16181.

10. See Senate, *Hearings on Criminal Laws*, pp. 91-98, and, generally, Ramsey Clark, *Crime in America*, New York, Simon and Schuster, 1970, pp. 330-337.

11. See American Civil Liberties Union, *Civil Liberties*, May 1967, p. 1, and December 1967, p. 7; also Jack Greenberg and Jack Himmelstein, "Varieties of Attack on the Death Penalty," *Crime and Delinquency* 15 (January 1969): 112-120.

12. See Sid Ross and Herbert Kuperferberg, "The Longest Week in One Man's Life," *Parade*, 4 May 1969.

13. 395 U.S. 238 (1969). See, for the constitutional argument, especially the Brief filed in the case by Gerald H. Gottlieb and Earl Klein, *amici curiae*.

14. *New York Times*, 12 December 1970, p. 56. The case is Ralph v. Warden, No. 13, 757 (4th Cir. 1970). As of this writing it was uncertain whether the state would appeal.

15. *New York Times*, 30 December 1970, p. 26.

16. (Albany, N.Y.) *Times Union*, 31 December 1970, p. 2.

17. Compare National Commission on Reform of Federal Criminal Laws, *Study Draft of a New Federal Criminal Code* (1970), pp. 307-308, and *Final Report* (1970), pp. 310-314. See also *Working Papers of the National Commission on Reform of Federal Criminal Laws*, Washington, D.C., G.P.O., 1970, II, "Memorandum on The Capital Punishment Issue," pp. 1347-1376.

18. See National Commission, *Draft of Criminal Code*, p. 310, and *New York Times*, 8 January 1971, p. 1.

19. See, e.g., *Baltimore Evening Sun*, 8 January 1971; Salt Lake *Tribune*, 9 January 1971.

20. *Philadelphia Inquirer*, 21 January 1971, pp. 1; also *Philadelphia Evening Bulletin*, 21 January 1971, p. 1. See also the press release from Attorney General Speaker of 25 January 1971.

21. See letter to Commissioner Allyn Sielaff from Attorney General J. Shane Creamer of 27 January 1971.

22. *Psychology Today*, November 1969, p. 56.

23. *Good Housekeeping*, November 1969, p. 24.

24. *The Death Penalty*, pp. 236-241.

25. See Hazel Erskine, "The Polls: Capital Punishment," in *Public Opinion Quarterly* 34 (1970): 290-307.

26. Erskine, "The Polls," p. 291.

27. Erskine, "The Polls," pp. 298-300.

28. See *The Challenge of Crime in a Free Society*, 1967, p. 143, note 1.

29. Senate, *Hearings on Criminal Laws*, p. 85.

30. See the notes cited in Chapter 3.

31. Thorsten Sellin, "Capital Punishment," *Federal Probation* 25 (September 1961): 3-11.

32. See *The Death Penalty*, at pp. 209-214.

33. See Ramsey Clark, *Crime in America,* p. 334.

34. See *The Death Penalty*, pp. 434-452.

35. Donal E.J. MacNamara, "Convicting the Innocent," *Crime and Delinquency* 15 (January 1969): 57-62, at p. 60.

36. See *Tempe* (Ariz.) *Daily News*, 27 July 1966, p. 9.

37. See CALM Newsletter, III, no. 6, September 1969, p. 3.

38. See Isidore Zimmerman, *Punishment Without Crime*, N.Y., Clarkson Potter, 1964.

39. See Rupert C. Koeninger, "Capital Punishment in Texas, 1924-1968," *Crime and Delinquency* 15 (January 1969): 132-141, at p. 141.

40. See Edwin Wolf, "Analysis of Jury Sentencing in Capital Cases: New Jersey, 1937-1961," *Rutgers Law Review* 19 (Fall 1964): 56-64.

41. H.A. Bedau, "Death Sentences in New Jersey, 1907-1960," *Rutgers Law Review* 19 (Fall 1964): 1-54, at pp. 18-21.

42. See especially the opinion in Maxwell v. Bishop, 257 F. Suppl, 710 (E.D. Ark. 1966), and the Brief for Petitioner, Maxwell v. Bishop, 1968 (Sup. Ct. No. 622), at pp. 11-24, and Appendix A.

43. Brief in Maxwell v. Bishop, p. 18.

44. Ibid., p. 19.

45. Ibid., p. 19.

46. See Legal Defense Fund, *Equal Rights* I (June/July 1970): 1.

47. See James V. Bennett, "A Historical Move," *American Bar Association Journal* 44 (November 1958): 1053-1054; Herbert L. Cobin, "Abolition and Restoration of the Death Penalty in Delaware," in *The Death Penalty*, pp. 359-373; Glenn W. Samuelson, "Why Was Capital Punishment Restored in Delaware?," *Journal of Criminal Law, Criminology and Police Science* 60 (1969): 149-151.

48. See the speech by Robert K. Holliday, "How to Save Lives with Pen and Paper," delivered 9 May 1965, in Brookline, Mass., and published in his column, "Our Chat," in *Fayette* (W. Va.) *Tribune*, 20 May 1965, p. 1.

49. Gerald H. Gottleib, "Testing the Death Penalty," *Southern California Law Review* 34 (Spring 1961): 268-281, and also *Capital Punishment,* Center for the Study of Democratic Institutions, 1967.

50. 375 U.S. 889 (1963), cert. denied.

51. "Declaring the Death Penalty Unconstitutional," *Harvard Law Review* 83 (June 1970): 1773-1819. This "reversed" the conclusions of the *Review*'s only previous entry into these waters; see Note, "The Cruel and Unusual Punishment Clause and the Substantive Criminal Law," *Harvard Law Review* 79 (January 1966): 635-655, at pp. 638-639. See also Sol Rubin, "The Supreme Court, Cruel and Unusual Punishment, and the Death Penalty," *Crime and Delinquency* 15 (January 1969): 121-131.

52. Goldberg and Dershowitz, op. cit., p. 1798.

53. 398 U.S. 262 (1970).

54. *National Prisoner Statistics*, No. 45, "Executions 1930-1968," table 1, p. 7.

55. 390 U.S. 570 (1968).

56. United States v. Jackson, 390 U.S. 570 (1968), at p. 581.

57. Cited in National Commission on Reform of Federal Criminal Laws, *Working Papers*, II, pp. 1348-1350.

58. 391 U.S. 510 (1968).

59. "Does Disqualification of Jurors for Scruples Against Capital Punishment Constitute Denial of Fair Trial on Issue of Guilt?," *Texas Law Review* 39 (May 1961): 545-567.

60. The evidence has not yet been published in full; for a summary, see my article, "The Courts, The Constitution, and Capital Punishment," *Utah Law Review* (May 1968): 201-239, at pp. 206-210. See also Hans Zeisel, *Some Data on Juror Attitudes Towards Capital Punishment*, University of Chicago Law School, 1968. The latest studies in this vein are reported and reviewed in George L. Jurow, "New Data on the Effect of a 'Death Qualified' Jury on the Guilt Determination Process," *Harvard Law Review* 84 (January 1971): 567-611.

61. See Spencer v. Beto, 398 F.2d 500 (5th Cir. 1968); Williams v. Dutton, 400 F.2d 797 (5th Cir. 1968); Rideau v. White, E.D. La., Baton Rouge Div., Misc. No. 970, decided 12 May 1969.

62. According to the LDF, in its Brief *amici curiae* in McGautha v. California and Crampton v. Ohio at pp. 14ff.

63. See Bedau, op. cit., *supra*, note 60.

64. H.A. Bedau, "Capital Punishment in Oregon, 1903-64," *Oregon Law Review* 45 (December 1965): 1-39; Bedau, "Death Sentences in New Jersey; Koeninger, "Capital Punishment in Texas"; Robert M. Carter and A. LaMont Smith, "The Death Penalty in California—A Statistical and Composite Portrait," *Crime and Delinquency* 15 (January 1969): 62-76; also, Ohio, Legislative Service

Commission, *Capital Punishment* (1961), and Maryland, Legislative Council Committee, *Report ... On Capital Punishment* (1962).

65. For parole, see John M. Stanton, "Murders on Parole," *Crime and Deliquency* 15 (January 1969): 149-155; and the digest of eight states' reports in H.A. Bedau, "Parole of Capital Offenders, Recidivism, and Life Imprisonment," in *The Death Penalty*, pp. 395-405. On incarceration, see Thorsten Sellin, "Homicides and Assaults in American Prisons, 1964," *Acta Criminologiae et Medicinae Legalis Japonica* 31 (1965): 139-143; and Thorsten Sellin, "Prison Homicides," in Sellin, ed., *Capital Punishment* (1967): 154-160.

66. "A Study of the California Penalty Jury in First-Degree Murder Cases," *Stanford Law Review* 21 (June 1969): 1297-1497.

67. Note, "Executive Clemency in Capital Cases," *New York University Law Review* 39 (January 1967): 136-192; Solie M. Ringold, "The Dynamics of Executive Clemency," *American Bar Association Journal* 52 (March 1966): 240-243.

68. Harvey Bluestone and Carl L. McGahee, "Reaction to Extreme Stress: Impending Death By Execution," *American Journal of Psychiatry* 119 (November 1962): 393-396; Tom Murton, "Treatment of Condemned Prisoners," *Crime and Delinquency* 15 (January 1969): 94-111; Select Senate Committee Established to Investigate and Study Conditions Existing on the Death Row Section of the Massachusetts Correctional Institution at Walpole, *First Report*, Senate No. 1589, July 1970.

69. Edwin Powers, *Parole Eligibility of Prisoners Serving a Life Sentence*, Massachusetts Correctional Association, Boston, Mass., 1969.

70. Quoted in H.A. Bedau, "The Struggle Over Capital Punishment in New Jersey," in *The Death Penalty*, p. 376.

Chapter 5
The Politics of Death

1. United States v. Jackson, 390 U.S. 570 (1968).

2. Witherspoon v. Illinois, 391 U.S. 510 (1968).

3. Maxwell v. Bishop, 398 U.S. 262 (1970).

4. McGautha v. California, 402 U.S. 183 (1971).

5. Crampton v. Ohio was decided by the Supreme Court as part of its decision in *McGautha*.

6. Aikens v. California, 70 Cal. 2d 369 (1969), cert. granted 403 U.S. 952 (1971). The *Aikens* case was mooted in the U.S. Supreme Court by the ruling in People v. Anderson (see note 11).

7. Furman v. Georgia, 225 Ga. 253, 167 S.E. 2d 628 (1969).

8. Jackson v. Georgia, 225 Ga. 790, 171 S.E. 2d 501 (1969).

9. Branch v. Texas, 447 S.W. 2d 932 (Tex. Cri. App. 1969).

10. State v. Funicello, 60 N.J. 60, 286 A.2d 55 (1972).

11. People v. Anderson, 6 Cal. 3d 628, 100 Ca. Rptr. 152, 493 P.2d 880 (1972).

Chapter 6
Challenging the Death Penalty

1. See James V. Bennett, "A Historic Move: Delaware Abolishes Capital Punishment," *American Bar Association Journal* 44 (1958): 1053; and Herbert Cobin, "Abolition and Restoration of the Death Penalty in Delaware," in *The Death Penalty in America* (rev., ed. H. Bedau, 1967), p. 359. Meltsner appears to omit mention of this defeat for abolition.

2. Apparently, Arkansas in 1968 was the first state to abolish "death row" as a separate detention entity within the state prison where executions were held. This change in Arkansas practice was accomplished by the prison administration directly, and not by legislative action. See Tom Murton, "Treatment of Condemned Prisoners," *Crime & Delinquency* 15 (1969): 94. Meltsner mentions this development.

3. "Abolition of Capital Punishment," *Hearings on H.R. 870 Before Subcomm. No. 2, Senate Comm. on the Judiciary*, 86th Cong., 2d Sess. (1960) [hereinafter cited as *Hearings on H.R. 870*]. Apart from some useful information on the death penalty in the District of Columbia, at pp. 179-181, no testimony or information from the federal government on the death penalty was submitted at the hearing. This is merely one instance of what I have elsewhere called "a deplorable neglect on the part of the Federal Government [in studying empirical questions raised by the death penalty]." "Capital Punishment," *Hearings on H.R. 8414 etc. Before Subcomm. No. 3, Senate Comm. on the Judiciary*, 92d Cong., 2d Sess. 192 (1972) [hereinafter cited as *Hearings on H.R. 8414*].

4. Meltsner lists various standing organizations which had taken policy positions against the death penalty prior to the NAACP Legal Defense Fund in 1967, but he does not mention how recently in most cases these policy decisions were taken. The earliest, that of the National Council of Crime and Delinquency, dates from 1963. See *Crime & Delinquency* 10 (1964): 105.

5. No complete register exists of policy statements on capital punishment by religious organizations in the United States. For a useful compilation, see Continuation Committee of the Friends Conference on Crime and the Treatment of Offenders, "What Do the Churches Say on Capital Punishment?" (1961) (privately printed pamphlet prepared for the Third Assembly of World Council of Churches, 18-25 November 1961).

6. The history of this remarkable organization has yet to be written. For representative statements by its spokesmen during the early 1960s, see the remarks by the then executive director of the American League to Abolish Capital Punishment (ALACP), Sara (Mrs. Herbert F.) Ehrmann, in *Hearings on H.R. 870* at p. 44, and the statement by Donal E.J. MacNamara, then president of ALACP, ibid. at p. 158. The only other nonsectarian organization represented at these 1960 congressional hearings against the federal death penalty was the Women's International League for Peace and Freedom (WILPF). See the testimony by Annalee Stewart, legislative secretary, WILPF, at p. 148. The years of educational work performed by both Ehrmann and MacNamara receive no more than passing mention by Meltsner along with that of other "maverick moralists," who publicly opposed the death penalty during the earlier, lean years. In his preface, Meltsner excuses himself in advance for whatever shortcomings his book as history may have, on the ground that "[f]ortunately, the death penalty draws swarms of writers and researchers." Ibid at xii. It might be more accurate to say that it has continuously drawn passing attention from swarms of journalists and close scrutiny from few first rate scholars.

7. The organization was the New Jersey Citizens Against the Death Penalty, Inc. (NJCADP). Meltsner mentions the vigil at the State House in Trenton, N.J., to stop three executions in 1960, which led to the formation of NJCADP, but he omits mention of the organization itself. For a brief account of its activities, see H.A. Bedau, "The Struggle Over Capital Punishment in New Jersey," in *The Death Penalty in America* pp. 374, 390-395 (rev., ed. H. Bedau, 1967). A similar but unincorporated group was the Clemency Committee of the New York Committee to Abolish Capital Punishment. For an account, see Harold Levine, "Last Chance on Death Row," *Saturday Evening Post*, 29 June-6 July 1963, at p. 76.

8. 408 U.S. 238 (1972). Originally, *certiorari* had been granted by the Court in *Furman*, Jackson v. Georgia, Branch v. Texas, and Aikens v. California, 403 U.S. 952 (1971). The main brief and the oral argument in these consolidated cases were presented by LDF as well as by all the *amici* on behalf of *Aikens*. However, since this case was subsequently dismissed as moot, 406 U.S. 813 (1972), *Furman* was moved up in its place along with *Jackson* and *Branch*.

9. Stewart v. Massachusetts, and companion cases, 408 U.S. 845, 932-941 (1972). The Court ordered the judgment in each case "vacated insofar as it leaves undisturbed the death penalty imposed, and the case is remanded for further proceedings." See also Moore v. Illinois, 408 U.S. 786 (1972).

10. The exact number of persons under sentence of death when *Furman* was decided is somewhat uncertain. Meltsner at 292-293, reports "631 men and 2 women . . . on the death rows of 32 states" at the time. He gives no source, and his total of 633 may be in error. National Prisoner Statistics temporarily ceased publication with Number 46, August 1971, "Capital Punishment 1930-1970" released in March 1972. It reported 608 persons under death

sentence as of 31 December 1970. In the *Furman* opinion itself, the Justices were understandably vague on the point. Only Justice Marshall, 408 U.S. at p. 316, and Justice Powell, at p. 417, referred to the number of persons then awaiting execution and both fixed it at about 600. Neither gives any source for this total; they, too, probably relied on nongovernmental sources. During 1971 and 1972, public information regarding persons under sentence of death, with all the fluctuations day by day in that figure, was available only from Citizens Against Legalized Murder, Inc. (CALM), whose energetic director was Mr. Douglas Lyons. His testimony on this subject may be found in *Hearings on S. 176 Before the Subcomm. on Criminal Law and Procedures, Senate Comm. on the Judiciary*, 90th Cong., 2nd Sess. 39 (1968); *Hearings on H.R. 8414* at p. 243; and *Hearing on S. 1, S. 1400, and S. 1401, Before the Subcomm. on Criminal Laws and Procedures, Comm. of the Judiciary*, 93d Cong., 1st Sess. 162 (1972). An employee of LDF during 1971-1972, Lyons has been rightly described by Meltsner as "a one-man band, the 1960s most active and effective abolitionist." He collected death row data by direct telephone contact with prison wardens around the nation and made it generally available through the CALM Newsletter. As there was no one in government to check on his information, and as the media continually sought this information, the data he released at frequent but irregular intervals came to be regarded as authoritative. See, e.g., *Miami Herald*, 17 January 1972, § A at 14, col. 3; *New York Daily News*, 16 January 1972, at 119, col. 3; *U.S. News & World Report*, 10 July 1972, at p. 25 (all citing CALM statistics). In the most recent (and probably final) issue of the CALM Newsletter, it is reported that as of 29 June 1972, there were 631 persons under sentence of death in the United States, including one or more women in two states (Florida and Pennsylvania). *CALM Newsletter* 6, October 1972, at p. 4. Meltsner thanks Lyons for assistance in preparing *Cruel and Unusual*, and especially for "checking facts," but is unclear where the error lies in the discrepancy between the tally in Lyons' CALM Newsletter (631 persons, including women) and in Meltsner's book (631 men and two women).

11. Anyone under sentence of death at the time *Furman* was decided whose sentence was imposed under a *mandatory* death penalty statute was not eligible for resentencing under *Furman*. Several such death sentences had been vacated in California prior to *Furman* under the ruling in People v. Anderson, 6 Cal. 3d 628, 493 P.2d 880, 100 Cal. Rptr. 152, cert. denied, 406 U.S. 958 (1972). How many such death sentences remained in other states at the time *Furman* was decided is unclear. At least one such case is known: Frank Tarver was sentenced to death on 2 May 1972, for felony-murder-rape under a mandatory death penalty, *Mass. Gen. Laws Ann.* ch. 265, § 2 (1970). See *Boston Record-American*, 30 June 1972, at p. 2, col. 6. As of this writing, he is still under sentence of death, pending appeal of his conviction.

12. By implication, it was the death penalty *per se* which Justice Brennan declared to be "inconsistent with all four principles" of punishment implied by the Eighth Amendment bar to "cruel and unusual punishment." 408 U.S. at

305. Likewise, Justice Marshall wrote that "the death penalty is an excessive and unnecessary punishment which violates the Eighth Amendment." Ibid. at pp. 358-359. The three other Justices in the majority explicitly withheld any application of their opinions to the death penalty *per se.* Ibid. at p. 257 (Douglas, J., concurring); at p. 306 (Stewart, J., concurring); at 310-311 (White, J. concurring).

13. Leon Radzinowicz, *A History of English Criminal Law and Its Administration from 1750* (1948). Volume 1 of this work, *The Movement for Reform*, is largely concerned with the history of capital punishment in England during the early nineteenth century, and it continues to be the paradigm of scholarship on this subject.

14. Meltsner is rather vague about the work Clark, Heffron, and he did during 1963-1965 in persuading the LDF to attack capital punishment. "It is not easy to trace the evolution of ... [its] policy," he writes. Ibid at p. 106. Meltsner devotes surprisingly little space to showing how consciousness was raised and the LDF maneuvered into open attack on capital punishment. Most of the first five chapters of his book—exactly one-third of the whole volume—are given over to a general background discussion of the history of the LDF, the death penalty in America, the civil rights struggles, and related matters. All this information is necessary to Meltsner's story, but there will be those who will want to know more about the inner workings of the LDF, as well as more about Clark, Heffron, and Meltsner.

15. Meltsner presents a thumbnail sketch of Amsterdam's career after 1963 as a consulting attorney with the LDF and of his involvement in the anti-death penalty campaign. For a colorful biographical sketch, see Frederick Mann, "Anthony Amsterdam: Renaissance Man or Twentieth Century Computer?" *Juris Doctor* 3 (January 1973): p. 30. Not surprisingly, Meltsner supplies more and better anecdotes. One indication of the enormous contribution which, in Meltsner's judgment, Amsterdam made to the LDF's campaign against the death penalty is that the index to *Cruel and Unusual* mentions Amsterdam with greater frequency than any other two people. Several reviewers of Meltsner's book have expressed annoyance at his hyperbolic praise for the legal team Amsterdam headed (a team which, of course, included the author himself). Their favorite target has been Meltsner's passing boast that the LDF's "office library . . . [was usually] graced . . . [by] shiny minds from the best law schools." Meltsner does insist that "brilliant lawyer" is "truly apt to describe Amsterdam," and coming after the high compliment paid earlier ("the most versatile and talented lawyer of [his] . . . generation"), we can hardly be surprised at the hagiolatry ("[his] voice seemed that of an angry prophet") that follows. Meltsner's language may be open to rhetorical criticism, but that is only a minor flaw in the book. As he shows, chapter by chapter, Amsterdam was the one who was responsible for planning the entire strategy, writing the briefs and presenting the oral arguments in all the major death penalty cases, and carrying the increasingly heavy burden

of the whole campaign, year after year. Beyond these lawyerly abilities of one in a thousand, Amsterdam was able to accomplish what he did because "[b]etween 1965 and 1972, he spent no less than forty hours a week, every week of every year, representing capital case defendants." Given such a staggering workload and the competence with which it was performed, it is little wonder that Meltsner can write of Amsterdam only in superlatives.

16. The last execution in the nation took place in Colorado on 2 June 1967, one month after the national conference arranged by the LDF in New York to organize and announce its campaign, and not quite two months after the temporary stay of execution of all Florida death row prisoners. Meltsner does not explain whether LDF did not seek, or whether it sought but failed to obtain, a stay of this execution on the strength of the class action stay already obtained in Florida.

17. Like Meltsner before him (in 1970), Himmelstein left the LDF to join the faculty of Columbia Law School in 1974. Although Himmelstein's name appears with frequency throughout the last two-thirds of Meltsner's book, it is extremely difficult to get an accurate picture of Himmelstein's talents and his contributions to the LDF campaign which lasted throughout the five years from *Adderly* to *Furman* and after.

18. 272 F. Supp. 530 (M.D. Fla. 1967).

19. I borrow this phrase from the title of the book by Burton Wolfe, *Pileup on Death Row* (1973) published within a month or two of Meltsner's book.

20. 398 U.S. 262 (1970).

21. Apart from Thorsten Sellin, Marvin Wolfgang (a former student of Sellin's, and subsequently his colleague and successor at the University of Pennsylvania) is one of the few leading criminologists in the United States who has done firsthand research on issues involving capital punishment. See M. Wolfgang, *Patterns of Criminal Homicide* (1958); Wolfgang, Kelly, and Nolde, "Comparison of the Executed and the Commuted Among Admissions to Death Row," *Journal of Criminal Law, Criminology, and Police Science* 53 (1962): 301. Most of the results of the research which Wolfgang and Amsterdam initiated in 1965 on rape and the death penalty have yet to be published. But see Wolfgang and Riedel, "Race, Judicial Discretion, and the Death Penalty," *Annals* 407 (1973): 119, 126-133.

22. 391 U.S. 510 (1968), (death sentence impermissible if jury that imposed or recommended it was chosen by excluding potential jurors simply because they objected to the death penalty).

23. According to Meltsner, it was the ruling in *Witherspoon* that provided the "first hard evidence that abolition was on the Supreme Court's agenda." The LDF did, however, supply an *amicus* brief in *Witherspoon,* and evidently it influenced the Court's decision. The other important non-LDF case was United States v. Jackson, 390 U.S. 570 (1968). As Meltsner points out, the initial belief

among the LDF attorneys, that the effect of *Witherspoon* would be to end all executions, was rapidly dashed by the way in which the lower courts gave narrow interpretation to its holding, including its retroactive application.

24. 402 U.S. 183 (1971).

25. 395 U.S. 238 (1969).

26. 438 F.2d 786 (4th Cir. 1970).

27. 6 Cal. 3d 628, 493 P.2d 880, 100 Cal. Rptr. 152, cert. denied, 406 U.S. 958 (1972). One of the tasks undertaken during the summer of 1971 in preparation of the brief in *Aikens* was research into appellate court decisions in the English-speaking world and elsewhere which had held capital punishment, in some sense or other, to be "unconstitutional." Meltsner prints extracts of a memorandum drawn up by Amsterdam outlining proposed research for the *Aikens* brief, but the extract includes no mention of this particular project. In the brief in *Aikens*, Appendix E, "Worldwide and National Trends in the Use of the Death Penalty," and elsewhere in the brief, the topic is also omitted. No mention is made of the subject in the brief or by Meltsner, presumably because the research failed to turn up any record of judicial opposition to the death penalty elsewhere in the world. Dr. Jan Stepan, reference librarian at the International Legal Studies Library, Harvard Law School, has suggested in conversation with me that this presumption may well be correct and has brought to my attention information regarding four nations which have enacted constitutional provisions regarding the death penalty. See *Bundesverfassungsgesetz* (Federal Constitutional Law) art. 85. (Austria, 1955), in 3 A. Peaslee, *Constitution of Nations* 48 (3d ed. 1968), ("Capital punishment in ordinary procedure is abolished."); *Basic Law of the Federal Republic of Germany*, art. 102 (1949), in Peaslee, at p. 385 ("Capital punishment shall be abolished."); *The Constitution of the Republic of Italy*, art. 27, para. 4 (1947), in Peaslee, at p. 504 ("The death penalty is not admitted save in cases specified by military laws in time of war."); *Political Constitution of the Portugese Republic*, art. 8, § XI (1933), in Peaslee, at p. 730 ("Nobody shall be punished by ... death except ... during a state of war with a foreign country, in which case the sentence must be carried out in the theatre of war. ...").

28. Gottlieb, "Testing the Death Penalty," *Southern California Law Review* 34 (1961): 268; it was reprinted in *The Death Penalty in America* (H. Bedau ed., 1964); "On Capital Punishment" (Center for the Study of Democratic Institutions) (1967); *Case & Comment* 72 (1967): 3; and *Crime & Delinquency* 15 (1969): 1.

29. Meltsner does not mention this. For the posture of the ACLU during 1964, see the memorandum prepared by Norman Dorsen, then chairman of the ACLU Due Process Committee, on capital punishment and subsequently published in his book, *Frontiers of Civil Liberties* (1968).

30. Brief of *amicus curiae* at p. 38, Boykin v. Alabama, 395 U.S. 238 (1969) [hereinafter cited as Boykin Brief] (emphasis in original).

31. Boykin Brief, at p. 39. This passage is not quoted by Meltsner.

32. Ibid. at p. 40. This passage is not quoted by Meltsner.

33. See Arthur J. Goldberg and Alan Dershowitz, "Declaring the Death Penalty Unconstitutional," *Harvard Law Review* 83 (1970): 1773; Sol Rubin, "The Supreme Court, Cruel and Unusual Punishment, and the Death Penalty," *Crime & Delinquency* 15 (1969): 121. H.A. Bedau, "The Courts, the Constitutions, and Capital Punishment," *Utah Law Review* (1968): 201; and the article by Greenberg and Himmelstein (note 34).

34. Amsterdam did sketch out his own argument in a brief essay published after but written before the brief in *Aikens* was filed. Amsterdam, "The Case Against the Death Penalty," *Juris Doctor* 2 (November 1971): 11. The article by Jack Greenberg and Jack Himmelstein, "Varieties of Attack on the Death Penalty," *Crime & Delinquency* 15 (1969): 112, antedates the writing of the amicus brief in *Boykin*, and devotes only two short paragraphs to Eighth Amendment issues.

35. Meltsner indicates that Justices Stewart and White were regarded as the crucial "swing" votes, and that of the two, the latter was expected to be the most difficult to persuade.

36. *New York Times*, 30 June 1972, at p. 2, col. 6. Meltsner does not mention this press conference, though he does mention the avowed determination of the Nixon administration to restore the federal death penalty. For a critical discussion of one minor point incorporated into the government's testimony on behalf of such legislation, see my article, "The Nixon Administration and the Deterrent Effect of the Death Penalty," *University of Pittsburgh Law Review* 34 (1973): 557.

37. H.A. Bedau, "Survey of the Debate Over Capital Punishment in Canada, England, and the United States," *Prison Journal* 38 (October 1958): 35, 39.

38. The deterrent effect of the death penalty in the post-*Furman* months and years has been under study by Frank Zimring. So far, no results from his study have been published. For an analysis of post-*Furman* criminal statistics, see Bowers, *Executions in America* (1974). The subject has been discussed most recently in Bedau & Currie, Social Science Research and the Death Penalty in America: An Interim Report 13 (Russell Sage Foundation, unpublished, 1973). Some evidence that punishment deters, as a function of its severity, has been assembled in *The Economics of Crime and Punishment* (S. Rottenberg ed., 1973). An unpublished paper by Isaac Ehrlich has applied this evidence to the death penalty, apparently confirming for the first time that there is some measurable deterrent effect of capital punishment superior to that of life imprisonment.

39. Meltsner, at p. 213.

40. See *Congressional Quarterly*, 28 May 1974, at p. 2.

41. H.A. Bedau, "A Social Philosopher Looks at the Death Penalty," *American Journal of Psychiatry* 123 (1967): 1361.

42. Meltsner attributes this phrase to Jacques Barzun; see Barzun, "In Favor of Capital Punishment," *American Scholar* 31 (1962): 181.

Chapter 7
New Research and Literature Since *Furman*

1. For criticism of the testimony in Congress by the Department of Justice in favor of a federal death penalty, see my article, "The Nixon Administration and the Deterrent Effect of the Death Penalty," *University of Pittsburgh Law Review* 34 (Summer 1973): 557-566.

2. See Gerald H. Gottlieb, "Testing the Death Penalty," *Southern California Law Review* 34 (Spring 1961): 268-281; Jack Greenberg and Jack Himmelstein, "Varieties of Attack on the Death Penalty," *Crime and Delinquency* 15 (January 1969): 112-120; Sol Rubin, "The Supreme Court, Cruel and Unusual Punishment, and the Death Penalty," *Crime and Delinquency* 15 (January 1969): 121-131; Arthur J. Goldberg and Alan M. Dershowitz, "Declaring the Death Penalty Unconstitutional," *Harvard Law Review* 83 (June 1970): 1773-1819.

3. The first efforts of this sort did not appear until *Furman* was decided. See Malcolm E. Wheeler, "Toward a Theory of Limited Punishment: An Examination of the Eighth Amendment," *Stanford Law Review* 24 (May 1972): 838-873; Larry Charles Berkson, *The Concept of Cruel and Unusual Punishment*, Lexington, Mass., D.C. Heath and Company, 1975.

4. H.A. Bedau and Elliott Currie, Social Science Research and the Death Penalty: An Interim Report to the Russell Sage Foundation, June 1973 (Typescript). Copies are on file in several law school libraries.

5. The proposed projects and the principal investigators were as follows: "Public Attitudes Toward the Death Penalty" (Neil Vidmar); "Change from Mandatory to Discretionary Death Penalties" (William Bowers); "Patterns of Prison Homicides" (Peter Buffum); "Legislative Reimposition of the Death Penalty" (Edward Bronson and Charles Price); "Differential Imposition of the Death Penalty for Rape" (Marvin Wolfgang and Marc Riedel); "The Death Penalty as an Inciter of Violence" (William Graves and Alan Kringel); "A Cost/Benefit Study of the Death Penalty" (Ronald Slivka). The research by Vidmar and by Wolfgang and Riedel was subsequently published (see note 8); so was that of Buffum, in the special issue of *The Prison Journal* 53, no. 1 (Spring-Summer 1973), devoted to capital punishment.

6. See Phoebe C. Ellsworth and Lee Ross, "Public Opinion and Judicial Decision Making: An Example From Research on Capital Punishment," in H.A. Bedau and C.M. Pierce, eds., *Capital Punishment in the United States*, New York, AMS Press, 1976, pp. 152-171.

7. As of 1976, only one portion of this project had been completed; see my article, "Felony Murder Rape and the Mandatory Death Penalty: A Study in Discretionary Justice," *Suffolk University Law Review* 10 (Spring 1976): 493-520; a somewhat different version appears in Bedau and Pierce, eds., *Capital Punishment in the United States*, pp. 54-75.

8. All of the essays published in this issue of *Orthopsychiatry*, plus fifteen others (including those by Vidmar and by Wolfgang and Riedel cited in note 7), appeared in book form a year later in Bedau and Pierce, eds., *Capital Punishment in the United States*.

9. See Report of the Governor's Study Commission on Capital Punishment, Israel Packel, Chairman, September 1973 (typescript).

10. By title and investigator, these studies were as follows: "The Effect of Mandatory and Discretionary Death Sentences on Commutations and Executions, 1915-1962" (Marc Riedel); "A Review of the Literature Contrasting Mandatory and Discretionary Systems of Sentencing Capital Cases" (John McCloskey); "A Study of Capital Sentencing of First Degree Murderers in Pennsylvania" (Marc Riedel); "Homicides in Pennsylvania Prisons, 1964-1973" (Peter Buffum); "Capital Punishment: A Deterrent for Major Crime?" (Richard Pakola and Robert Sadoff); "A Report on the Questionnaire Administered to Life Term Inmates at State Correctional Institution, Graterford" (Marc Riedel); "A Content Analysis of Public Hearings of the Governor's Study Commission on Capital Punishment" (Marc Riedel). A revised version of the paper by Riedel on content analysis appears also in the special capital punishment issue of *The Prison Journal* (see note 5).

11. William J. Bowers, *Executions in America*, Lexington, Mass., D.C. Heath, 1974, p. 158.

Chapter 8
Are Mandatory Capital Statutes Unconstitutional?

1. See James R. Browning, "The New Death Penalty Statutes: Perpetuating a Costly Myth," *Gonzaga Law Review* 9 (Spring 1974): 651-705; and Note, "Discretion and the Constitutionality of the New Death Penalty Statutes," *Harvard Law Review* 87 (1974): 1690-1719.

2. The "Capital Punishment" series in *National Prisoner Statistics*, discontinued by the Bureau of Prisons after the August 1971 issue, resumed publication in December 1974 under the auspices of the Law Enforcement

Assistance Administration. However, the only source during 1975 for information on prisoners in the United States on death rows at that time was the unofficial tally maintained by the LDF and released at irregular intervals. The release of 6 January 1975 listed 187 persons in seventeen states under death sentence; the release of 10 June 1975 listed 283 persons in twenty-five states. Nonwhites amounted to 59 percent of the total in each instance.

3. See Marvin E. Wolfgang and Marc Riedel, "Race Judicial Discretion, and the Death Penalty," *The Annals* 407 (May 1973): 119-133.

4. This information was initially reported in The Harris Survey of June 1973 and confirmed in Neil Vidmar, "Retributive and Utilitarian Motives and Other Correlates of Canadian Attitudes Toward the Death Penalty," *The Canadian Psychologist* 15 (October 1974): 337-356, and in Austin Sarat and Neil Vidmar, "Public Opinion, the Death Penalty, and the Eighth Amendment: Testing the Marshall Hypothesis," *Wisconsin Law Review* (1976): 171-206. A different explanation, attaching greater weight to public fears of victimization, has been advanced in Charles W. Thomas and Samuel C. Foster, "A Sociological Perspective on Public Support for Capital Punishment," *American Journal of Orthopsychiatry* 45 (July/August 1975): 641-657.

5. Charles L. Black, Jr., *Capital Punishment: The Inevitability of Caprice and Mistake*, New York, W.W. Norton and Company, 1974, p. 21.

6. 282 N.C. 431, 194 S.E. 2d 19 (1973). See also "State Courts and the Death Penalty After *Furman v. Georgia*," State Courts Report Series Pub. No. NCSC R0004, April 1973.

7. Brief for the United States as Amicus Curiae, Fowler v. North Carolina, No. 73-7031, October Term, 1974, p. 35.

8. See Reply Brief for Petitioner, Fowler v. North Carolina, No. 73-7031, October Term, 1974, Appendix E, Peter Passell and John B. Taylor, "The Deterrent Effect of Capital Punishment," Columbia University Discussion Paper 74-7509, March 1975 (typescript); in a revised form it appears in H.A. Bedau and C.M. Pierce, eds., *Capital Punishment in the United States*, New York, AMS Press, 1976, pp. 359-371.

9. Ehrlich's research originally appeared as "The Deterrent Effect of Capital Punishment: A Question of Life and Death," Center for Economic Analysis of Human Behavior and Social Institutions, Working Paper No. 18, November 1973 (typescript); it subsequently appeared under the same title in *The American Economic Review* 65 (June 1975): 397-417.

10. Evidence for a counter-deterrence or "brutalization" effect of capital punishment is far from conclusive; however, see William J. Bowers and Glenn L. Pierce, "The Illusion of Deterrence in Isaac Ehrlich's Research on Capital Punishment," *Yale Law Journal* 85 (December 1975): 187-208, at p. 205 note 45.

11. Fowler v. North Carolina was eventually decided in July 1976; see 96 S. Ct. 3212 (1976).

Chapter 9
New Life for the Death Penalty

1. Gregg v. Georgia, 49 L.Ed. 2d 859 (1976).
2. Woodson v. North Carolina, 49 L.Ed. 2d 944 (1976).
3. Proffitt v. Florida, 49 L.Ed. 2d 913 (1976).
4. Jurek v. Texas, 49 L.Ed. 2d 929 (1976).
5. Roberts v. Louisiana, 49 L.Ed. 2d 974 (1976).

6. Jack Greenberg, *Cases and Materials on Judicial Process and Social Change: Constitutional Litigation*, St. Paul, Minn., West Publishing Co., 1977, p. 659.

7. See *Poverty Law Report* 4, no. 3 (Summer 1976): 3; and " 'Team Defense' Uses New Methods to Avoid Death for Clients," the *New York Times*, 5 December 1976, p. 60.

8. See Neil Vidmar and Phoebe Ellsworth, "Public Opinion and the Death Penalty," *Stanford Law Review* 26 (June 1974): 1245-1270; and Austin Sarat and Neil Vidmar, "Public Opinion, and the Death Penalty, and the Eighth Amendment: Testing the Marshall Hypothesis," *Wisconsin Law Review* (1976): 171-206. Both these essays are reprinted in H.A. Bedau and C.M. Pierce, eds., *Capital Punishment in the United States*, New York, AMS Press, 1976.

9. See the *New York Times*, 15 July 1976, p. 3. For a general discussion of the recent campaign to abolish the death penalty in Canada, see David Chandler, *Capital Punishment in Canada*, Toronto, McClelland and Stewart, 1976.

Chapter 10
Epilogue: A Right to Die by Firing Squad?

1. Thomas Szasz, "The Right to Die," *The New Republic*, 11 December 1976, pp. 8-9.

2. *The New York Times*, 15 November 1976, p. 24.

3. Thorsten Sellin, *The Death Penalty*, Philadelphia, The American Law Institute, 1959, p. 65.

4. Bernard L. Diamond, "Murder and the Death Penalty: A Case Report," in H.A. Bedau and C.M. Pierce, eds., *Capital Punishment in the United States*, New York, AMS Press, 1976, pp. 445-457, at p. 456. Diamond's article originally appeared in *The American Journal of Orthopsychiatry* 45 (July/August 1975): 712-722.

Index

Index

Abolition: arguments against, 6-8; arguments for, 6-8, 13-44, 54-55; bills, 69, 81; campaign, xiii-xiv, xvii-xviii, 70-72, 83-85; de facto, xix, 19, 20, 26; history of, xviii, 59-63, 83; judicial, 25; jurisdictions, 4-5 (table); legislation, 68-70; movement, xiii, 6, 119; opposition to, 8, 69; by referenda, 4, 64; religious groups favoring, 4; sentiment for, 15; unpopularity of, 69
ACLU. *See* American Civil Liberties Union
Adderly v. Wainwright, 13, 84
Aggravating circumstances, 25-27, 82, 111, 113
Aikens v. California, 79
Air piracy, 59
Alabama, 61, 112
Alaska, 5, 68, 81
Allocution, right of, 70, 77
American Civil Liberties Union (ACLU), xiii, xiv, xix, 5, 13, 16, 29, 60, 86, 99, 100, 121
American Correctional Association, 6, 60
American Journal of Orthopsychiatry, 97
American Law Institute, 25, 26, 82, 124
American League to Abolish Capital Punishment, 6, 71, 82, 102, 127n, 144n
American Orthopsychiatric Association, xviii, 97, 124
Amsterdam, Anthony G., xvii, 78, 79-80, 83, 85, 86-89, 92, 104-107, 109, 111
Annals of the American Academy of Political and Social Science, The, 100
Appellate courts, xiii, 11, 14, 21, 25, 44, 63, 69, 81. *See also name of individual state*; U.S. Court of Appeals; U.S. Supreme Court
Arizona, 5, 116; persons under death sentence in, 61, 112
Arkansas, 23-24, 63, 68, 76, 116; persons under death sentence in, 112
Arroyo, Miguel, 67
Assassination, 59, 64
Assault: aggravated, 2, 114; on police, 53; on prison guards, 7; by prisoners, 34, 75
Attica, 75, 80
Attorney General. *See* U.S. Department of Justice
Authoritarian personality, 18

Banishment, 38, 80
Barrett, Nicole, 122
Beccaria, Cesare, 38
Benoy, Jean A., 107
Bentham, Jeremy, 54
Bicentennial, U.S., 119
Bifurcated trial. *See* Trial
Bill of Rights. *See* U.S. Constitution
Black, Charles L., Jr., xvii, 99-100, 105
Black, Hugo L., 14, 28, 31, 78, 85
Black Codes, 131n
Blackmun, Harry A., 86
Blacks, xviii, 68, 76, 83, 103. *See also* Negroes; Race
Blackstone, William, 43
Bork, Robert H., 106-107, 111
Bowers, William J., 100-101
Boykin v. Alabama, 62, 70, 71, 85, 86, 87-88
Brennan, William J., Jr., 80, 88, 91, 113, 115
Brown, Edmund G., 63
Brown v. Board of Education, 12
Brutalization, 56
Burden of proof, 45, 57-58
Burger, Warren E., 92, 103, 117

157

Burger Court, 115
Burglary, 1, 28, 78, 114

Cadena temporal, 32
Cahill, William T., 78
California, 8, 25, 26, 30, 34, 60, 62, 69, 78, 85, 93, 97, 99; persons under death sentence in, 61, 112; Supreme Court of, 17, 19, 21, 78, 80
Calvert, Roy, 102
Camus, Albert, 100
Canada, 60, 65, 98, 101
Capital punishment: abolition of (*see* Abolition); administration of, 6, 15, 31, 84; alternatives to, 38, 50, 124; attitudes toward, 8, 15, 65, 82, 115 (*see also* Opinion, public); bills to restore, 93; campaign to abolish (*see* Abolition); constitutionality of, xiv-xv, 11-44, 111-119; as deterrent, xv-xvi, 6, 7, 39-40, 45-58, 64, 65-67, 89, 94, 100-101, 104, 107-109, 117; discretionary (*see* Discretion); for juveniles, 41; jurisdictions authorizing, 4, 13, 59, 81, 111; mandatory (*see* Mandatory capital punishment); modes of inflicting (*see* Execution); offenses punishable by, 1-2, 34; for prison killings, 75; referenda on, 4, 64; restoration of, 5 (table), 89, 93, 103, 106; statutory, 13; study commissions on, 8, 65-66, 98, 102. *See also* Death Sentence
Capital Punishment (McCafferty), 98-99
Capital Punishment (Sellin), xiii
Capital Punishment in the Twentieth Century (Calvert), 102
Capital Punishment in the United States (Bedau and Pierce), xviii, 124
Capital Punishment: The Inevitability of Caprice and Mistake (Black), xvii, 99, 105
Capote, Truman, 1

Carnal knowledge, 1
Carter, Jimmy, 114
Center for Criminal Justice (Harvard), 93
Center for Research in Criminal Justice (U. Illinois), 93
Center for Studies in Criminology and Criminal Justice (U. Pennsylvania), 93
Center for the Study of Law and Society (UC Berkeley), 93
Center for the Study and Reduction of Violence (UCLA), 93
Certiori, writ of, 27, 72
Challenge of Crime in a Free Society, The, 1, 39. *See also* President's Commission on Law Enforcement and Administration of Justice
Challenges, peremptory, 19, 20
Chessman, Caryl, 30, 33, 60, 99, 101
Circumstances, aggravating and mitigating, 25-27, 82, 111, 113; logic of, 27. *See also* Discretion
Citizens Against Legalized Murder, 62, 145n
Clark, Leroy, 83
Clark, Ramsey, xiii, 6, 62
Clemency, executive, 21, 73, 104, 118-119, 123
Colorado, 5, 35, 62, 64, 115, 116; persons under death sentence in, 61, 112
Commutation, xiii, 60, 63, 81. *See also* Clemency, executive
Connecticut, 8; persons under death sentence in, 61
Conscientious scruples, 16, 71
Constitution. *See* U.S. Constitution
Convictions, reversal of, 27
Cop killers, 23
Counsel: appellate, 28; court-appointed, 23, 31; post-appellate, 29, 62; trial, 28; volunteer, 27-28
Courts. *See* Appellate courts; Trial; U.S. Court of Appeals; U.S. Supreme Court
Crampton v. Ohio, 71, 74, 77

Creamer, J. Shane, 63
Crime rate, 89, 108
Crimes, capital, 2, 34
Criminal justice, 1, 72
Criminologists, 46, 54, 124
Cross-examination, right against, 77
Crosson, Robert F., 18
Cruel and unusual punishment, xiii-xix, 14, 32-41, 79-80, 85, 86-89, 103, 111, 114-115; and evolving standards of decency, 86, 114; logic of concept, 36-40; research on, 94-95; and retribution, 117-118. *See also* Eighth Amendment
Cruel and Unusual: The Supreme Court and Capital Punishment (Meltsner), xvi, xvii-xviii, 81-90, 99
Cruelty, 36-37
Cushing, Richard Cardinal, 5
Cuyahoga County Criminal Court (Ohio), 18

Darrow, Clarence, 71, 101
Death penalty. *See* Capital Punishment; Death sentence; Execution
Death Penalty in America, The (Bedau), xiii, xvi, 64
Death Penalty Inquiry, The, 102
Death row, abolition of, 143n. *See also* Death sentence
Death sentence: appellate review of (*see* Appellate courts); arbitrary, 117-118; commutation of (*see* Clemency, executive); delay in carrying out, 3-4, 34, 60; effect upon persons under, 29, 33-34, 73; persons under, 3 (table), 4, 30, 59, 60 (table), 61 (table), 74, 76, 81, 82, 103, 112 (table), 115, 121; race of persons under, 76, 103-104, 112 (table); reversals of, 82; time served under, 30; unjust (*see* Justice, miscarriages of); women under, 112 (table). *See also* Capital punishment; *names of states*
Declaration of Independence, 42
Defendants, indigent, 28, 82

Delaware, 5, 59, 69, 81; persons under death sentence in, 61, 112
Dershowitz, Alan M., 70, 87
Desecration of a grave, 35
Deterrence: conference on, 93; of crimininal homicide, 51-52; defined, 46-48, 136n; differential, 7-8, 39, 50-53; evidence on, xv-xvi, 7, 51-55, 65-67, 101, 108, 117; vs. incapacitation, 39; of life term prisoners, 49-50, 75-76; vs. prevention, 46; theory of, 54-55
Diamond, Bernard L., 97, 124
Dignity, human, 32; of man, 80
DiSalle, Michael, 101
Discretion, 104-106; guided, 95, 100, 103, 113; jury, 21-27; sentencing, 1-2, 13, 19-20, 81, 103, 114-115; standardless, 99-100; unguided, 91. *See also* Cricumstances, aggravating and mitigating
Discrimination, racial, xviii, 6, 22, 24, 67-68, 84, 103-104
District of Columbia, 4, 59, 62, 81, 97; persons under death sentence in, 61
Dorsen, Norman, 29
Dostoyevsky, Fyodor, 33
Douglas, William O., xix, 31, 80, 91, 109
Douglas v. California, 28
Due process of law, 12, 14, 27-31, 42, 62, 70, 71, 81. *See also* Fifth amendment
Duffy, Clinton, 101

Ehrlich, Isaac, 108
Eighth amendment, xiii, xiv, 14, 32-41, 77, 80, 82, 85-89, 91, 94-95, 103, 115. *See also* Cruel and unusual punishment
Electric chair, 63
Electrocution, 34, 35
Elfenbein, Donald, 97
Elliott, Robert, 101
England, 33, 35, 98, 102
Equal protection of the laws, xvi, 11,

Equal protection of the laws (cont.) 14, 21-27, 62, 70, 71, 81. *See also* Fourteenth amendment
Ervin, Sam J., 63
Escobedo v. Illinois, 31
Eshelman, Byron, 101
Espionage, 2
Europe, 99
Execution: modes of inflicting, 34, 86; for murder, 2, 13; for rape, 6
Executioners, 101
Executions: decline in, xiii, 2-3, 30, 82; as deterrent, xvi, 89, 107-108; under federal authority, 13; frequency of, 36, 81; as incitement to violence, 108, 124; moratorium on, xiii, xix, 70, 74, 76, 83-84, 89, 93, 100, 115, 122; number of, 2, 3 (table), 13, 60 (table), 100; resumption of, xiv, 115, 121; under state authority, 13, 100
Executions in America (Bowers), 100-101
Executive clemency. *See* Clemency, executive
Expiation, 6
Eyewitness: I Saw 189 Men Die in the Electric Chair (Reid), 101

Fairness, 72, 121. *See also* Justice
Fattah, Ezzat, 101
Federal Bureau of Investigation, 2, 6
Federal death penalty, 71, 82, 98. *See also* United States capital statutes
Federal Kidnapping Act, 71
Federal Probation, 66
Federalism, 119
Felonies, 4
Fifth amendment, 14, 71. *See also* Due process of law
Firing squad, 34, 121, 124
Flogging, 14, 38, 80
Florida, 62, 67, 84, 93, 113, 115, 116; persons under death sentence in, 61, 112
Florida State University, 93
Ford Foundation, 97

Fourteenth amendment, 12, 14, 27, 77, 82, 91. *See also* Equal protection of the laws
Fowler, Jesse T., 103
Fowler v. North Carolina, xiv, xviii-xix, 97, 103-109
Francis, Willie, 34
Frankfurter, Felix, 29
Furman v. Georgia, xiii, xiv, xvii, 82-83, 85-89, 91-92, 103, 106, 109, 111, 115

Gallup poll, 4, 15, 65, 82, 93
Gas, lethal, 34, 35
Gelles, Richard, 97
Georgia, 35, 100, 113, 115, 116, 118; persons under death sentence in, 61, 112
Gideon's Trumpet (Lewis), 84
Gilmore, Gary Mark, xiv, xix, 121-125
Goldberg, Arthur J., xv, 12, 39, 70, 83
Good Housekeeping, 64
Gottlieb, Gerald H., xiv, 70, 86
Great Britain, 60, 65. *See also* England
Greenberg, Jack, xv, 79-80, 83, 115
Gregg, Troy, 118
Gregg v. Georgia, xiii, xiv, xix, 111-119
Griffin v. Illinois, 28, 29
Griswold v. Connecticut, 42

Haag, Ernest van den, xv-xvi, 45-58
Habeus corpus, 4, 27
Hamilton v. Alabama, 29
Hanging, 33, 34, 38
Harlan, John Marshall, 78, 84, 85
Harris Survey, 4, 15
Hart, Philip A., 59, 62, 98
Harvard Law Review, 36, 70
Harvard Law School, xv, 84, 93
Hawaii, 5, 68, 81
Hearnes, Warren, 63
Heffron, Frank, 83
Hill v. Nelson, 13
Himmelstein, Jack, xi, xv, 83, 92
Hobbes, Thomas, 42
Holliday, Robert K., 69

Holmes, Oliver W., Jr., 32
Homicide, criminal, 51-52; judicial, 90; rates, 7, 51-52. *See also* Murder
Hoover, J. Edgar, 6
Horvath, Csaba, 67

Idaho, 112
The Idiot (Dostoyevsky), 33
Illinois, 52, 64; persons under death sentence in, 61
Impeachment, right against, 77
Imprisonment, 8, 38-39, 76; as retribution, 117. *See also* Life imprisonment
Incapacitation, 39
In Cold Blood (Capote), 1
Indiana, 61, 112
Innocent persons. *See* Justice, miscarriages of
Iowa, 4, 5, 21, 59, 68
Isolation, 39

Jewish Advocate, The, xvii
Johnson v. New Jersey, 31
Judicial abolition, 25; initiative, 11; responsibility, 21; restraint, 29, 36, 41, 119; review, 12
Jurek v. Texas, 113, 114
Juries: attitudes toward death penalty by, 15-16; blue ribbon, 19; death-qualified, 16-21, 26; execution-prone, 19; impartial, 14, 15-21; research on, 21; scrupled, 71; standards in sentencing for, 7, 113
Justice, 118, 121; individual, 125; miscarriages of, xvi-xvii, 7, 30, 67-68, 73, 94; precepts of, 40-41; retributive, 117-118
Juveniles, 33, 41

Kalven, Harry, 21
Kansas, 5, 28; persons under death sentence in, 61; Supreme Court of, 22
Kastenmeier, Robert W., 98
Kentucky, 61, 112
Kidnapping, 1, 2, 64, 71, 77

Kleindienst, Richard G., 93
Kluger, Richard, xviii
Koestler, Arthur, 101
Kohlberg, Lawrence, 97

Lafayette, Marquis de, 67
Law enforcement, 8; personnel, 6. *See also* Police; Prison guards; Wardens
Lawes, Lewis E., 101-102
LDF. *See* NAACP Legal Defense and Educational Fund
Levi, Edward H., 106
Lewis, Anthony, 84
Lex talionis. See Life for life
Liberties, civil, 12, 13
Life, sanctity of, 6
Life imprisonment, 6, 8, 24, 49, 75, 113, 114; worse than death, 38-39, 121. *See also* Imprisonment
Life for life, 2, 121
Locke, John, 43
Louisiana, 34, 114; persons under death sentence in, 61, 112
Lyons, Douglas, 62, 100, 145n

McCafferty, James A., 98
McClellan, John L., 63, 98
McGautha v. California, xvi, 71, 74, 77, 84-85
MacNamara, Donald E.J., 67
Mackey, Philip English, xviii
Maine, 5, 81
Mandatory capital punishment, xix, 1, 19-20, 25, 59, 81, 92, 93, 95, 100, 103-109, 111, 114, 118; as deterrent, 100; jurisdictions, 59; research on, 97, 98
Man's Judgment of Death (Lawes), 101
Manslaughter, 20, 67
Marshall, Thurgood, 91, 113, 115, 116
Maryland, 8, 20, 77; persons under death sentence in, 61, 112
Massachusetts, 8, 46, 64, 69, 70, 97; persons under death sentence in, 61; Special Commission to Investigate the Effectiveness of Capital Punishment as a Deterrent, 65

Maxwell, William L., 23-24
Maxwell v. Bishop, 23-24, 68, 70-71, 77, 84
Meltsner, Michael, xv, xvii-xviii, 81-90, 99
Mental disease, 26
Michigan, 4, 5, 8, 52
Minnesota, 5, 81
Miranda v. Illinois, 31
Mississippi, 61, 112
Missouri, 5, 63; persons under death sentence in, 61
Mitigating circumstances, 25-27, 82, 111, 113. *See also* Discretion
Model Penal Code, 25-26, 82
Monge, Luis, xix
Monroe, John, 23
Montana, 112
Multer, Abraham J., 59
Murder: degrees of, 1; executions for, 2, 13; felony, 26, 78, 118; first degree, 2, 4, 6, 78, 103; for hire, 117; persons under death sentence for, 61 (table), 112 (table); by prisoners, 26, 75-76, 114, 117; punishment for, 1; rate, 2; second degree, 20; and suicide, 97, 123-124. *See also* Homicide
Murderers: characteristics of, 116; as housemen, 101; as parolees, 8, 73, 124; as prisoners, 8, 73; retribution to, 117-118

NAACP Legal Defense and Educational Fund (LDF), xi, xiii, xiv, xv, xvii-xviii, 5, 13, 23, 60, 62, 70-71, 76, 78, 83-90, 92, 111, 115, 116, 121
Narcotics violation, 35
Nation, The, xvii
National Association for the Advancement of Colored People (NAACP), xviii
National Association of Attorneys General, 93
National Coalition Against the Death Penalty, xix

National Commission on Reform of Federal Criminal Laws, 63, 69
National Council on Crime and Delinquency, 5-6, 60
National Governors Conference, 63
National Prisoner Statistics, 3, 5, 60
Nationality Act, 32
Nebraska, 61, 112
Negroes, 7, 23-24, 68, 112. *See also* Blacks
Nevada, 34, 61, 112
New Hampshire, 61
New Jersey, 6, 16, 21, 25, 27, 73, 78-79, 82; Commission to Study Capital Punishment, 8; persons under death sentence in, 61; Supreme Court of, 20, 22-23, 26, 27
New Mexico, 34, 59, 68; persons under death sentence in, 112
New York, 4, 5, 8, 26, 34, 97; persons under death sentence in, 59, 61, 67, 112
New York Times, The, 75, 123
New Yorker, 18
Newsweek, 121
Ninth amendment, 14, 42-43
Nixon, Richard M., 89, 93
Nixon Administration, 85, 93
North Carolina, 59, 103-107, 114, 118; persons under death sentence in, 61, 112
North Dakota, 5

Oberer, Walter G., 18, 71
Offender/victim relationship, 23-24
Ohio, 8, 18, 101, 116; persons under death sentence in, 61, 112
Oklahoma, 61, 112
Opinion, public, 4, 6, 15, 64-65, 104, 116-117. *See also* Capital punishment, attitudes toward; Gallup poll; Harris Survey, Roper poll
Oregon, 4, 5, 13, 59, 64, 65, 68, 124; Supreme Court of, 16-17

Pain, concept of, 35, 36-37

Paine, Thomas, 42
Parole, 73, 124
Patterns of Criminal Homicide (Wolfgang), 55
Pennsylvania, 4, 26, 63, 67; persons under death sentence in, 61, 112; Report of the Governor's Study Commission on Capital Punishment, 98; Supreme Court of, 21-22
Penologists, 8
People v. Anderson, 78, 80, 85, 99
Perjury, 1, 20
Philippines, 32
Pierce, Chester M., xviii
Pileup on Death Row (Wolfe), 99
Plea bargaining, 97, 105
Police, 5, 64, 69; assault and homicide of, 23, 52, 53; murder of, 67, 75
Polls, opinion, 64-65, 102, 104. *See also* Gallup poll; Harris Survey; Opinion, public; Roper poll
Powell, Lewis F., Jr., 78, 80, 113, 115
Powell v. Alabama, 28-29, 99. *See also* Scottsboro Boys
Prejudice. *See* Discrimination, racial
President's Commission on Law Enforcement and Administration of Justice, xiii, 1, 4, 7, 34, 38, 65. *See also Challenge of Crime*
Prison guards, 7, 75-76
Prisoners: assault by life term, 52; homicide by life term, 75
Proffitt v. Florida, 113, 114
Proposition 17 (California), 93
Protestant, denominations favoring abolition, 4
Psychology Today, 64
Public defender, 31
Public Interest, The, 104
Puerto Rico, 4, 5
Punishing Criminals (van den Haag), xv
Punishment: aims of, 12; capital (*see* Capital punishment); corporal (*see* Flogging); cruel and unusual (*see* Cruel and unusual punishment); as deterrent (*see* Deterrence); functions of, 46, 47-48; proportional to offense, 32, 40-41; purposes of, 39, 117-118

Race, 23, 67-68; persons under death sentence by, 76, 103-104, 112 (table). *See also* Blacks; Discrimination, racial; Negroes
Radzinowicz, Leon, 83
Ralph v. Warden, 63, 77, 85
Rape, xv, 1, 2, 5, 6, 12, 28, 40, 63, 64, 68, 77, 78, 83, 84, 104, 114; attempted, 34; and deterrence, 40; execution for, 22, 71; persons under death sentence for, 61, 76, 112
Reagan, Ronald, 59
Recidivism, 8
Referenda, 4, 64
Reflections on the Guillotine (Camus), 100
Reflections on Hanging (Koestler), 101
Rehabilitation, 8, 39
Rehnquist, William H., 78
Reid, Don, 101
Remedies: post-appellate, 28; post-conviction, 29-31
Research, xii, xvi-xviii, 18, 23-24, 66, 67-68, 73, 75, 82, 83, 91-102, 104, 108, 116
Retentionists, 6, 8, 66
Retribution, 104, 117-118, 119, 124, 134n. *See also* Justice; Punishment
Revenge, 76
Rhode Island, 5, 8, 70, 75; persons under death sentence in, 112
Right, of allocution, 70, 77; to commence sanity proceeding, 29; to counsel, 29; against cross-examination, 77; to die; forfeiture of, 43, 76, 121; against impeachment, 77; to life, 42-43; against self-incrimination, 77
Rights: civil, 12, 32; constitutional, 66-67; natural, 119; offender's, 29-30; and remedies, 30; retained, 14, 42; retroactive application of, 28-29; unalienable, 42

Robbery, 1, 62, 70; armed, 2, 114, 118; persons under death sentence for, 61-62 (table)
Roberts v. Louisiana, 114
Robinson v. California, 32
Rockefeller, Winthrop, 63
Roper poll, 4, 15
Rosenberg, Ethel and Julius, xvi-xvii
Rousseau, Jean-Jacques, 42
Royal Commission on Capital Punishment, 102
Rudolph v. Alabama, xv, 12, 83
Russell Sage Foundation, xviii, 93, 96-97

Sanity proceedings, right to commence, 29
Schneir, Miriam and Walter, xvii
Schwartz, Louis, 63
Scottsboro Boys, 28, 72, 76, 99
Select Committee on Capital Punishment, 102
Self-incrimination, right against, 77
Sellin, Thorsten, xiii, xvi, 7, 8, 66, 89, 100, 124, 136n
Sentence, death. *See* Death sentence
Sentencing: bias in, 73; standards in, 27, 113; standardless, 70-72, 77, 84. *See also* Discretion; Mandatory capital punishment
Seventh amendment, 19
Sex, 2; persons under death sentence by, 76, 103, 112 (table)
Simple Justice (Kluger), xviii
Sing Sing Prison, 67, 101
Sixth amendment, 14, 19, 71
Smith, Edgar, 101
Social scientists, xiv, xviii, 92-93, 97-98, 100, 108, 116
Solicitor General. *See* U.S. Solicitor General
Solomon, George F., 97, 124
South Carolina, 67; persons under death sentence in, 61, 112
South Dakota, 5, 61
Southern Poverty Law Center, 116
Speaker, Fred, 63

Standards, 21, 25-27, 37-38, 80, 113-114. *See also* Sentencing
Stanford University, 97
State v. Funicello, 78-79
State v. Waddell, 106
Statistics, 2, 23-24, 53
Stevens, John Paul, 113, 115
Stewart, Potter, 80, 88, 91, 107, 113-117
Straus, Murray, 97
Studies in Homicide (Wolfgang), 55
Study commissions, 98; in Massachusetts, 65; in New Jersey, 8; in Pennsylvania, 98; Royal Commission, 102; Select Committee, 102. *See also* President's Commission on Law Enforcement and Administration of Justice
Study of the Deterrent Effect of Capital Punishment with Special Reference to Canada, A (Fattah), 101
Suicide, 123; by execution, 123-124; murder as, 97
Supreme Court. *See* U.S. Supreme Court
Survey research, 93. *See also* Opinion, public
Szasz, Thomas, 123

Team Defense, 116
Teeters, Negley, 100
Tennessee, 5; persons under death sentence in, 62, 112
Texas, 15, 67, 100, 101, 115, 116; persons under death sentence in, 62, 112
Train robbery, attempted, 34
Train wrecking, 35
Treason, 1, 5, 20
Treatment, 36
Trial: single-stage or unitary, 71, 72, 77, 84; special verdict in capital, 113; two-stage, 26, 82, 111, 113, 116
Trop v. Dulles, 32, 86
Tullock, Gordon, 104

Uniform Crime Reports, 2, 3
United Nations Educational Scientific and Cultural Organization (UNESCO), 43
United States: capital statutes of, 4, 59, 63; executions in, 100; persons under death sentence in, 81, 112 (table)
U.S. Congress, 6, 11, 14, 59, 81, 93, 103, 115; House Judiciary Committee, 98
U.S. Constitution, Bill of Rights, xv, 12, 13, 14, 36, 77, 79, 104. *See also individual amendments*
U.S. Court of Appeals, 23, 63, 77
U.S. Department of Justice, xiii, 6, 106-107, 109; Attorney General's office in, 62, 71, 72, 81-82
U.S. Senate, 62; Judiciary Committee, 98
U.S. Solicitor General, 72, 106, 107, 108, 111
U.S. Supreme Court, 3-4, 11-44, 62, 82-90, 111-119; oral argument before, xiii, 70-72, 74, 78-80, 104-109
United States v. Jackson, 71, 77, 78-79
Utah, xiv, 34, 121-125; persons under death sentence in, 62, 112

Vargas, Anastacio, 67
Velasquez, Jose, 67
Vengeance, 6, 76
Vermont, 4, 5, 59, 68
Victims, 26, 68, 117
Virgin Islands, 4, 5
Virginia, 6; persons under death sentence in, 62, 112
Voices Against Death: American Opposition to Capital Punishment, 1787-1975 (Mackey), xviii

Wake County (N.C.), 105
Wardens, 29, 101
Warren, Earl, 37
Warren Court, 77
Washington, 5, 62
Wechsler, Herbert, 26
Weems v. United States, 32
West, Louis Jolyon, 124
West Virginia, 4, 5, 59, 68, 69
Whipping, 14, 38, 80
White, Byron R., 80, 88, 91, 115
Whites, 2; under death sentence, 112 (table)
Wilson, Cody, 18
Wisconsin, 5, 81
Witherspoon v. Illinois, 71, 77, 84
Wolfe, Burton H., 99
Wolfgang, Marvin E., 23-24, 55, 68
Woods, John C., 123-124
Woodson, Tyrone, 118
Woodson v. North Carolina, xix, 113-119
Wright, Donald, 80
Wyoming, 35; persons under death sentence in, 62, 112

Yale Law School, 93

Zeisel, Hans, 21
Zibulka, William, 100
Zimmerman, Isidore, 67

About the Author

Hugo Adam Bedau is Austin Fletcher Professor of Philosophy at Tufts University, Medford, Massachusetts. He graduated with the B.A. summa cum laude from University of Redlands, and was awarded the M.A. degree from Boston University and Harvard University and the Ph.D. from Harvard. He taught at Dartmouth, Princeton, and Reed before coming to Tufts in 1966, and was a Liberal Arts Fellow at Harvard Law School in 1961-62. He is the co-author, with Edwin M. Schur, of *Victimless Crimes: Two Sides of a Controversy*, co-editor, with Chester M. Pierce, of *Capital Punishment in the United States*, and editor of *Justice and Equality, Civil Disobedience: Theory and Practice,* and *The Death Penalty in America.* He has written many articles, essays, and reviews in the professional journals of law, philosophy, and the social sciences.